# ISRAELI REJECTIONISM

# KEEP IN TOUCH WITH PLUTO PRESS

For special offers, author updates, new title info and more there are plenty of ways to stay in touch with Pluto Press.

Our Website: http://www.plutobooks.com

Our Blog: http://plutopress.wordpress.com

Our Facebook: http://www.facebook.com/PlutoPress

Our Twitter: http://twitter.com/plutopress

**Pluto**Press
www.plutobooks.com

# Israeli Rejectionism
## A Hidden Agenda in the Middle East Peace Process

Zalman Amit

and

Daphna Levit

PlutoPress
www.plutobooks.com

First published 2011 by Pluto Press
345 Archway Road, London N6 5AA and
175 Fifth Avenue, New York, NY 10010

Distributed in the United States of America exclusively by
Palgrave Macmillan, a division of St. Martin's Press LLC,
175 Fifth Avenue, New York, NY 10010

www.plutobooks.com

British Library Cataloguing in Publication Data
A catalogue record for this book is available from the British Library

ISBN     978 0 7453 3029 7    Hardback
ISBN     978 0 7453 3028 0    Paperback

Library of Congress Cataloging in Publication Data applied for

This book is printed on paper suitable for recycling and made from fully
managed and sustained forest sources. Logging, pulping and manufactur-
ing processes are expected to conform to the environmental standards of
the country of origin.

10 9 8 7 6 5 4 3 2 1

Designed and produced for Pluto Press by
Curran Publishing Services, Norwich

Printed and bound in the European Union by
CPI Antony Rowe, Chippenham and Eastbourne

# CONTENTS

Introduction      **1**

1   **Palestine – homeland for the Jews?**      **13**
    The Peel Commission: A first stab at partition      18
    The Biltmore Conference      21

2   **The partition of Palestine**      **23**
    Creation of the state      27
    Initial secret contacts      30

3   **Early initiatives**      **35**
    Young officers' revolution in Egypt      38
    Cross-border hostilities intensify      41
    Ben Gurion resigns      42
    *Esek habish* – the mishap      46
    Lavon out, Ben Gurion in      49
    Egypt nationalizes the Suez Canal      53
    The 1956 war      54

4   **The lull in hostilities. 1956–67**      **58**
    Early peace initiatives      60
    Egypt, Iraq, and Syria form a confederation      62
    Ben Gurion's final resignation      63
    Conflict over water      65

5   **The aftermath of the June 1967 war**      **70**
    Settlements      71
    Another round of initiatives      74
    Israel's terms of negotiation      75
    The Khartoum summit      76
    UN Resolution 242      76
    From Eshkol to Golda      77
    The War of Attrition      78
    Palestinians intensify the struggle      79
    Nasser dies      81

6   From Yom Kippur to Lebanon                         85
    Yatzhak Rabin, fifth prime minister                87
    The *Mahapach*                                     89
    Carter's initiative                                90
    Sadat in Jerusalem                                 92
    Camp David I                                       94
    The Egypt–Israel Peace Treaty                      95
    Sadat assassinated                                 96

7   From Lebanon to Oslo                               98
    The Begin doctrine and the bombing of Iraq's nuclear
    plant                                              99
    Sharon wages war                                  101
    The Sabra and Shatila massacre                    103
    Super hawk prime minister                         104
    The First *Intifada*                              106
    Post-*Intifada* intransigence                     108
    Madrid, another failure                           110

8   The PLO as a peace partner?                       112
    Oslo                                              113
    Rabin's deliberate ambiguity                      114
    The atrocity of Dr. Goldstein                     116
    Oslo on the wane                                  116
    Rabin assassinated                                117
    Peres briefly PM                                  119
    Netanyahu in power                                121
    Likud's first concessions                         122
    The River Wye Plantation                          123
    Netanyahu calls for new elections, and Barak wins  124

9   Barak leaves no stone unturned                    126
    A generous offer shatters the peace camp          127
    Talks with Syrians rather than Palestinians       128
    From a Syrian to a Palestinian failure            129
    The focus back on the Palestinians: Camp David II  130
    The Right of Return                               135
    The Second *Intifada*                             136
    What actually happened at Taba?                   137

10  Peace on a downhill slope                         140
    Sharon presents his government                    141
    Egypt proposes peace via Jordan                   143

The Mitchell Committee report                          143
Targeted assassinations intensify                      145
Rehavam Zeevi is killed                                146
General Zinni's mission: another hapless US effort     147
Operation Defensive Shield versus the Saudi peace plan 149
Arafat is forced to restructure the PA                 152
The road map                                           152
The Ayalon–Nusseibeh initiative                        153
The Geneva Accord                                      154
The Gaza disengagement subterfuge?                     155
Arafat dies and Abbas rises                            158
Elections, elections                                   160

Conclusion                                             163

Chronology of peace                                    167
Notes                                                  175
Bibliography                                           194
Index                                                  200

*In memory of Ann – an inspiration!*

# INTRODUCTION

How do two people, one a behavioral neuroscientist and the other a financial analyst, end up joining forces and writing a book about the political history of the Middle East? We were born over a decade apart, our parents or grandparents migrated to Palestine from very different European countries, and our socio-economic backgrounds were quite dissimilar, yet the similarities in our inculcated values and the critical stages of our development are striking.

No matter what part of the world their parents came from, Jews born in the 1930s and 1940s and raised in British Mandatory Palestine, which later became the State of Israel, shared very similar education curricula, belief systems, and even political ideology. The pressure to conform in small communities is always high, but in the Jewish community of the pre-state period it was enormous.

The Jewish community in Palestine during the 1930s and the 1940s consisted of fewer than 500,000 people, barely the size of a small city today. For this community, the authority of the Jewish institutions, whose spokesman was the Jewish Agency, was widely accepted over that of the official British Mandatory government. There were several political parties comprising the Jewish Agency, but its effective blending of political views provided the prescription for a homogeneous upbringing and early indoctrination of the younger generation born in what was commonly called Eretz Israel (the land of Israel).

The majority of the community were non-religious, and most children attended secular schools. There were few differences in the structure of education or the mode of socialization of the pupils in the schools. This uniformity extended to the religious schools as well. A unique feature of the education system was the presence of a parallel, non-academic, and highly political system, the pioneer youth movements. Among the youth movements operating within the mainstream of the Jewish community, two were the largest by far: the socialist youth movement or Labor Youth, under the patronage and supervision of the Histadrut (the Jewish Federation of

1

Labor), and the non-socialist, more centrist movement of the Scouts. The youth movements had an unofficial but powerful affiliation with the school boards, and a comprehensive system of recruitment operated throughout the country effectively until the 1950s and 1960s.

Elementary school principals encouraged their young students to consider joining a youth movement, and would even introduce the representatives of one or other of the movements. Joining was a major rite of passage, and although schools applied no recruitment incentives, the social pressure to join was ferocious. Youth movements operated in practically all towns or villages during the pre-state and the early years of the post-state era.[1]

New members were invited to attend frequent branch activities, which were a mixture of social activities and political indoctrination. The more political meetings were talks given by the counselors, group discussions, or presentations by one of the youths. They invariably focused on the history of the kibbutz movement, of Zionism, and of socialism. The history and geography of the land, and the ties of the Jewish people to it, were foremost in these talks. As the young members grew older, the level and intensity of these activities increased.

Conformity was a crucial value, and extended to many aspects of life. The uniform, for example, was important, and all mainstream youth movements maintained a strict adherence to a dress code. Members attending any activity would dependably wear the uniform shirt, which for both of us at different times was a blue shirt with red laces at the collar. Another youth movement required the same blue shirt but with white laces. One could easily identify fellow members of the group everywhere in the country.

The more dedicated members, with leadership potential, were identified over their first two or three years of membership, and a select few were offered the position of counselor. This was an enormous vote of confidence in their commitment to the movement and their comprehension and knowledge of the movement's values, principles, and ideology.

Zalman Amit accepted such an offer, and dedicated a considerable amount of time and effort to the job. Both of us, Zalman as a counselor and Daphna Levit as an ordinary member, were absolutely convinced that we were the vanguard of socialist Zionism serving the neophyte state, and that it relied on our support for its existence.

When the members of a youth movement group who were

seriously devoted to its ideals reached their last year of high school, many would traditionally make a commitment to join a specific kibbutz. In the pre-state era they might have established an entirely new kibbutz, and its members would have been expected to join the Haganah, the underground force of the Jewish community, or the Palmach – the elite force of the Haganah. The Palmach placed them in specific kibbutzim for one year of service, which was a mixture of military and agricultural training, after which they were invited to apply for membership of the kibbutz.

Soon after the end of the 1948 war, the Palmach was disbanded. Military service at the age of 18 became mandatory, but the disappearance of the Palmach created an enormous problem for the kibbutz movement. It endangered the flow of dedicated, indoctrinated youth committed to the idea of Zionism and its implementation in the framework of a kibbutz. There was serious apprehension that graduates of the pioneering youth movements who would be disconnected from the movement for two years of service in the army would not return to the kibbutz womb.

As a result of fierce negotiations between the kibbutz movements, their affiliated political parties, and the army, a new military brigade was established: the Pioneering Combat Youth (Nachal). Its unique character was that it allowed youth movement groups to join the army as a unit, but also allowed individual soldiers to volunteer. As in the pre-state Palmach, every Nachal unit spent most of its army years on a base established at a kibbutz, and its military service was a combination of agricultural and military training. Each Nachal unit had to assign about 15 percent of its members to regular military service. They were usually streamed into officer training programs or other military assignments. Another 10 percent of the members were assigned to work in the youth movement, usually as emissaries.

Upon their discharge from military service in the Nachal, members of the unit, now as civilians, were expected to join the kibbutz to which they were assigned. However, during the years of training and military service there was attrition. Some assigned to full military service did not return to the kibbutz, and others eventually decided against membership. In the initial years of the Nachal, most did join and became members of the kibbutz. The indoctrination was powerful in all cases, and even affected young people who did not grow up in the pioneering youth movement and did not serve in Nachal units.

Loyal, committed and devout Zionists were the products of

intense indoctrination by the *yishuv* (the Jewish community in Palestine) in the pre-state era, and government control over all information available during the early years of the state. The pressure to conform affected all, including academics and those in the defense forces, who were always given carefully selected and pre-interpreted information.

Censorship prevalent in Israel was primarily military censorship, which was enshrined in law. But there was also a more subtle censorship employed by the newspaper editors' committee. This committee served as a liaison between the press and the censors who represented the political leadership of the state. It was common for the prime minister or the defense minister to meet with the committee and request they not publish some potentially disturbing fact. These requests were invariably couched in terms of state security and Israel's international status. The editors' committee was a voluntary body, and regardless of the personal integrity of its members, it was obedient and rarely balked at acceding to the requests. During the Six Day War of 1967 and at the end of her military service in the Nachal, Daphna was transferred to the Military Spokesman Office in the Press Liaison Office. Journalists, local and foreign, who did not absolutely conform to the requirements of the censor, were usually given fewer privileges and less access, or even total denial of access, to militarily sensitive areas and people.

Despite the difference in our ages, we both entered post-army and post-kibbutz civilian life with a very similar set of beliefs and convictions. Most of our peers, even those who had not joined the movement and had not been completely immersed in the socialist version of Zionism, were largely committed to the same basic Zionist ideology. The powerful system of indoctrination produced generations of high-school graduates who were taught Jewish history and citizenship in the schools, and socialist or non-socialist Zionist ideology in the youth movements. The atmosphere in the street, the influence of the radio, the newspapers, the literature, and the theater augmented this uniformity of thought.[2] It was a very successful system, and although there were exceptions, the vast majority of young Israelis exposed to this system were effectively indoctrinated. They believed the message that the system delivered, were committed to it, and mostly were willing to give their lives for it. Many still do.

We were no different. We believed wholeheartedly that Zionism was the national liberation movement of the Jewish people. We also believed that Jews, wherever they live, belonged to the same people;

that some two thousand years ago after their defeat by the Romans, the Jews were forced into exile where they lived for centuries, dreaming of the day they would return to their beloved homeland.

A somewhat more complicated, but no less prevalent, belief was that at the onset of the Zionist project, at the turn of the 20th century, the land of Israel was actually empty. This belief, first articulated by Lord Shaftsbury and popularized by a British Zionist, Israel Zangwill,[3] was complicated by the fact that there was plenty of evidence to the contrary. The country was not actually empty, and an authentic, multi-layered community was living in hundreds of villages, towns, and several cities.[4] In our own minds we resolved this apparent contradiction by considering the people residing in Mandatory Palestine as primitive, non-productive, reactionary, and existing in a feudal society. They shunned modernity and did little to improve the living conditions on the land. Consequently we believed most of the land was a combination of desert and malaria-infested swamps. It was the early Zionists who risked and sacrificed their lives to drain the swamps, irrigate the desert, and make the land livable. We believed all this, we sang (and danced) about it, and we never doubted it.

We also completely believed in the right of the Jewish people to national self-determination. We had to ignore contradictions inherent in our position, and the arguments of Marx, Lenin, and Stalin[5] that the Jews do not constitute a people. To solve this problem we turned to Katzenelson, Borochov, and Tabenkin,[6] who argued with equal force that the Jews were a people with definite rights. Throughout their history the Jews had been forced to disperse, but since they did not assimilate and remained "faithful to their roots," their national right to self-determination was evident.

Just as we were absolutely convinced that the Jews had a historic right to return to their ancient homeland, we also believed that the Arabs living in Palestine and constituting the vast majority of the population up to the 1948 war had no right to national self-determination. After all, people including Marie Sirkin and M. S. Arnoni[7] argued heatedly that most of the Arabs were actually newcomers to the land. They had drifted into it from the neighboring Arab countries because of the economic boom created by the Zionists who were actively developing the land.

Our priorities were clearly expressed in the slogan of our youth movement badge: Labor, Defense, and Peace. We believed that Jews residing in Palestine and later Israel, aided by the resources of Jews everywhere, had the right to defend themselves against hostile

Arabs. This defense included the right to acquire land by force, taking advantage of loopholes in the Ottoman law that remained operative during the early years of the British Mandate. We regarded the policy of the wall and the tower (*Choma U'Migdal*)[8] underlying this approach to land acquisition just as morally compelling as all other Zionist principles. We simply could not imagine ideals more lofty or lives more worthy than serving our newly born country by becoming members of a kibbutz, developing the land, and protecting its borders.

We were peripherally aware that the conquest of most of Mandatory Palestine occurred at a high cost to the Jewish population. We were even aware of the fact that the war demolished the Arab community in the country and much of its population disappeared almost overnight. Along with the rest of our Jewish community, we convinced ourselves that it was *entirely their fault.* *They* did not accept the UN partition plan; aided by the armies of five independent states, *they* attacked a one-day-old state. We considered their defeat a justified miracle. Besides, we believed we never really forced them to leave. Their leaders had ordered them to abandon their homes in order to return victorious accompanied by the armies of their brethren from the neighboring Arab countries.

Like many Israelis who grew up in the 1940s and 1950s, we considered the years after military service as the best years of our lives. It is a rare privilege to participate in the building of a new-born country, particularly one for which, we were convinced, its people had longed over thousands of years. As both of us reached military age after the establishment of the state, we almost felt deprived of the opportunity to participate in the fight for its creation.

Zalman was recalled to military service (in the Reserves) when the 1956 war broke out. For him it was a moment of indescribable happiness. This was the chance to experience a right of passage and honorably serve his nation. At that time he never suspected that Israel might have been involved in a war largely conducted by two European colonial powers, England and France, over control of the Suez Canal.

At the end of this war Israel was in possession of the entire Sinai peninsula and the Gaza Strip.[9] Zalman was decommissioned in the Sinai. This was a huge benefit, and allowed him to explore the newly conquered territory. He found it appealing to the point that he considered leaving his kibbutz to establish a new kibbutz in the Sinai. To avoid the guilt of betraying the kibbutz he had just joined, he convinced himself that it would only be for a short while before he would return home. But then Ben Gurion capitulated to US pressure[10] and ordered a retreat from both the Sinai peninsula and the Gaza Strip. Zalman was enraged, and even considered Ben Gurion a traitor.

Five years later Zalman was sent to Canada as an emissary of the United Kibbutz Movement sponsored by the Jewish Agency. Jewish youth movements in the diaspora were affiliated with the various kibbutz movements and through them with Israeli political parties. When he began his studies at McGill University he was the national director of the Students Zionist Organization of Canada.

In the mid-1960s Allan Pollack, a professor of history and an active member of American Professors for Peace in the Middle East (APME), was the guest speaker at a seminar Zalman attended. Professor Pollack had just returned from a trip to the Middle East sponsored by APME, and amazed Zalman by stating that one of the stops was Amman, Jordan, where the group had met with King Hussein. The king had apparently assured his visitors repeatedly that he was committed to pursuing peace with Israel, and that he communicated his commitment and his intentions to contacts in Israel. Professor Pollack was no radical left-winger, and yet he claimed in no uncertain terms that he believed the king's sincerity and earnestness.

Prior to this encounter Zalman had been totally confident that Israel unwaveringly wanted peace and would never miss an opportunity to explore such possibilities. He was equally certain that the Arabs never wanted peace and took every opportunity to scuttle any Israeli initiative to start peace negotiations. In other words, he never doubted the famous words of Israel's celebrated foreign minister, Abba Eban, "They never miss an opportunity to miss an opportunity."

Another jab in Zalman's Zionist armor occurred during a Jewish jamboree, a yearly gathering of Jewish summer camps in eastern Canada, which he directed for several years. Hundreds of children attending Jewish summer camps participated in this event. One emissary from Israel spent several evenings with Zalman in increasingly heated discussions about the Middle East. After Zalman gave a fairly lengthy tirade of standard left-wing Zionist beliefs about Israel's commitment to peace and the uniform rejection of peace by all the Arab states surrounding Israel, the emissary's response was astonishing. His new friend said, "Do you really believe this?" Actually, he claimed, Ben Gurion had never wanted peace; he did not think peace served the interest of the young state. He consistently sabotaged any peace initiative launched by the Arabs. The friend claimed that as early as 1952, Nasser had launched a serious peace initiative via an acquaintance, Yerucham Cohen,[11] who was Yigal Alon's adjutant. The details of this initiative, as well as Ben Gurion's views on peace, will be discussed in Chapter 3. Ben Gurion was not interested, and undermined the effort with a retaliation operation in Gaza led by a young paratrooper, a major named Ariel Sharon. Enraged by the killing of unarmed Egyptian soldiers, Nasser stopped the contacts with Cohen, and soon afterwards he signed the first Egyptian–Soviet arms deal.[12]

A committed Zionist, Zalman had great difficulty believing the story. It was incomprehensible that just three years after the establishment of the State of Israel there had been any peace initiative that was cavalierly rejected by Israel. But cracks in the armor continued to widen.

Then came the pre-emptive war of 1967. Daphna was obediently serving her term in the army, with not a doubt about the righteousness of Israel's objectives. She served as a press liaison officer in the days immediately following the Six Day War (the 1967 war), and accompanied journalists as they watched Palestinian refugees crossing the Allenby Bridge in flight, and visited an UNRWA refugee camp in what is now referred to as the West Bank. This caused her some discomfort about Israel's activities, but this only made any sense in hindsight. At this time Zalman was in Canada, and because the Israeli information machine effectively portrayed Israel as a country about to be overrun by enemy armies, he volunteered to serve.

The results of this war are well known. Rather than being in any grave danger of attack, Israel demolished the joint forces of Syria, Jordan, and Egypt in six days. Israel then occupied the Sinai peninsula and the Gaza Strip, which it had conquered from Egypt, the West Bank and East Jerusalem, conquered from Jordan, and the Golan Heights, conquered from Syria.

Initially we both regarded the outcome of this war with what could be described as euphoria. We were absolutely convinced that the only possible political outcome of this war would be the end of the conflict. Finally, and for the first time, Israel had a territorial incentive of the kind the recalcitrant Arab states could not refuse. Within Israel there was a growing demand to pursue a quick route to peace. Most notable was the call by Yitzhak Ben Aharon, the former secretary general of the Labor Federation (Histadrut), to take a unilateral step and declare peace.[13] But the strategy actually implemented was that of "do nothing," advocated by Moshe Dayan.

He called it the telephone strategy:[14] the Arabs would have to start negotiating – they had no alternative – and therefore Israel need do nothing other than wait by the telephone for a call from the Arabs. The call never came.

Several events took place in the year that followed that irrevocably changed our perception of the dynamics of the conflict. Within days after the war, on June 14, 1967, Israel destroyed the entire Mugrabi neighborhood facing the Western Wall to make room for a huge plaza. This provided space in front of the wall for throngs of Jews to pray without the presence of any Arabs in the vicinity.[15] Then on June 25, Israel announced a unilateral annexation of East Jerusalem, ostensibly to protect the road to Jerusalem. Under direct orders from Yitzhak Rabin, Israel expelled the residents of three non-combative villages located at the Latrun enclave.[16] This was the same Yitzhak Rabin who later became a figurehead for peace.

The first settlements in two of the largest Palestinian cities, Hebron and Nablus, were established under the direct sponsorship of Yigal Alon and Shimon Peres, two Labor leaders vying for the job of prime minister.[17] Additional settlements soon followed. Defense minister Moshe Dayan claimed that Sharm El Sheikh was actually more important than peace,[18] and radical right-wing groups such as Gush Emunim and the Greater Israel Movement came into being. Both of these groups rejected any negotiations and advocated relinquishing not one inch of what they described as liberated land.[19]

Independently and without knowing each other, both of us were stunned. All this made no sense. Israel was single-handedly throwing away a definitive opportunity to end the conflict. The combination of the establishment of the settlements together with Dayan's statement about the triviality of peace spoke volumes about what the leading triumvirate of the day (Alon, Peres, and Dayan) thought about the importance of peace and the urgency of taking advantage of the post 1967 war situation: peace was not their highest priority.

The contention that Israel was the party opposed to peace, and had always been opposed to peace, initially sounded outrageous. But if it was true, then everything we had believed in since we joined the youth movement could not be true. It is difficult for adults to be forced to re-examine all their past convictions, but all the indications pointed in this direction. When a historic opportunity presented itself to end the conflict and normalize the relationship with its neighbors, Israel sabotaged the opportunity. We had to face the possibility that Israel was simply not interested in making peace with its neighbors.

The events of the post 1967 war era forced us to undertake this painful journey of re-examining our most fervent beliefs since the very early days of the Zionist movement in Palestine. Our journey benefited from and coincided with the appearance of the New Historians. These were a group of historians, along with a group of non-conformist journalists, who took a more critical approach to the official history of the state. Some could take advantage of newly declassified critical archival material which now became available to researchers. We immersed ourselves in their writings.

Our conclusion was as painful as it was clear. Ever since the first proposal by the British Peel Commission (in 1936),[20] Israel had rejected peace options. Wherever possible it scuttled proposals that were placed on the table by Arab leaders. It agreed to the UN partition proposal, but even that now seems to be expediency, with the Israeli leadership conscious of the possibility it would be discarded at the first opportunity. After the signing of the armistice agreement in 1949, which legalized Israel's acquisition of an additional 22 percent of Mandatory Palestine,[21] the attitude among most of the Israeli leadership became even more hostile to any idea of peace. This was particularly true of Ben Gurion.

Suddenly the subject of Israel's right to the land somehow attached itself to talk of Israel's ultimate victimhood. The Holocaust increasingly emerged as a ubiquitous justification for anything Israel did. It served a multitude of purposes as the occupation of the territories conquered by Israel in 1967 became more oppressive and the settlement movement grew in strength. We gradually became more involved in the peace movement, which was also gathering some momentum.

With a short hiatus beginning in 1993, during the Oslo peace talks and quickly ending with the assassination of Prime Minister Rabin, we saw a persistent progression towards Israel becoming an oppressive occupier. It prevented any step taken towards the recognition of the rights of the Palestinians for a state of their own, and moved slowly to acquire as much of the land and water of the West Bank and Gaza as possible. The suggestion made to us several decades earlier that Israel's strategy was to avoid peace at all costs became unavoidably apparent.

We began discussing the need to write a book focused specifically on Israel's negation of the entire concept of peace with the Palestinians early in the 2000s. But it was Operation Cast Lead in Gaza at the end of 2008 that made us unquestionably ready to begin writing this book.

Over the years much has been written about peace in the Middle East. In what way then does this book make a unique contribution to our understanding of the peace process?

No one can deny the fact that all the efforts to bring about peace and end the Palestinian–Israel conflict have failed. The unanswered questions are why they failed, and why they continue to do so. This is apparently a debate about cause and effect. For some the failure of the peace process is related to the Israeli occupation and the growth of the settlement movement. Others argue that Palestinian violence is what led to the failure of peace. Ehud Barak and Dennis Ross argued that the responsibility for the failure lies with the Palestinians, who rejected Barak's generous offers during Camp David II.[22] Still others suggest that the growth of Islamic fundamentalism and its dominance among the Palestinians is the cause of the failure. The common denominator among these attempts to explain the failure is that the conflict and its consequences are seen as the cause, and the resultant failed peace process is the effect.

This book takes a different position. It argues that there is no peace between Israelis and Palestinians after 62 years because Israel never wanted to achieve peace with its Palestinian neighbors. In recognition of political expediencies and political realities, Israel has consistently proclaimed its commitment to peace, but its consistent strategy was to sabotage any real possibility of peace. It did so because its leadership has always been convinced that peace is not in Israel's interest. We argue that this began even before the establishment of the State of Israel. Indeed, one can detect this conviction even among the early Zionist leaders such as Herzl.

The reason for the rejection of peace varied over the years depending on those in power at any given point in time. Nevertheless, the conviction that peace is not in Israel's interest has been flawlessly consistent. It is you, the reader, who will have to undertake the task of deciding whether our contention is valid.

## A NOTE

This is not a history book. It is a position paper. It presents our position about the central question underlying this book: Why, 62 years after the establishment of the State of Israel, is there no real peace between this state and its neighbors? Our position is that Israel was never primarily interested in establishing peace with its neighbors unless such a peace was totally on its own terms.

Israel has signed two peace agreements. One with Egypt was

imposed on it, and the other, with Jordan, was signed to acknowledge that there was no animosity between the two states. There is still a state of war or a state of occupation between Israel and all its other neighbors. We argue that maintaining the state of belligerence is preferable to Israel than a peace agreement that would require territorial concessions and compromises regarding refugees.

To write a book of this kind we used historic material and relied on historic sources. We made every possible effort to check and double-check the accuracy and validity of these sources.

We were often asked whether we could be objective. Our response has consistently been that we are not and do not wish to be objective. Our stated position and our effort to describe it forced us on many occasions to be polemic. We hope that we have presented our position accurately. If we did, the effort was worth it.

## ACKNOWLEDGMENTS

We would like to thank all those who supported us in the process of writing this book. We would particularly like to acknowledge the help of Norman White, Ismail Zayid and Patricia McKenzie who read the manuscript and gave us useful suggestions. Special thanks go also to Zeev Rafael, who provided us with valuable source information. Finally we would like to recognize the help of Haggai Matar, without whom we could not have done it.

# 1
# PALESTINE – HOMELAND FOR THE JEWS?

Israel's persistent resistance to the implementation of peace with its Palestinian neighbors has roots that go back to the early days of the Zionist movement and the nascent notion of establishing an independent homeland for the Jews.

The desire for a homeland was the product of fierce struggles for national independence that erupted in several European nations at the end of the 19th century. These often involved violence directed at all minorities who were perceived as outsiders or as collaborators of the oppressing regimes. Jewish communities caught in the midst of these struggles, particularly in Eastern Europe, became targets of much of that violence.[1]

A growing conviction that there could be no future for Jews in Europe was reinforced by nationalistic winds blowing throughout Europe, and further reinforced by several prominent anti-Semitic incidents such as the Alfred Dreyfus affair.[2] For an increasing number of Jews the obvious solution to the problems they were facing in Europe was the establishment of an independent Jewish state, possibly outside of Europe. This idea was unusual at that time, as no other group of independence seekers considered establishing a state in a place distant from that in which they were actually living. The expectation that potential future citizens of the new state would assemble from many different countries, with different backgrounds and a multitude of languages, was also unique. Although Yiddish and Ladino were two languages some of these future citizens would have in common, they were connected primarily by religion and the belief that all Jews originated from their ancient homeland in what was now known as Palestine. Therefore many of those seeking a free and independent Jewish state assumed that the preferred location should be that ancient homeland on the shores of the Mediterranean.

The idea of uprooting communities and moving them to an unknown foreign region may have been influenced to some extent by the institution of European colonialism, which commenced in the 15th century when powerful countries began to send explorers to find and conquer new lands. At the 1878 Congress of Berlin, Britain's Prime Minister Disraeli said that Bismarck's idea of progress was to seize someone else's territory.[3] Acquired by force, these territories became the property of the invading country. This was the fabric of European history. Although European Jews were often subjected to plunder and persecution themselves, the Zionists among them did not shrink from plans to take over a country to which they were connected by a rather weak historical narrative. Early on they knew very little about the contemporary realities of the land they claimed was their homeland: its geography, resources, or economy. Even less did they know about the people actually residing in that land, their origins, numbers, and way of life, and in the true spirit of the colonial era, they did not think it mattered. Theirs was a higher purpose.

The World Zionist Organization was founded at the first Zionist Congress in Basel, Switzerland, which took place from August 29 to August 31, 1897. Its leaders, Theodor Herzl, Max Nordau, and Menachem Usishkin among others, did not contemplate any negotiation with the primitive population of Palestine about the future status of a Jewish homeland. In 1895 Herzl wrote in his diary, "We shall try to spirit the penniless populations across the border by procuring employment for them in the transit countries while denying them employment in our own country."[4]

In a very real sense the seeds of the Middle East conflict were sown in those early days of the Zionist movement. Some of its leaders publicly claimed that the ancient Jewish homeland was an empty country. This became the leading slogan of the Zionist movement, "A land without people for a people without land," first articulated by Lord Shaftsbury in his memoirs in 1854, and later popularized by the Jewish British writer, Israel Zangwill in an article in 1901.[5] If the country were actually empty there would be no need to negotiate any agreement that would both acknowledge the rights of that population and legalize the Jewish presence in the country. However, in 1920 Zangwill stated, "We must be prepared either to drive out by the sword the tribes in possession, as our forefathers did, or to grapple with the problem of a large alien population."[6]

He knew the land was populated. Theodor Herzl, the uncontested leader of the Zionist movement, was widely self-educated about the demographics of the land, and knew that there was an extensive native population in Palestine.[7] In his writings he expressed the thought that a transfer of most of the native population was desirable. In his efforts to gain the support of the European powers for the Zionist idea, he offered to serve as their colonial spearhead in the battle against "barbarism."[8] Another Zionist leader, Moshe Smilansky, articulated this prevalent sentiment: "We must not forget that we are dealing here with a semi-savage people, which has extremely primitive concepts."[9]

In the period between the First Zionist Congress in August 1897 and the First World War, Herzl and his successors endeavored to buy the homeland from the moribund Ottoman Empire. No attention was given to possible responses from the native Palestinian population. To Herzl's chagrin, ultimately neither the Jewish magnates who were to provide the funds nor the Ottoman government would meet the Zionist challenge. Some Zionist leaders attributed Herzl's ill health and premature death in 1904 to this failure.[10]

After the defeat of the Ottoman Empire in 1918, and the conquest of the Middle East by the British, the prospects for an independent Jewish state improved considerably. The League of Nations gave Britain the mandate to administer the affairs of Palestine, which intensified the Jewish lobbying efforts. These efforts moved from Turkey to Britain, and the point man on behalf of the Zionists was Chaim Weizman. As a chemist, Weizman developed a new method for the manufacture of acetone, which helped the British produce ammunition for their First World War effort. By the beginning of the war, Weizman got to know many political leaders, including Winston Churchill and Arthur James Balfour. Many years later Lloyd George described the Balfour Declaration as a prize awarded to "his court Jew." Whether it was given because Britain was grateful for his contribution to the outcome of the war, or because he had successfully identified the interest of the Zionists with those of the British, is unresolved. Balfour wrote, "Zionism, be it right or wrong, good or bad, is of far profounder import than the desires and prejudices of the 700,000 Arabs who now inhabit that ancient land."[11]

In the Balfour Declaration, the first official recognition of the national aspirations of the Jews, the foreign secretary, Lord Arthur James Balfour, announced on November 2, 1917 that:

on behalf of His Majesty's Government, the following declaration of sympathy with Jewish Zionist aspirations which has been submitted to, and approved by, the Cabinet.

His Majesty's Government view with favour the establishment in Palestine of a national home for the Jewish people, and will use their best endeavours to facilitate the achievement of this object, it being clearly understood that nothing shall be done which may prejudice the civil and religious rights of existing non-Jewish communities in Palestine, or the rights and political status enjoyed by Jews in any other country.

The Declaration did not specify the political structure of this homeland, while it did emphasize the commitment to the protection of the rights and interests of the local population. At this time Britain was making additional agreements across the newly conquered Middle East that often contradicted each other. But on the surface, it appeared that Britain was now committed to safeguarding the interests of both the Jews and the Arabs.

For the Zionist movement, the Balfour Declaration was a momentous event. It was the first official recognition of Jewish aspirations, and it was issued by the government of the United Kingdom, which had wrenched this part of the world out of Ottoman control. Moreover, the United Kingdom had the mandate from the League of Nations to administer it for the time being. One could not ask for a more critical support for the Zionist dream of building a Jewish state.

Despite what seemed like intended British ambiguity in the wording of the Declaration, the Zionist leadership interpreted the Balfour Declaration unambiguously. They saw it as unquestionable support for the establishment of an independent, sovereign Jewish state. Their preferred interpretation of the words "In Palestine" was the entire area between the Jordan River and the Mediterranean Sea.[12] Some Zionist leaders believed that the borders of the future state would include portions of TransJordan, Syria, and Lebanon.[13] Since the indigenous Arab residents in this territory were not consulted, the Balfour Declaration commitment to the protection of their rights received short shrift if any at all. From the early years of the British Mandate, no serious effort was made to reach agreement with the local Arab community, which would obviously have involved a territorial compromise. The strategic goal was to acquire the entire area of Palestine, and at the same time transfer the bulk of the population to the neighboring Arab countries.

The Balfour Declaration and the Jewish–Zionist reaction to it provided fuel for the emerging and then ongoing Arab rebellion against the Jewish influx. Consistent with the pattern of ignoring the local Palestinian community, Chaim Weizman attempted to broker a deal directly with the Hashemite family and the leader of this tribal aggregate, Prince Faisal. Encouraged to do so by the British government, Faisal initially issued a statement supportive of the Jewish national presence in Palestine, and on January 3, 1919 an official deal between Weizman and Faisal was struck. The unreceptive reaction of the Palestinian population, and of the Arab population in the neighboring countries, overwhelmed Faisal – who had no legitimate right to negotiate on behalf of the Palestinians – and he quickly concluded that the deal he had signed was not feasible, and the separation of Palestine from Syria was not acceptable. His revised position was that Zionist aspirations were incompatible with Arab ideology.[14] Both Weizman and Faisal were detached from the reality on the ground, and could anticipate neither the reactions of the Palestinian Arabs nor those of a substantial portion of the Zionist leadership. Since neither had any real authority to negotiate, the life of the Faisal–Weizman deal was very short.

This incident reinforced the image of Zionism as a version of British colonialism in the eyes of the Palestinians and of other Arab nationalist movements. It added fuel to the nationalist Palestinian fires feeding the unfolding Arab rebellion, which was aimed primarily against British rule over Palestine. But the rebellion also opposed the influx of Jewish immigrants in the post-First World War years, which persisted with no consideration for their wishes and rights, and was perceived as an existential threat.

The stage was set for the emergence of the violence that marked the entire period from the Balfour Declaration to the UN Partition Resolution. The conflict involved three parties with mutually exclusive agendas. The British government had to pit the two other sides against each other to maintain its control over Palestine, which was validated by the Mandate given by the League of Nations. The local Palestinians, increasingly alarmed by the growing Jewish presence in the land, perceived the British Mandatory government to be supportive of the Zionist efforts. Responding to the Zionist reluctance to seek a compromise, they resorted to escalating violence in defense of their homes and community. The Jewish community was led by Zionists with the stated goal of establishing an independent Jewish state in the entire area between the Jordan River and the Mediterranean Sea. This party to the conflict, by far the smallest, was not interested in reaching a compromise with the local population, whom they considered to be primitive.

Despite the colonial tendencies of the Zionist leadership, they knew that the road to an independent Jewish state must traverse, at least officially, some geopolitical compromise.[15] The acceptance of such a territorial compromise was a necessary step towards the acquisition of "a land without people." One essential component of their aspiration was the conviction that transferring the Arab population out of Palestine could solve the demographic problem facing the emergent Jewish state. The Zionist leadership spoke of a voluntary transfer but allowed for the possibility of a forceful one, should the former not be attainable.[16]

During the 1930s the Arab rebellion intensified. About 6,000 Arabs and 450 Jews died, mostly in violent internecine disturbances, but more than 1,500 of these Arabs were killed by the British and some by the Jews.[17] The bloody conflict forced a rude awakening on the part of both the British government and the *yishuv* (the Jewish community living in Palestine during the pre-state era). Initially the British Mandatory government tried to forcefully suppress the rebellion, an effort supported by the *yishuv*. However, the Jewish/Zionist leadership gradually realized that Arab objection to the establishment of a Jewish state in Palestine would not easily diminish. Progress in this quest required the support of the western world, and particularly the United Kingdom and the United States. The Zionist leadership knew that they could only obtain such support by expressing their desire for a territorial compromise in Palestine. At the same time, the British government itself recognized the necessity for compromise to protect the British Mandate in Palestine. In May 1936 a royal commission, named for its chairman, Lord William Robert Peel, was established.

### THE PEEL COMMISSION: A FIRST STAB AT PARTITION

The premise underlying the commission's work was that the conflict could not be resolved within the confines of one state, and the deliberations introduced the concept of the partition of Palestine.[18] The Commission report, published in July 1937, proposed the partitioning of Palestine into two states: the Jews would be allotted about 20 percent of the territory (approximately 5,000 square kilometers), comprising parts of the Galilee, the Jezreel valley, and most of the coastal plain; the Arabs would be allotted most of the rest of the territory, with the exception of several small pockets including

Jerusalem, a corridor between Jerusalem and Jaffa, and a strip along the Red Sea, all of which would remain in British control.

The Arabs rejected the recommendations of the Peel Commission, while the Jews endorsed and accepted the partition of Palestine.[19] The official Jewish support for partition was enthusiastic. Both Weizman and Ben Gurion appeared before the commission to express their support. Weizman said, "The Jews would be fools not to accept it even if the land they were allocated were the size of a tablecloth."[20] The Palestinian leader, Haj Amin el Husseini, appeared before the Commission to explain the Arab rejection of the concept of partition.

The *yishuv* position set the stage for almost all future attempts to settle the Arab–Jewish conflict. Once the leadership accepted that partition of Palestine was the most realistic proposal and that the western powers were generally favorable to the concept, they positioned themselves in support of the idea. This was generally considered a necessary step towards the accomplishment of the ideal goal: the acquisition of the territory of Palestine. At every junction in the long and arduous road of the Arab–Israeli conflict, the Zionists expressed a moderate position without abandoning the goal of acquiring as much as possible of the area west of the Jordan River, and doing whatever possible to eliminate or massively reduce the Arab population residing there.

A clear expression of the Zionists' intentions can be seen in a letter that Ben Gurion sent his son Amos in October 1937. He explained the need to support the partition proposal, but emphasized that he saw partition merely as a beginning. The ultimate goal was a Jewish state in the entire land. He wrote confidently that this goal would be achieved in time.[21]

Among its recommendations, the Peel Commission proposed that the Arab portion of Palestine be joined to TransJordan. More importantly, the Commission recommended that most of the Arab population in the future Jewish state, roughly equal to the number of Jews, be transferred to the projected Arab state. It described the transfer as a *voluntary measure*; however, it stipulated that the British government would carry out a *compulsory transfer* if necessary.[22]

Ben Gurion endorsed this enthusiastically. In the letter to his son Amos, he explained that the importance of the proposed transfer of population outweighed all the shortcomings of the partition proposal.[23] In his diary he spoke of the "gigantic importance" of the proposal, and claimed that the Balfour Declaration would pale by comparison.

The idea of transfer did not originate in the Peel Commission report. Zionist leaders introduced it frequently during the first four decades of the 20th century, and considered it inescapable. Nevertheless practically all the *yishuv* leaders expressed a desire to live side by side, in peace, with the Arab neighbors. Since the same leaders expressed these two diametrically opposed views, it is hard to determine whether the desire for coexistence was sincere, or whether they simply understood the tactical advantage of a duplicitous attitude. With the escalating violence in the 1920s and certainly at the outbreak of the 1936 Disturbances, the support for coexistence weakened. By the outbreak of the Second World War many continued to speak about coexistence but hardly any believed it possible.[24] The Zionist leadership believed that transfer was just and moral; that the need of the Jews for a state large enough to accommodate the global Jewish population far outweighed the rights of the Palestinians.[25] These sentiments were uttered quite frequently and openly, and the Arabs soon became aware of them. When Amir Faisal, a Hashemite leader of the Arab Rebellion against the Turks, complained about this in a meeting in Paris on April 15, 1919, Zangwill became the convenient scapegoat to be blamed for the idea, and he was dismissed as an outsider.[26]

Throughout the first half of the 20th century, the Zionist leadership maintained this inherently contradictory position: expressing desire for coexistence on the one hand while simultaneously planning that Palestine – in its entirety – serve as the territorial base for the future Jewish state.[27] The Jewish leadership received with tremendous excitement the Peel Commission mention of a possible forcible transfer. Ben Gurion understood its implications and even thought it possible that the British would carry it out. He knew that if the British did not carry it out, the Jews would have to do it, and thereby engage in both the expansion of their territorial boundaries and the transfer of the Arab population. He anticipated that TransJordan would eventually become part of the future Jewish state. But his declared position continued to be that Palestine could accommodate both peoples.[28]

The Zionist Congress of August 1937 debated at length partition and transfer, the two primary recommendations of the Peel Commission. While a significant group of delegates argued against division of the homeland, the majority passed a resolution in favor of partition. An open and frank debate about the necessity of transfer also took place. Ben Gurion addressed the Congress on August 7, and informed the delegates that partly due to the activities of the Jewish National

Fund (JNF), transfer had already occurred in the Jezreel valley and other places. The JNF was the land acquisition and control agency of the *yishuv*. But transfer on a much larger scale would have to be undertaken for the widespread settlement of Jews. He boldly informed the delegates that the recommendation for transfer must come from the Commission rather than from the Zionist leadership, but he had previously written to his son that the *yishuv* would have to do the transfer themselves, should the British refuse to carry it out.[29]

During the years of the Second World War both Weizman and Ben Gurion became more strident and definitive about the right of the Jews to an independent, sovereign state. Weizman outlined the boundaries of this state, which encompassed the entire area west of the Jordan River.[30]

## THE BILTMORE CONFERENCE

In May 1942, during the war, Weizman and Ben Gurion met with a group of American Zionists at the Biltmore Hotel in New York. This became known as the Biltmore conference, and it passed a resolution "that Palestine be constituted as a Jewish Commonwealth integrated in the structure of the new democratic world,"[31] which later served as the basis for the demand to establish a Jewish state in the entire area of Palestine. The notion of coexistence with the Arabs was a secondary, superficial concern rather than an actual political goal. Consistent with either an unintentional or a deliberate policy of duplicity, the notion that Palestine would be partitioned and the Jewish state would be established on only part of it was implicit in the deliberations of the Biltmore conference.[32]

The full extent of the Holocaust was not known at the time of the Biltmore conference. As more information about this catastrophe became available, it provided important reinforcement for two apparently contradictory endeavors. On the one hand there was a growing recognition that global support for the establishment of an independent Jewish state required the partition of Palestine, as first articulated by the Peel Commission. On the other hand, the Holocaust gave importance to the acquisition of as much territory as possible to allow the immigration of all surviving European Jews. Since accurate information about the dimensions of the massacre was unavailable, Zionist leaders foresaw many millions of European Jews migrating to Palestine. There is ample support for the conclusion that partition was considered tactical while expansion by land acquisition and transfer were strategic.[33]

At the outset of the Second World War, in the face of mounting resistance by the Arabs, the British government published a White Paper[34] which proposed severe restrictions on Jewish migration to Palestine. Partly as a result of this change of attitude, the 20th Zionist Congress passed a resolution in 1945 to initiate a campaign of active opposition to British rule. This was against the wishes of Chaim Weizman, a staunch supporter of the British. The ensuing Jewish revolt coordinated the armed underground Jewish forces of the Etzel, Lehi, and the much larger Hagannah.

The mounting opposition from both the Arabs and the Jews over-whelmed the British government, or as the British governor general told Ben Gurion, "Our people are fed up with all this."[35]

In February 1947 the British government returned its Palestine Mandate to the United Nations, the heir of the League of Nations which had originally granted it. The United Nations set up yet another committee, which after extensive deliberations recommended the partition of Palestine to the UN General Assembly.

# 2 THE PARTITION OF PALESTINE

With a surprising two-thirds majority, the General Assembly of the United Nations approved the partition of Palestine into two independent states, a Jewish state and a Palestinian state, on November 29, 1947. Jerusalem and its holy places were to remain under an international protectorate. For the first time since the Second World War the United States and the Soviet Union supported the same resolution. Thirty-three UN members voted in favor of the resolution, thirteen voted against, and ten members abstained. More than any previous political event, this UN decision laid the foundation for the establishment of the State of Israel.

For those involved in the creation of a Jewish state, the years between the end of the Second World War and the UN partition decision were marked primarily by the impact of the horrors of the Holocaust. The UN General Assembly might not have approved the partition of Palestine were it not for the shock of the Holocaust. And had Britain anticipated that the United Nations would restore its mandate on Palestine after it had surrendered it, it underestimated the magnitude of this shock.

This period between two world wars also marked the ascendancy of David Ben Gurion to the position of undisputed leader of Jewish Zionists worldwide. Over the years Ben Gurion's political and ideological views underwent many substantial changes, but he effectively represented the attitudes and aspirations of the majority of the Zionist movement.

Ben Gurion was an odd product of his era, the late colonial era and the rise of Marxist-socialist ideology. In his early years he appears to have sincerely believed in cooperation between Jews and Arabs in the process of building the two communities in Palestine. He also seemed firmly against any dispossession of Arabs, and expressed the view that Jewish objectives could not come at the expense of even one Arab child losing his land. But he unequivocally opposed any suggestion to form a binational state such as the one proposed by the first president of the Hebrew University, Yehudah

Leib Magnes, of the group of Jewish intellectuals Brit Shalom, which included Martin Buber. In their plan the Arabs would be the majority but the Jewish community and cultural rights of both communities would be guaranteed.[1]

Ben Gurion held that it would be possible to convince the Palestinian Arab leadership to accept the establishment of an independent Jewish state in Palestine with a constitutionally guaranteed Jewish majority. Despite his socialist and secular background, he was greatly influenced by biblical history. The boundaries of the future Jewish state he envisioned were flexible but included, at various times, territory from the mountains of Lebanon or from the Litany River to El Arish in the northern Sinai desert; from the Mediterranean Sea to the desert in what is now Lebanon, Egypt, and the Kingdom of Jordan. The Negev and Arava areas to the Red Sea were also perceived as part of the future state.[2]

Before the UN partition vote Ben Gurion had initiated a series of encounters with moderate Palestinian Arab leaders. First and most notable among them was Mussa Alami, a wealthy Palestinian who was well respected and considered honest, decent, and moderate. It is difficult to imagine that a politician as shrewd as Ben Gurion could have been so profoundly naïve to believe that moderate Arab leaders could be persuaded to give up all their own national aspirations. To Alami's skeptical question 'What's in it for the Arabs?' Ben Gurion expounded on the economic measures the Jews would take to improve the life of the Arabs.[3] Mussa Alami recommended that Ben Gurion meet the leaders of the nationalist Syrian-Palestinian Istiklal movement living in Geneva. Ben Gurion presented his vision of a Jewish state extending over Palestine and TransJordan as well as parts of Syria, Lebanon, and Egypt to Jabri and Arslan, who were leading Arab nationalists. The two angrily dismissed the proposal as a nonsensical insult.

Ben Gurion's proposals to the Arab leaders may well have represented his true beliefs and his conception of the fundamental goal of the Zionist movement. As a pragmatist he was willing to consider a variety of partial solutions. But none of the solutions, even those he probably found extremely exciting, dissuaded him from the ultimate goal: a Jewish state in all of Palestine and adjoining areas in the neighboring Arab countries. His overriding ambition was to achieve the ingathering of all the Jews of the world in a sovereign, independent state of their own.[4]

Throughout the pre-state era Ben Gurion supported the achievement of peace between the Zionist movement and its Arab neighbors. But as the response of the Arabs to the influx of Jews to Palestine grew increasingly violent in the late 1920s and the 1930s, Ben Gurion became more reluctant to compromise. He expressed the view that the price of peace would be much too high, and it would force the Jews to give up too much land and resources. In his own words, "There are tens of millions of Arabs around the land of Israel and they will never accept a Jewish Palestine."[5]

Unlike Weizman and most of the Zionists who bitterly opposed the recommendations of the Peel Commission, Ben Gurion endorsed them. He obviously understood that it would not be otherwise possible to recruit global support for a Jewish state even on the territorially limited concept of Mandatory Palestine. Therefore his support for what he considered an interim solution, partition, was unwavering. But it was never absolute and unconditional. It was only the first step towards the ultimate goal. In 1947, after Britain relinquished the Palestinian Mandate, the UN Commission recommended partition, which Ben Gurion enthusiastically supported. He campaigned for the proposal in the Zionist movement and within his own party. His declared that this was an interim step without which the Jewish state would not become a reality.[6]

Ben Gurion gave increasing consideration to a massive transfer of the Arab population as the only realistic guaranty for the presence of a Jewish majority. The concept of *transfer*, the removal of a local native population to make room for an incoming colonizing population, was not unusual during the colonial era. On several occasions, Ben Gurion claimed that the idea of transferring Palestinians to the neighboring countries was justifiable. He would have undoubtedly preferred a voluntary transfer facilitated by Jewish money or by successful purchase of Arab lands. But a transfer by force was not ruled out as a necessary alternative.[7]

Ben Gurion's underlying strategy during the years of debate around the concept of partition, particularly immediately after the Second World War, was to gain control of as much territory as possible with the fewest possible Arab residents. This was essential for the re-establishment of the Kingdom of Israel on the territories that Ben Gurion imagined were its biblical boundaries. To facilitate this goal the tactics employed were to acquire more land through purchase or conquest, to refuse any plan for permanent borders for the future state, and to rely on biblical history as the basis for the Zionist claim. In Israel's Declaration of Independence, Ben Gurion refused to acknowledge the role of the United Nations. He avoided any mention of the UN General Assembly decision on the establishment of the Jewish state in the Declaration of Independence, or of the UN-sponsored partition boundaries. He revealed his stance at an earlier appearance before the Peel Commission when he responded to a statement made by one commissioner that the British Mandate was the bible of Zionism, by countering, "In the name of the Jewish people ... the Bible is our Mandate." This position also kept the possibility of expansion open.[8]

An intriguing chapter in the early crusade to establish the Jewish state was the relationship between the Zionist leadership and Abdullah, the king of TransJordan. This relationship went as far back as the 1920s, and intensified during the critical post Second World War years from 1946 to the king's death in 1951.[9]

Many prominent individuals participated in the talks with Abdullah, including Golda Meir, Ezra Danin, Reuven Shiloah, Moshe Dayan, Elias Sasson, and Walter Eitan. Most expressed respect and admiration for the king, for his honesty and reliability. The king's motives for reaching an agreement with the Jewish leadership appear to have been uncomplicated: he was a Hashemite who had received a negligible portion of territory from the British conquerors at the end of First World War, and he hoped talks with the Jews would serve to expand his own kingdom by annexing the future Palestinian state to TransJordan.[10] He knew that all the parties to the talks, even the British, shared a common enemy in the Palestinian grand mufti.

The king's desire for peace was apparently based on the subsequent annexation of the Palestinian territories and other, more minor demands. Over time, however, pressure by the rest of the Arab world and by the growing number of Palestinians in his own kingdom had an escalating effect. He spoke of the increasing limitations on his ability to maneuver, and admitted this to his Jewish interlocutors.[11] The Jewish participants in the talks nevertheless supposed that an agreement with Abdullah was a realistic possibility.

The position of the Jewish leadership, and particularly of Ben Gurion and Moshe Sharet, was more complex. Ostensibly, and possibly sincerely, they wanted peace with TransJordan. But they understood the price of such a peace agreement, and the majority of the Zionist leadership was unwilling to pay such a price. They feared, as did Ben Gurion, that every piece of land given to the Arabs in the process of negotiating peace would reduce the ability of the Jewish state to absorb Jewish immigrants (*Olim*).

This position was inherently contradictory: on the one hand the desire for peace, and on the other hand the overwhelming desire to expand the boundaries of the new state. Ben Gurion expressed the belief that it would be possible to reach an agreement, initially with the Palestinians and later with Jordan, whereby huge tracts of land belonging to the Palestinian state, Jordan, Egypt, and Syria would become part of the Jewish state. He persistently claimed the Arabs would agree to such a peace deal. But even one of Ben Gurion's biographers questioned the sincerity of this incredible position.[12]

Eventually Ben Gurion must have realized that the Arabs would never accept his ideas about the boundaries of the Jewish state. While he knew that the Jews must adopt a pro-partition stand, he continued to see partition as a temporary proposal, to be corrected over time and probably by force. A peace agreement based on territorial compromise was not in the interests of the new state.

Several peace proposals came up immediately before and more came after the 1948 war, but in July 1949 Ben Gurion gave the following response to a journalist's query: "I am not in a hurry, and I can wait ten years. We are under no pressure whatsoever."[13] Even modest partition plans presented the Zionist leaders with intractable problems. According to the UN partition plan, more than 40 percent of the population of the future Jewish state would be Arabs. Demographic growth would unavoidably lead to an Arab majority in the new Jewish state in a relatively short period of time.[14] The boundaries drawn by the United Nations would have to be extended, but it became equally imperative to the Jewish negotiators that the new state would have the fewest Arab residents possible, if any at all.[15] Ben Gurion repeatedly considered *transfer*, the voluntary or forceful removal of Palestinian residents out of the new state and into the surrounding Arab states, as early as the 1930s.[16]

The fundamental issue underlying Ben Gurion's political platform was *Aliyah*, the ingathering in Israel of all or most of the Jews. Ben Gurion occasionally even expressed the need to deliberately keep the state of war ongoing.[17] Peace was always a matter of *Realpolitik* and not in the interest of the nascent Jewish state. Most of the Zionist leaders, including Moshe Sharet and Chaim Weizman, shared this position.

## CREATION OF THE STATE

On May 15, 1948 the British Mandate over Palestine officially ended. The British army evacuated the region, and on the same day, at a meeting of the Jewish Temporary State Council, Ben Gurion announced the establishment of the State of Israel. Also on that day several regular Arab armies entered the territory that was designated to become two independent states.

To show support for the UN partition resolution (Resolution 181), the Zionists could have simply taken control of all the territories allotted to the Jewish state and if required over time defended it. By so doing they would have taken the high ground both morally and militarily. But peace in accordance with international law, as reflected in the UN decision, was not highest on the agenda for the Zionist leadership. The official Israeli version is that war was imposed on the Jews by a much superior alliance of Arab states. The most common metaphor used was that of David and Goliath, with the Jewish side depicted as David fighting for his life against an Arab Goliath. The Jewish defeat of the Arabs was portrayed as a miracle of biblical proportions.

The New Historians had a different interpretation of events. Avi Shlaim[18] suggested that the initial round of fighting in 1948, from May 15 to the first truce on June 11, was a struggle for survival, but the situation soon changed dramatically. During the truce, in blatant violation of UN resolutions, Israel ignored the weapons embargo and moved significant amounts of military hardware from the Soviet bloc into Israel. This decidedly shifted the balance of power in Israel's favor. Shlaim and other New Historians such as Pappe and Morris agree that in the 1948 war the Haganah, with approximately 35,000 soldiers, had at its disposal more troops than all the Arab forces combined, which had between 20,000 to 25,000.[19] Most historians, old and new, agree that the Jewish troops were much better trained and far more motivated.

The Zionist narrative about the 1948 war contends that the unprovoked Palestinians and their Arab neighbors attacked Israel, with the intention of destroying the day-old state and throwing all Jewish residents into the sea. This contention absolved Israel of any responsibility towards the Arabs, the UN resolutions, and international law. Israel was accordingly free to pursue its goals with no regard to previous resolutions. Along with the belief that Jewish goals and national boundaries were mandated by the Bible, this conviction allowed Israel to do whatever was necessary to bolster its stability and continuity. One necessary measure was to prevent the Palestinians becoming a majority in the Jewish state. Ben Gurion was apparently prepared to go to great lengths to achieve this goal, and was recorded saying, "It would be good if a general conflagration took place."[20] However the only solution ever suggested by

Ben Gurion in this regard was *transfer*. In 1947 prior to the UN decision on partition, he predicted the successful outcome for Israel of a military confrontation between the Jews and the Arabs.[21]

Various plans were made to be used against the Palestinians after the British left. These plans were given alphabetical titles. Plan C was the amalgamation of plans A and B, which were developed in 1946. Plan D, better known as Plan Dalet,[22] called for the removal of the Palestinian population from the entire area coveted by the Zionist leadership. Simha Flapan, the earliest of the New Historians, referred to this plan as "a master plan for ethnic cleansing."[23] There were two critical points in Plan Dalet. One was the destruction of the infrastructure of Palestinian villages and larger population centers such as Haifa, Tiberias, and Safad; the other was the expulsion of the Arab population from the area soon to become included in the designated Jewish state. Plan Dalet was officially adopted on March 10, 1948. However military operations to destroy Arab villages began in December 1947. These were supposedly launched in response to Arab attacks on buses and shops during the protests against the UN partition decision. Although the pre-Plan Dalet Jewish operations were somewhat disorganized, they were sufficiently severe to result in the departure of around 75,000 people.[24]

A long time after this, in the winter of 2005, at a conference of the Israeli Society of Military History held at Kfar Ha'makabia near Tel Aviv, the topic was the Nachshon operation to clear the road to Jerusalem. Alon Kadosh, a historian, explained how the Palmach typically operated:

> They advance on a village and when they reach its outskirts, they blow up one or two houses. Usually the Arabs get the message and evacuate the village. If they don't, the Palmach advances a little further and blows up a few more houses, preferably with some people in them. After that there is no question that the Arabs get the message and leave in a hurry.[25]

Following the adoption of Plan Dalet, military activities intensified. The main targets were Palestinian urban centers, all of which were successfully occupied by the Jewish forces by the end of April 1948. Approximately 250,000 Palestinians were displaced during this phase of Jewish military operations.[26] This was no war of a Jewish David desperately defending itself against an Arab Goliath. Over half of the Palestinian refugees were created prior to the onset of the 1948 war. Much of the territory that became the State of Israel following the armistice agreements was already in Jewish hands and cleared from its Arab residents before the war.[27] These facts contradict the official argument that Israel's intention prior to May 15, 1948 was to abide by the partition resolution and achieve peace and coexistence with the Arabs.

In February 1948 the US administration proposed alternatives to avoid the escalation of belligerence, which the UN partition resolution might well have promoted. The initial suggestion was to postpone the partition and install a trusteeship for a period of five years. On May 12, 1948, just three days prior to the onset of the 1948 war and the official establishment of the State of Israel, they proposed a cease-fire of three months. The Jewish leadership rejected both proposals.[28]

The war that broke out on May 15, 1948 between Israel and Egypt, Syria, Jordan, Lebanon, and Iraq precipitated the process that led to the expulsion of almost half the Arab population of Mandatory Palestine. The pretense of adherence to Resolution 181 was then also abandoned. This war accelerated the implementation of Plan Dalet, the acquisition of as much of Mandatory Palestine as possible with the fewest possible Arab residents. At the official end of the war a series of armistice agreements were signed on the island of Rhodes, and Israel found itself in possession of 78 percent of Mandatory Palestine and a Palestinian population of a mere 175,000, a significant decrease from more than one million who resided in these areas prior to the war.

## INITIAL SECRET CONTACTS

While the war was in progress, secret negotiations were taking place, initiated by King Farouk of Egypt, with the intention of working out a peace agreement. The king's message to the Israelis was that Egypt would be willing to sign a peace treaty in return for territorial concessions in the Negev. The negotiations with Egypt began around the end of September, during the second truce. Kamal Riad, a Farouk court official, met with Elias Sasson of Israel to determine Israel's readiness for a peace treaty. Sasson penned a draft treaty, which was submitted to the Egyptians. But while these negotiations were happening, Ben Gurion actively supported a cabinet decision to renew military activities in what became the Yoav operation, the resumption of fighting after the truce.

Some time later, Ben Gurion sent Sharet, who oversaw the negotiations, a telegram in which he said, "Israel will not discuss peace involving the concession of any territory. The neighboring states do not deserve an inch of Israel's land .... We are ready for peace in exchange for peace."[29] One interpretation of this utterance is that Israel would be interested in peace only if its neighbors accepted all its acquisitions of land and population changes beyond any UN resolution or any other international mandate.

In November the Egyptians renewed their peace initiatives, which were based on the retention of the Gaza Strip and some territory in the Negev. Ben Gurion, supported by a majority of ministers, rejected the Egyptian proposal. Soon after, between December 1948 and January 1949, Israel embarked on Operation Horev, the last military operation of the 1948 war. It ended with the retreat of the Egyptian army from all of Palestine except the Gaza Strip.[30]

During the latter part of 1948 the first UN mediator, the Swedish Count Folke Bernadotte, became actively involved. He was appointed as mediator in Palestine on May 20, 1948, only a few days after the official war began. He achieved an open-ended second truce within ten days of the end of the first. On June 28 Bernadotte submitted his first peace proposal, suggesting that Palestine and TransJordan form a union with the following boundaries:

> most of the Negev would be Arab territory; most of western Galilee would be Jewish territory; Jerusalem would be Arab territory with municipal autonomy for the Jewish community and guaranteed protection for the holy places; Haifa would be a free port, and Lydda a free airport.

Despite the lack of enthusiasm for Bernadotte's first proposal, he proposed yet another, which essentially abandoned the concept of a union. On September 16, 1948 he suggested that the boundaries of the two states be renegotiated by the parties themselves or by the United Nations, and these new negotiated boundaries should take precedence over the November 29, 1947 partition. He specifically enjoined the right of innocent people uprooted from their homes to return, and recommended that the second truce be replaced by a formal peace. Many details of the first proposal were also included in the second.

The government of Israel was not enthusiastic. Ben Gurion was preoccupied with a political campaign following Israel's accomplishments in its Ten Day Operation, or the first ten days of fighting after the second truce collapsed. He was particularly concerned that Count Bernadotte's peace proposals would serve as the background of the second truce. His main concern was that the truce and Bernadotte's proposals would stall the advancement of Israeli forces and prevent further conquests.[31]

Count Bernadotte was assassinated on September 17, 1948 by members of the Jewish militant group the Stern Gang (*Lehi*), an event which led to the disarmament of the Gang. Several of their members were arrested but no one was charged and none served any sentence. Although forced to condemn this murder, the government of Israel was not overly grieved over the disappearance of this man who was determined to bring peace.

Nor did his death bring an end to subsequent peace initiatives, all of which failed. On March 30, 1949 Colonel Husni al-Za'im, the Syrian army's chief of staff, took control of his country in a bloodless coup. Although he only lasted five months in this capacity, he proposed a serious peace agreement with Israel. In mid-April al-Za'im asked for a direct meeting with Ben Gurion, which Ben Gurion refused, just as he had previously refused to meet with King Abdullah of Jordan. Al-Za'im was executed shortly afterwards. His proposal had been to skip the armistice stage and to go directly for a peace deal with Israel.[32] He suggested that Syria absorb between 250,000 and 500,000 Palestinian refugees. Ben Gurion refused to make any concessions, demanding that Syria first recognize the existing frontier and sign an armistice agreement. Peace could come later. Apparently Ben Gurion made most decisions alone, and the rest of the leadership seems to have known nothing about al Za'im's proposal. The Israeli public knew even less.[33]

In a prophetic cable, James Keeley, the US ambassador to Damascus, wrote:

> Unless Israel can be brought to understand that it cannot have all of its cake (partition boundaries) and gravy as well (area captured in violation of truce, Jerusalem and resettlement of Arab refugees elsewhere) it may find that it has won Palestine war but lost peace. It should be evident that Israel's continued insistence upon her pound of flesh and more is driving Arab states slowly (and perhaps surely) to gird their loins (politically and economically if not yet militarily) for a long-range struggle.[34]

The agreement between Israel and Syria, the last armistice agreement to date between Israel and an Arab state, was signed on July 20, 1949. But there were many other peace proposals made during and after the 1948 war. Dr. Ralph Bunche, previously Count Bernadotte's chief aide and later his replacement as chief UN mediator, led the negotiations, which mostly took place on the island of Rhodes. The armistice agreements previously signed were between Egypt and Israel on February 24, between Lebanon and Israel on March 23, and between Jordan and Israel on April 3. Ben Gurion insisted that these agreements were restricted to ending the hostilities, and despite some opposition from Israel's military leaders he was prepared to abide by them.[35]

Disputes over the interpretation of the agreements quickly followed. The United Nations assigned the resolution of the differences and the creation of formal peace treaties to the Palestine Conciliation Commission (PCC). It invited both Israel and the Arabs to a conference in Lausanne, which began in April and, with several interruptions, extended to September 1949. Israel and probably Jordan were reluctant participants since their main focus at that time was on the results of the war and the division of Palestine. Under pressure from the PCC, Israel reluctantly agreed to take back 100,000 Palestinian refugees. The real additional number was 70,000 since Israel had already agreed to accept 30,000 refugees. Ben Gurion was strongly opposed to the considerable number of returnees, while the Arabs and the Americans wanted a much bigger number. Ben Gurion's intransigence inevitably led to the failure of the Lausanne conference.[36] Following this failure the pace of peace negotiations slowed, although negotiations between Israel and Jordan continued.

These talks got under way in November 1949, and could have served two purposes for Israel. One was the possibility of achieving a deal with Jordan, but even more important was the hope that such a deal might lead to further deals with Lebanon or Egypt, strictly on Israel's terms. Actually the talks had no possibility of success. Ben Gurion's left-wing coalition partners were suspicious of the talks, since they considered King Abdullah a puppet or a servant of the British government. The right-wing parties objected to the talks because they would probably require land concessions on Israel's part. Ben Gurion shared both the left's suspicions and the right's objections to giving up any part of the whole of Mandatory Palestine.[37] Whatever breakthroughs occurred in the talks, they were invariably followed by setbacks. One main sticking point appeared to be the Jordanian demand for a land corridor to the sea.

The second phase of the talks with Jordan began in mid-January 1950 and resulted in the initialing of a non-aggression pact signed on February 24. This pact was the brainchild of the king, and was accepted by the Israeli cabinet as a basis for further negotiations. The king saw it as a turning point in the negotiations, but just four days later another setback occurred.[38] Growing opposition from the king's own government was progressively limiting his ability to maneuver. A suspension of the talks produced a deadlock, which in turn led to increased military activities or aggressive retaliatory attacks by Israel in response to Palestinian incursions. There was a growing dissatisfaction with the status quo, and increasingly Moshe Dayan and others spoke of the possibility of a conquest of the entire area west of the Jordan River. The main opponent to these ideas was Moshe Sharet, who refused to consider that the loss of a single Israeli soldier was acceptable to feed the appetite for expansion.[39]

In April 1950 Jordan annexed the West Bank. At the suggestion of the king, the talks resumed in December and centered mostly on the implementation of Article 8 of the armistice agreement, which related to Israel's access to Jewish institutions that were now under Jordanian control. Ben Gurion expressed his growing doubts about the desirability of a settlement with Jordan. In a conversation with Reuven Shiloah he listed many reasons for his doubts. One of these was, "Do we have an interest in committing ourselves to such ridiculous borders?"[40]

Ben Gurion's reluctance to achieve a political settlement with Jordan was the deciding factor in the failure of these talks, although they continued right up to Abdullah's assassination. The king's determination to reach agreement was sufficiently strong that he offered to go to Jerusalem to meet Israel's prime minister in person. His offer received no more than a stony silence. Although the king needed a major offer in order to overcome resistance to any deal with Israel in his own country, Ben Gurion was willing to make no more than minor concessions.[41] On Friday July 20, 1951 a Muslim extremist assassinated King Abdullah outside the al-Aksa Mosque. Ben Gurion considered this an opportunity to gain control over the entire area of Mandatory Palestine.

The assassination of the King marked the end of active negotiations between Israel and Jordan for some time. Ben Gurion's desire for territorial expansion was enhanced, as were his doubts about the desirability of any deal with the Arab world.

# 3

# EARLY INITIATIVES

After the assassination of King Abdullah, the outcome of the 1948 war and the armistice agreements signed in 1949 were the primary determinants of the ongoing conflict.

Foremost among the consequential issues was the creation of the Palestinian refugee problem. The various armistice agreements created a new geopolitical reality on the ground by recognizing Israel's control of 78 percent of the territory of Mandatory Palestine. Over 700,000 former residents of areas now included in the State of Israel lived along the armistice boundaries – the Green Line – within clear sight of intensive Jewish resettlement activity occurring in what had a short time previously been their land.

This situation unavoidably resulted in a continuous state of instability and recurring incidents of violence along those boundaries. Conflagrations occurred in different locations along the border when refugees would cross into what was now Israel to harvest their own fields, which they had planted prior to the war. Or they would steal Jewish crops now growing in what they regarded as their fields or livestock now adopted by Jewish residents. Some refugees tried to cultivate the land where Jewish settlements did not yet exist. Sometimes the forays were undertaken simply to visit family members who remained behind. Although Israel's contention was that the violence was planned and initiated by hostile Arab governments, most of the violence was triggered by individual Arab border crossings, which on some occasions could have been motivated by basic revenge. The infiltrators were initially referred to by Israel as *mehablim* (which means saboteurs). On the Palestinian side the term *fedayun* (or suicide troops) was gradually adopted, and it was then increasingly also used by the Israelis.

The early 1950s saw a significant number of casualties on both sides, but the number of deaths on the Arab side far exceeded those suffered by the Jews.[1] Censorship laws prevalent in Israel during that period kept the residents of Israel unaware of the real nature and motivation of the *fedayun* activities. The majority of the Jewish citizens were convinced that they were subjected to deliberate, planned attacks by Arab government forces. The official and the only Israeli position available in newspapers and on radio was that these infiltrators were funded, equipped, trained, and directed by the Egyptian government. According to the official sources their purpose was to create panic on the Israeli side.[2]

Between 1951, when the king was assassinated, and 1954 the most relentless tension along the border occurred between Israel and Jordan. The large number of Palestinian refugees along the border compounded Jordan's internal political instability. But there were also conflicts with Egypt, which heated up in 1955, and Syria.[3] Against the background of instability and violence, there were many peace initiatives which predominantly came from the Arab side of the conflict. Earlier peace negotiations held between the Jordanian king and a cast of official Jewish representatives were followed by the scuttled Syrian proposal of Husni al-Za'im. Between 1951 and up to the Sinai war in 1956, the Egyptians were the primary instigators of peace initiatives.

The Egyptian peace initiatives should be considered on the background of Israel's response to *fedayun* activities. As expressed by Ben Gurion a few years later,[4] the official Israeli version was that Israel always acted strictly in self-defense: Israel was committed to keeping the armistice agreements to the letter, but if the other side did not abide by the agreement, Israel felt free to act as it saw fit.

Israel's strategy was defined as retaliation, and most commonly enacted by a company-sized force or larger, with artillery going into action across the border. Sometimes the air force joined on a bombing mission. If, as Israel contended, Arab governments launched the *fedayun* activity, Israel was merely responding to these provocations and was retaliating appropriately to violations of its sovereignty.[5] Israel, accordingly, had the right to cross the various Arab borders. The retaliations reached a peak in 1955 but continued sporadically to 1960. Evidence suggests that retaliation was often motivated by a geopolitical and territorial agenda and was not a simply defensive response to Arab cross-border raids. At times retaliation was used to sabotage or put an end to peace opportunities.[6]

The first retaliation operation was taken against Syria on April 5, 1951 after an Israeli military patrol disguised as civilian police was sent into el Hamma, which was an uncontested Syrian location. The Syrians reacted violently to this provocation and as a result seven Israeli soldiers were killed.[7] Israel then bombed Syrian army installations in the Demilitarized Zone (DMZ). Officially the reason for the operation was the killing of the seven Israelis. But even members of the Knesset Committee for Defense and Foreign Affairs severely criticized the Israeli air bombardment, as did most western powers including the United States. The armistice agreement between Syria and Israel recognized a DMZ along the boundary between the two countries, which Israel wanted to control.[8] However the area included very few Israeli settlements and a large number of Arab farmers cultivated it. The DMZ was also the focus of a struggle between Syria and Israel over control of water resources. Israel provoked confrontations with Syrian farmers in the hope that they would leave the zone. When the Syrians initiated the shooting, it was often triggered by Israeli provocations.[9]

In November 1951 Adib Shishakly, the deputy chief of staff of the Syrian army, seized power in Syria. Shishakly was apparently interested in reaching an agreement with Israel, and attempted to resolve the DMZ problem by a formal division of this territory. Moshe Dayan represented Israel in a meeting on October 1952 when the Syrians proposed a division of the DMZ. Israel did not reject the proposal but wanted to abandon the armistice agreement, whereas the Syrians were only willing to amend the existing agreement.[10] Moshe Sharet found the Syrian position reasonable and the Israeli position rigid and legalistic. Although Ben Gurion did not entirely agree with Sharet, the meetings were no longer continued in the presence of UN observers, who had always been in attendance since the Armistice agreements..

In a meeting on April 13, 1953 the Syrians proposed giving Israel 70 percent of the area comprising the DMZ. This generosity of the Syrian offer made an agreement seem imminent. But Moshe Dayan consulted with Israel's water expert Simha Blass, who advised Dayan not to accept the offer because "it did not suit Israel's irrigation and water development plans."[11] Blass's views on the issue were discussed in cabinet, which concluded that the negotiations should continue with the intention of accommodating his demands. The cabinet decision, despite its endorsement of continuation, marked the end of the negotiations between Israel and Syria over the future of the DMZ.[12] The tension between the two countries over the DMZ remained an ongoing irritant despite the fact that there was some willingness on the Syrian side for further talks.

## YOUNG OFFICERS' REVOLUTION IN EGYPT

Another peace initiative occurred after King Farouk of Egypt was overthrown by a military coup of the Free Officers Movement. In 1948 King Farouk had sent the Egyptian army into Palestine, and Gamal Abdel Nasser served in the 6th Infantry Battalion as deputy commander of the Egyptian forces in Falluja, which was quickly surrounded by Israeli forces. Yerucham Cohen, a young Yemenite Jew, served as adjutant to Israel's commander, General Yigal Alon. The Egyptian and Israeli deputies met to secure a ceasefire to bury the bodies left on the battlefield, and a surprising friendship was struck in the Falluja pocket, not far from Gaza. In one of their coordination meetings Nasser expressed the fear that the Egyptians would never get out of Falluja alive. Cohen allegedly assured Nasser that he would survive the siege and go on to have his own children.

After the 1948 war Yerucham Cohen was appointed as a representative to the armistice negotiations. On one occasion an Egyptian delegate brought him a message from Lieutenant-Colonel Nasser. Nasser's daughter had just been born and he remembered Cohen's reassuring words in Falluja. Cohen sent baby clothes to Nasser's daughter, and Nasser later reciprocated with a gift of chocolates, from the famous Groppi Coffee House in Cairo.

Late in 1952 or early in 1953, while General Muhammad Naguib was still the official ruler of Egypt, Cohen met with Uri Avnery, the dean of the Israeli peace camp and publisher of the political weekly *Ha'olam Ha'zeh*. Cohen expressed the view that the real power in Egypt was in the hands of his friend Gamal Abdel Nasser. Avnery published this, and a couple of months later so did *Time Magazine*.

Cohen told Avnery another story, which he published. When Nasser deposed Naguib and took over control of Egypt he sent Cohen an invitation to visit him in Cairo. Despite Avnery's advice to grab the opportunity, Cohen as a law-abiding citizen sought approval from the Israeli Foreign Ministry, which forbade him to go. The official Israeli argument was that the Egyptians should employ proper channels, if they wanted to talk. The Israeli Foreign Ministry refused to encourage non-official contacts. Although it initiated no peace-related dialogue of its own, it disrupted initiatives that came from the other side. Two years later Nasser again invited Cohen to meet in Senegal or some other African country that was not Egypt. Cohen sought approval from the Foreign Ministry, which again forbade him to go. Yerucham Cohen and Gamal Abdel Nasser never met again.[13]

According to Avnery's analysis, Nasser wanted to explore peace options after assuming power, and considered Yerucham Cohen a suitable contact to work with. Avnery suspected that Nasser did not have a clear agenda but was interested in all options. The Foreign Ministry's rigidity put an end to this episode. Interestingly, Cohen himself never included this incident in his own book.[14] Nasser continued to pursue contacts for unofficial discussions about peace until the 1967 war, and many of these initiatives were reported and published by Uri Avnery in *Ha'olam Hazeh*.[15]

But these were not the first attempts made to end the conflict. A short while after the Free Officers Movement took power in Egypt in July 1952, Shmuel Divon, the first secretary at the Israeli embassy in Paris, approached the top man in the Egyptian embassy, Ali Shawqi, with a proposal from the Israeli government. The Israelis wanted secret talks to explore the possibility of peace between the two countries. The Egyptian response was ambiguous: Egyptian diplomats conveyed goodwill but simultaneously Egypt sharpened its verbal attacks on Israel in the United Nations. At a meeting attended by a number of senior officials in his office, Ben Gurion was doubtful about the possibility of contact with Egypt. He stated that Israel's desire for peace with Egypt had limits. He conceded that it was one of Israel's interests, but certainly not the most important. He considered the relationship between Israel and American Jewry as more pressing for Israel than peace with the Arabs.[16]

Nevertheless, in October 1952, Divon made contact with Abdel Rahman Sadeq, the Egyptian press attaché in Paris, newly appointed by the Revolutionary Command Council (RCC). The content of these meetings was channeled directly to the RCC. Sadeq reported directly to Nasser, who was now in charge of contacts with Israel at the RCC. Nasser instructed Sadeq to request Israeli support in obtaining US economic aid for Egypt's efforts to gain control of the Suez Canal from the United Kingdom.[17] Nasser insisted that these contacts between Israel and Egypt remain secret.

Shmuel Divon, assigned the job of communicating with the Egyptians, presented Israel's reply to Sadeq. The Israelis essentially welcomed the establishment of contacts but demanded that Egypt abide by the armistice agreement and accept the clause allowing Israeli passage through the Gulf of Aqaba and the Canal. Israel would support Egypt's desire to remove the British from the Canal Zone on condition that Egypt improve relations between the two countries.

In a meeting on May 13, 1953, Sadeq showed Divon a letter signed by Nasser, which proposed maintaining a low profile for the contacts with Israel and the elimination of aggressive vocabulary on Egypt's part as the primary step. Nasser clarified that Egypt had no belligerent intentions towards Israel, and encouraged Israel to use its influence with the United States towards the removal of British forces from the Canal Zone. Nasser considered this a significant step towards a peace settlement with Israel, and believed it would lead to a re-examination of Israel's rights of free navigation in the canal. Israel and Egypt were guided by their own agenda for the continuation of talks between them. Egypt's position, as articulated by Nasser, was to significantly reduce the level of belligerence between the two countries and to employ Israel's influence in the United States to bring about the departure of the British. Israel seemed primarily interested in obtaining navigation rights in the Red Sea and the Suez Canal, which had hitherto been closed to its shipping. Israel was also interested in having a relationship with Egypt apart from the rest of the more belligerent Arab world.[18]

Nasser's letter, shown to Divon on May 13, was the first time Egypt clearly articulated the intention of improving its relationship with Israel, moving to a final settlement and peace between the two countries. Ben Gurion perceived Nasser's proposals as disadvantageous for Israel, and wanted Sharet, the foreign minister, to inform the Egyptians that Israel insisted on guarantees of free navigation or it would provide no assistance with the United States.

Sharet's response to Nasser may not have been as harsh as Ben Gurion would have wished, but it made very few concessions. Sharet may have determined that it was expedient to exploit Egypt's circumstance to determine whether Egypt was serious about moving towards a final settlement.[19]

By the end of 1953 hope of progress from the Divon–Sadeq talks in Paris had died completely. Nasser had on several occasions stated that Egypt had no belligerent intentions towards Israel, but in Israel he was consistently portrayed as an enemy of the State of Israel whose primary goal was the destruction of the Jewish state. This duality was consistent: despite Israel's implied support for Egypt's desire to gain control of the canal, and its vague offer to help Egypt achieve this, in 1953 Israel was already secretly exploring the possibility of a joint operation with Britain and France to take over the Sinai desert, thereby helping Britain and France regain control of the Canal Zone.[20]

## CROSS-BORDER HOSTILITIES INTENSIFY

Cross-border activities continued throughout 1953 in the DMZ between Syria and Israel, and across the Israeli borders with Jordan and Egypt. On August 28 Israel carried out a major retaliation operation in the Palestinian refugee camp El Boreij, in the Gaza Strip. Nineteen Palestinian refugees, among them seven women and four children, were killed. Eighteen others were wounded. The IDF spokesman denied the Egyptian claim that the casualties were the result of an Israeli military operation. However, the Joint Egyptian–Israeli Armistice Committee heard the claims of both sides and condemned Israel for a violation of the armistice agreement. The Israeli public was not told of the operation. But on September 2, the *Ha'aretz* newspaper published an editorial about the deliberate silence of the Israeli authorities, claiming that the Israelis could only learn about the operation by listening to Arab media sources. *Ha'aretz* concluded that this operation was retaliation for the murder of five Israelis who had crossed the border with Jordan, and were spotted and killed by the Jordanian Legion. This Israeli newspaper forewarned that the world would not side with Israel when it understood that unarmed Palestinians, among them women and children, were killed in the Israeli operation. Although both sides were guilty of bloody violence, the disproportionate Israeli response would merely raise the level of anger and desire for revenge across the borders, and would do nothing to reduce the tension and violence there.[21] Israel chose to retaliate in Gaza, an area under Egyptian control, although the Jordanian Legion in Jordan had allegedly committed the provocation. This raises doubt about the actual motive for retaliation.

On October 14, just six weeks after the El-Boreij incident, Israel attacked the village of Kibya, which is located across the border in Jordan. About 50 people were killed and many others were injured. Dozens of houses were destroyed. The declared reason for this bloodbath was the killing of a woman and her two children in the village of Yehud.

On October 19, Ben Gurion justified the operation in a radio broadcast by blaming the Jordanian government. He claimed that despite Israel's best efforts, the Jordanian forces continued their murderous raids into Israel. In self-defense, he stated, Israeli border residents had attacked the village of Kibya, which was a main hub for the marauding gangs. On behalf of the government, the prime minister regretted any loss of life but insisted that the Jordanian government was responsible. He vehemently rejected any suggestion that the operation was actually carried out by a military unit of 600 soldiers, and concluded his speech by saying, "We carried out a thorough investigation and it is absolutely clear that not one military unit was absent from its barracks during the night of the attack on Kibya."

Seventeen years later, however, this was contradicted in an official publication of the Israeli Public Relations Authority:

> In a series of retaliatory operations – in the North (the Kineret Operation), on the Jordanian border (Kibya & Hossan) and on the Egyptian border (Gaza, Han Euniss & Kountilla) the IDF hit centers from which the Fedayun were sent or Israel was fired upon.[22]

The Kibya operation was carried out by Commando Unit 101, and led by a young and ambitious Paratroop major, Ariel Sharon.[23]

A week after the Kibya attack, on October 21, the French newspaper *Le Monde* contended that the operation in Kibya was designed to prevent a shift in the balance of power in the Middle East and to change the US attitude towards Israel.[24] If this analysis was correct, the El Boreij and Kibya operations failed. The frequency of cross-border raids from Egypt and Jordan did not diminish at all, and the relationship between Israel and the United States significantly worsened. The Security Council condemned Israel harshly, and other western powers rejected Ben Gurion's version of events.[25] Although there is no direct evidence to prove there was any deliberate attempt to sabotage Arab attempts to settle the conflict, Ben Gurion and many of his cabinet colleagues showed no regret for the impact these operations had on the prospects for peace.

### BEN GURION RESIGNS

A month later, on December 7, Ben Gurion resigned all his ministerial duties and retired to his retreat in Sdeh Boker. Moshe Sharet replaced him as Israel's second prime minister. Before Ben Gurion's departure he made a number of significant government appointments: Pinhas Lavon was confirmed as minister of defense, Shimon Peres was appointed director general of the Ministry of Defense, and Moshe Dayan was appointed chief of Israeli Defense Force (IDF) staff. The appointment of this hawkish trio made any progress towards peace unlikely.

In March 1954 Israel was shaken by an attack on an Israeli bus in Ma'aleh Akrabim, in which twelve passengers were killed. The identity of the perpetrators was not known, but after twelve days the IDF attacked the Jordanian village Na'hlin and killed ten people. Nine days later the village of Hossan was attacked, causing more casualties.[26]

During this turbulent period there was a division in the Israeli leadership about the approach towards the Arabs. The two leaders representing the factions across the divide were Ben Gurion and Moshe Sharet. Both had been prime ministers prior to the 1956 Sinai war, but they differed in their attitudes to negotiation. Ben Gurion could be described as a messianic hawk who distrusted the Arabs. He expressed the conviction that Arab hatred of Jews is undeviating. Sharet was a moderate who favored negotiation, spoke Arabic, and respected the culture. Nevertheless both refused to consider the return of Palestinian refugees to their homes, and were equally determined to hold on to lands that legally belonged to the Palestinians. Apparently the only change in the status quo that they would consider was the expansion of Israel's boundaries at the expense of its neighbors. For both, concessions towards the Arabs were considered too high a price to pay for peace.

Pinhas Lavon replaced Ben Gurion as defense minister following his resignation, and this essentially amounted to the planting of a time bomb under Sharet's premiership.[27] Golda Meir described Lavon as one of the most capable if least stable member of Mapai (Israel's Workers' Party – later Labor), and he was a curious appointment. He had been considered a doveish moderate, but his involvement in defense issues promptly transformed him into an uncompromising hawk. Most considered Lavon an unsuitable candidate for the Defense Ministry, and people tried to no avail to convince Ben Gurion of their concern.[28]

The goal that quickly became apparent, shared by Lavon and Dayan, was to expand the boundaries of Israel by force and in every possible direction. Lavon openly declared that he considered the status quo bad for Israel, and that any peace settlement was bound to be disadvantageous to Israel. He believed that Israel's best strategy was a state of neither peace nor war. This would be the best starting point for achieving future territorial goals. Therefore Israel should prevent a peaceful settlement of the Arab–Israeli conflict, object to any suggestions of concessions, and react with military force to any hostile act.[29]

In a meeting of Mapai's Central Committee in April 1954, Lavon said, I want war and I wish there were no Americans or British since without them we could achieve our war goals.[30]

As the new IDF chief of staff, Dayan was well matched with Lavon. A political army chief, he was totally loyal to Ben Gurion, and with his colleague Shimon Peres he regularly traveled to Sdeh Boker to consult with the *Old Man*. Dayan shared Lavon's position that Israel's survival depends on deterrence and power; that the only way was the way of the sword. Both men were committed to expanding Israel's control over the entire area west of the Jordan River to complete what had not been achieved during the 1948 war. A military man, Dayan considered the use of force as a positive contribution to Israel's deterrence power .[31] Dayan and Lavon became the key promoters of a policy of relentless retaliation, using force often against civilians. He positioned himself as the advocate of collective punishment for any Arab village suspected of aiding infiltrators or *fedayun*.[32]

Prime Minister Moshe Sharet was a moderate, cautious man, and his year at the helm was challenging. The policies of the Ministry of Defense, supported by the retired Ben Gurion, in 1954 prevented any peace effort. Grave concerns in Israel were raised by the agreement of the British to withdraw from the Suez Canal. The relationship with the United States was worsening as the United States increasingly focused on strengthening its pro-western alliance with Egypt and Iraq. Along the borders infiltrations and incidents of sabotage increased, which the UN supervisory organization was not able to stop. Complicating matters was Lavon's rejection of Sharet's authority over defense issues. Lavon did not report to his prime minister on matters related to defense policy and military operations, and basically ignored the entire cabinet. He made no attempt to gain their confidence or approval.[33]

On January 31, 1954, Lavon organized a convention of Mapai ministers with Dayan, the new chief of staff. According to Sharet's diary, Dayan discussed various plans for direct action at this meeting. One was to send an Israeli ship to defy the blockade in the Gulf of Aqaba and thereby provoke the Egyptians to use force to prevent its advancement. Dayan wanted to use the provoked Egyptian response as the basis of an air attack and the conquest of Ras el Naqb, deep in Egyptian territory. Another proposal was to force open the coast road south of Gaza. An incredulous Sharet wondered whether he was aware these tactics would lead to war with Egypt, and Dayan clearly admitted that he was. The list of plans included actions against Syria. Backed by the other cabinet members, Sharet rejected these proposals outright. Nevertheless, he worried about his new chief of staff working in cooperation with Lavon, the defense minister.[34]

In the spring of that year General Naguib of Egypt was replaced by Nasser, and Adib Shishakly of Syria was overthrown in a military coup. Ben Gurion was invited to a meeting at which Lavon proposed both an operation to separate the Gaza Strip from Egypt and an invasion of the DMZ between Israel and Syria. Whereas Sharet openly opposed these plans, Ben Gurion unfolded his scheme to attack Lebanon and establish a Christian-Maronite state in the north that would serve the interests of Israel. When Sharet vigorously objected to this too, Ben Gurion accused him of cowardice.[35]

The split in the Israeli leadership was between Ben Gurion, Dayan, and Lavon on the one hand, and the more moderate Sharet, who was supported by the cabinet. The military leaders were becoming increasingly determined to fight their Arab neighbors, who were obtaining weapons from the west. They wanted to confront the Arabs before they become any stronger, although at this time no Arab state was overtly preparing for a war, or apparently interested in pursuing one. On May 12 at a political committee meeting, Sharet argued that saying Israel wanted peace was not enough. The government and the IDF had to act accordingly. Even if Israel were to conquer the entire area west of the Jordan River, Sharet argued that it was unlikely the large Arab population of these newly conquered areas would leave, and he did not relish the annexation of the rest of Mandatory Palestine and its millions of residents.[36]

Sharet's restraining influence, along with the deployment of forces by the Jordanian Legion, effected a temporary lull in retaliatory operations. Instead of overall confrontation, the military leaders resorted to a strategy of small cross-border incursions attacking Jordanian army positions. They explained these to the cabinet as responses to Arab incursions into Israel. In an interview with the pro-Israeli British journalist John Kimche, Dayan admitted this. When the journalist relayed this information to Sharet, he claimed that UN reports were more accurate than those produced by the Israelis. In a July meeting of the IDF general staff, Lavon declared that during his tenure as minister of defense the IDF had carried out more than 40 military operations, which had included the laying of mines, the destruction of houses, and assassinations.[37]

While Sharet was working on plans for practical cooperation with Israel's neighbors,[38] the military continued their aggressive engagement policies. Dayan reported these activities to Ben Gurion, who reportedly asked, "What do you want? War?" Dayan explained that although he did not actually wish to initiate a war with the neighbors, he was not opposed to having a war. His view was that Israel must persist with its plans: the diversion of the Jordan River and the opening of the Straits of Aqaba. If the Syrians or the Egyptians were to resist, Israel would have to respond.[39]

## ESEK HABISH – THE MISHAP

Against the background of this growing tension between Dayan and Sharet, a calamitous event began to develop in July. This event was named *esek habish*, which translates into the mishap. The mishap was defined by power struggles, disagreements over security jurisdictions, bitter personal animosities, and intrigue.

The Israelis were concerned that the agreement between the Egyptians and the British over the withdrawal of British forces from the Suez Canal could present a problem by removing the British barrier between Egypt and Israel. Israel's military wanted to derail the agreement, while some in the Foreign Ministry believed that by liberating his country from foreign forces, Nasser would resume his exploration of a settlement with Israel. While the diplomats encouraged the reopening of a dialogue, the military was designing plans to nullify the agreement. A unit of Israeli military intelligence activated a Jewish espionage ring to carry out a series of clandestine operations in Egypt. On one occasion an explosive device intended for a movie theater showing British and American movies activated prematurely and its carrier was caught. His detention led to the capture of the rest of the members of the group. They were all tried, two committed suicide, and two were subsequently executed. The rest were sentenced to lengthy jail terms.

There were investigations in Israel about who was responsible for this disaster. These led to forged documents and perjured testimony, as everyone involved tried to implicate others, and there was even the suspicion of betrayal by an Israeli agent.[40]

At the time, censorship prevented the incident from being reported in Israel. Israelis knew that something bad had happened, but they did not know much else. What was given a great deal of public attention was a debate about who gave the order to carry out this operation. Lavon was accused, but he maintained that the operation had been directed by military officers in an attempt to discredit him personally. Neither Lavon nor the army officers involved demonstrated any regret about the botched operation. Their stated concern continued to be preparation for further war. Lavon suggested that Israel cancel the armistice agreement with Egypt and conquer the Gaza Strip. The officers produced other suggestions intended to provoke a war with Egypt.[41]

In September Israel sent a small ship flying the Israeli flag, the *Bat Galim*, to traverse the Suez Canal on its way to Haifa. The Egyptians were not likely to permit the ship's passage, and it was indeed stopped at the southern entrance to the canal. The purpose of this undertaking was to attract international public attention, to pressure the British to reconsider the Anglo–Egyptian agreement. Another purpose was to recruit the influence of the United States and the other western powers on Egypt to open the Straits of Tiran to Israeli navigation. The British–Egyptian agreement nevertheless was signed and the United States, encouraged by its progress in developing a pro-Western alliance in the Middle East, refused to get drawn into Israel's game plan.[42]

On September 27, soon after the *Bat Galim* attempt, a flock of Israeli sheep strayed onto the Jordanian side of the armistice boundary. Israel claimed they had been stolen in Israel and taken to Jordan. Jordan insisted that the sheep had just strayed into Jordan. Dayan wanted to use force, claiming that failure to do so would be interpreted as weakness on Israel's part. Sharet insisted that UN observers be brought in to resolve the issue peacefully.[43] Twelve days later and with great effort by the UN team, the flock was returned and handed back to its owners. The UN team nicknamed this affair Operation Bo-Peep as not one shot was fired. The result could have been very different if resolution had been left in the hands of the military.[44]

There were many other opportunities for demonstrations of force. On December 8 five Israeli soldiers captured inside Syrian territory admitted that their mission had been to retrieve a telephone-bugging device previously planted by another Israeli squad. Israel, however, claimed that the soldiers were kidnapped inside Israeli territory. The United Nations investigated and confirmed Syria's position. Israel then forced a Syrian civilian airplane to land in Israel. Defense Minister Lavon intended to use the plane and its passengers as bargaining chips in the negotiations to free the Israeli soldiers. An international outcry forced Israel to release the airliner within 48 hours. Unfortunately one of the Israeli soldiers captured committed suicide while in Syrian captivity, and Israel immediately accused the Syrians of barbarity, kidnapping, and torture.[45]

Angered by this incident, Sharet issued a very sharp rebuke

accusing both the military leadership and Lavon of stupidity and shortsightedness. With hawkish pressure for a non-confidence motion against Sharet mounting, he responded by publicly revealing some of the truth about the capture of the soldiers and the forced landing of the Syrian civilian airliner. But on January 18, 1955, infiltrators from Jordan killed two Israeli tractor drivers. Sharet realized that now he would have to accede to the demand for retaliation, which was aggravated by tension inside Israel and an uninformed desire for revenge. There was a great deal of confusion in Israel about the real responsibility for the series of catastrophic events: the *esek habish*, the sheep incident, the capture in Syria, and the suicide of one soldier.[46]

Nasser was still apparently willing to resume a dialogue with Israel. Before non-Arab listeners he reiterated that there would be peace with Israel, and he kept the Divon–Sadeq channel open. According to the Egyptian interlocutor, Abdel-Rahman Sadeq, Nasser believed that Sharet had had no part in the *esek habish*.[47] Sharet's immediate goal was to free the spy ring members, but he was willing to cooperate in the Divon and Sadeq talks, which were not restricted to this issue. Among the topics under discussion was the possibility of economic cooperation between Israel and Egypt. Through their people in Paris, Sharet and Nasser engaged in an exchange of unsigned letters. In one response to Sharet dated December 21, 1954 Nasser expressed appreciation for Sharet's understanding of Egypt's sincere desire for a peaceful solution.[48]

While the Divon–Sadeq talks were ongoing, another channel of communications opened. The Jewish British Labour MP Maurice Orbach visited Cairo and met with Nasser twice, on November 24 and December 16, 1954. The brief Orbach presented had been prepared by officials in the Israeli Foreign Ministry loyal to Sharet, and covered a wide range of topics. Among them was a very important appeal to save the lives of the *esek habish* participants. Nasser responded that, under the circumstances, he was unable to interfere in the judicial process, but promised to do all he could to ensure that the sentences would not be overly harsh. He also told Orbach that the ship *Bat Galim* would be released but not allowed to cross the canal, and that non-Israeli ships carrying cargo destined for Israel would be allowed passage. Nasser promised Orbach that Egypt would make every effort to prevent border incidents on the condition that Israel would do the same, and agreed to high level talks as long as strict secrecy would be kept.[49] Orbach's report asserted that Colonel Nasser wanted peace and felt that within a year or two, or perhaps sooner, in six months time, they might be able to make approaches on a proper basis, and thus make it possible for peace to be secured.[50] Nothing came out of this initiative. On January 27, 1955 the Egyptian military court found eight members of the spy ring guilty and sentenced two of them to death. A few weeks earlier one of them had committed suicide in his prison cell. Given the strict censorship formerly imposed on the affair, the Israeli public knew nothing about what had happened, and was outraged by the Egyptian verdict. Sharet immediately stopped the talks about to unfold in Paris, saying "We will not negotiate in the shadow of the gallows."[51] Israeli opinion, as reflected in the memoirs of one participant in the talks, was that Nasser was dishonest and said different things to different people depending on his convenience.[52]

Avi Shlaim has argued that documentary evidence did not support this view and that Nasser lived up to most of his commitments. He released the ship *Bat Galim*, he curbed the propaganda campaign, and he stopped cross-border incursions. Nasser never promised that there would be no death sentences for the captured spies. He had clearly stated that he could not interfere in the legal proceedings. Just before the sentencing, several members of the Muslim Brotherhood who had committed terrorist acts were sentenced to death by an Egyptian court and were executed. Nasser was in no position to commute the death sentence on Israeli spy agents.[53]

Nasser forwarded a message through the CIA that although he could not commute the death sentences, he was still willing to proceed with the talks despite their high risk to him. Sharet refused, and called the talks off despite American pressure on Israel to participate. Sharet's contention was that Nasser's dishonesty and duplicity on the sentences proved that he was not a serious partner for peace negotiations.[54] What would have happened had Israel responded positively and the proposed meetings taken place cannot be known. Nevertheless Nasser offered Israel a chance to negotiate and Israel rejected it.[55]

## LAVON OUT, BEN GURION IN

Lavon resigned following the *esek habish*, and Ben Gurion returned to the government as minister of defense on February 21, 1955. One week later, on February 28, a Gaza raid with the military code name Black Arrow took place. Two paratroop companies under the command of Ariel Sharon attacked the Egyptian headquarters near

Gaza. The building was destroyed, 38 Egyptian soldiers were killed, and 31 were wounded. Israel's losses amounted to eight soldiers dead and nine wounded. This was the largest military encounter between Israel and Egypt since the signing of the armistice agreements.[56]

After the incident, an IDF spokesperson issued the following statement:

> On Monday evening (28.2.) an IDF unit was attacked near the Israeli–Egyptian Armistice boundary across from Gaza City. A fierce battle was triggered between the Egyptian force and the Israeli army unit. This battle began on Israeli territory and continued into the Gaza strip. The enemy force was repelled.[57]

The statement submitted by the Israeli delegation to the United Nations claimed that an Egyptian unit had crossed the border near Gaza, engaging an Israeli defense patrol, which drove the Egyptian soldiers back. Israel complained about the incident to the UN Security Council on March 4. Most Israelis knew nothing about the incident and had no reason to doubt the official version. Four years later, in October 1959, the military correspondent from the *Ma'ariv* newspaper published the full details of the incident. In the report, which included names, photos, the exact timing and the text of the operations order, the operation was described as a large-scale incursion into Egypt against an Egyptian *fedayun* center.

Furthermore, the chief of staff waited for the unit to return from the operation at dawn. After the battle he read the troops a letter from the prime minister congratulating them for their skills at battle, in both planning and execution. There is a clear contradiction between the planned operation this account describes and an unplanned encounter with an Egyptian unit that had penetrated into Israel.

The *Ma'ariv* articles talk about retaliation against a *fedayun* center and about the incursions of Nasser's *fedayun* during the years preceding the 1955 Gaza operation. But they did so several years later, and added to the general confusion about the event. The first *fedayun* incursion into Israel actually occurred at the end of August of that year, or six months after the operation. At the time of the operation most Israelis were unfamiliar with the term *fedayun*.[58]

Many commentators claim that this operation resulted in a Egyptian–Czech arms deal which, in turn, led to the outbreak of the 1956 war. It also led to the cessation of dialogue between Israel and Egypt and thereby delayed the peace between Israel and Egypt by about two decades, until long after Ben Gurion was no longer in power.[59]

One of Israel's arguments in defense of the operation was Egypt's refusal to join the western-oriented Baghdad Alliance. The treaty underlying this alliance was signed on February 24, 1955, or four days before the Gaza operation.[60] But it is the contention of the authors that the main reason for the Gaza operation was Ben Gurion's determination to bury any possibility of peace with Egypt, which would unavoidably be based on territorial and demographic compromises on both sides.

The tension between Israel and Egypt continued unabated, with both sides complaining almost daily to the United Nations. Shots were fired and mines laid, and the UN Armistice Committee would alternate its condemnations. After a series of violent encounters along the border, Israel carried out an operation on the Khan Yunis police fortress on August 31, which resulted in many casualties. To maintain pressure on Egypt, a few weeks later Israel deployed military forces in the DMZ near Nitzana.[61] The New York correspondent for *Ha'aretz* at the time suggested that some of the violence was intended to assist the United States in its endeavors to pressure Egypt to join the western alliance.[62] But if this was the purpose, it did not work because the Baghdad Alliance was widely unpopular. Instead of joining it Egypt turned to the east for assistance; hence the Czech–Egyptian arms deal.

In an interview with a reporter of the American weekly *Time* in 1955, Nasser said, "Until the 28 of February I felt that peace was coming. The borders between Egypt and Israel were quiet from 1952. However, when the Jews attacked Gaza my feelings changed, and I signed the deal with Czechoslovakia."[63]

Nasser announced the signing of the arms deal on September 27, 1955 on Radio Cairo. The reaction in Israel was a media frenzy, with newspapers and radio creating the impression that a newly and massively armed Egypt would immediately attack Israel and throw the Jews into the sea. Political parties from all sides were calling for a pre-emptive strike, before the Egyptian army could acquire competence in the use of their new weapons. On October 18, Menachem Begin, the leader of the opposition, declared "we must conduct an operation to prevent the war of extermination planned against us."[64]

On November 2, Ben Gurion once again presented his new coalition to the Knesset. On the background of increased border hostilities, he said:

In order to prevent the dangers in the current unruly situation I am prepared to meet the Prime-Minister of Egypt and any other Arab ruler, as soon as possible, to work out a mutual agreement without pre-conditions. The government of Israel is ready for a peace agreement and political, cultural and economic co-operation between Israel and its neighbors for a long time to come.[65]

This speech received much attention in Egypt, and the official *Al Ahram* newspaper devoted its front page to it. Soon after the paper went to print, Israel launched an attack on Sabha in the Nitzana area. Ben Gurion offered to negotiate peace with Nasser only hours before launching this attack in which 50 Egyptian soldiers were killed and 49 were taken prisoner.[66]

It is probable that when Ben Gurion officially spoke about a meeting with Nasser, he had already signed the battle order for the Sabha/Nitzana operation. Two weeks later the IDF attacked Syrian army posts on the north-east coast of the Sea of Galilee, which resulted in 56 Syrians being killed, 9 wounded and 30 taken prisoner. Since this attack was preceded by no violent incident it surprised most Israelis, including Zalman Amit, who participated in the operation as a reserve soldier.[67] Although there was criticism, it was not directed against retaliation but against the poor timing of this operation. Apparently Ben Gurion again had not consulted his cabinet colleagues, and they later claimed to have learned about it from the newspapers.

The numbers of casualties in 1955 given in Table 3.1 are taken from the official report of the UN Truce Supervision Organization (UNTSO) presented on January 19, 1956 as an official document of the UN Security Council.

**Table 3.1** Israeli, Egyptian, and Syrian casualties in 1955

|  | Dead | | Wounded | | Prisoners | |
|---|---|---|---|---|---|---|
|  | Soldiers | Civilians | Soldiers | Civilians | Soldiers | Civilians |
| In Israeli–Egyptian incidents: | | | | | | |
| Israel | 32 | 15 | 108 | 10 | 3 | – |
| Egypt | 196 | 20 | 166 | 22 | 80 | – |
| In Israel–Syrian incidents: | | | | | | |
| Israel | 6 | – | 12 | 3 | – | – |
| Syria | 45 | 17 | 20 | 6 | 36 | 4 |

Source: UN Security Council, SCOR No. S/3685.

In 1956 Israel conducted only one large-scale incursion across the armistice boundary with Egypt, on April 5 when it responded to several *fedayun* incursions by bombarding the refugee camps in the Gaza Strip and hitting the market place in Gaza City.[68]

## EGYPT NATIONALIZES THE SUEZ CANAL

On July 26, Egypt nationalized the Suez Canal, despite a massive campaign to persuade it not to do so. Britain and France protested. Along with the preparations for war a disinformation campaign was also started.

In September and October, Israel conducted four incursions into Jordan (Rahwah, Garandal, Hossan, and Kalkilia), but none in retaliation to Egyptian *fedayun* incursions. Jordan was in an unstable, tense political situation, and the Israeli leadership was quoted in the press as wanting to liberate occupied homeland territories from the clutches of the artificial creature called the Kingdom of Jordan.[69] The beleaguered government of Jordan was not responsible for any terrorist incursions, and was actively trying to prevent them.[70]

On September 15 Radio Cairo broadcast a report from the Egyptian newspaper *El-Sha'ab:*

> The Israeli attack on the Garandal is nothing but part of a detailed plan prepared in London, Paris and Tel Aviv against all the Arabs.[71]

On September 28, Radio Cairo broadcast this statement:

> We want to emphasize that these actions will not scare us and will not drag us into war … we inform all the Jews living in Israel that we want peace. However, we want to solve the Middle East problems according to the wishes of the people of the region.[72]

On the Israeli side an editorial of July 9, 1956, in *LaMerhav*, a newspaper affiliated with one of the major partners in the coalition, stated:

> Everything predicts that the day of reckoning with regards to the fate of Jordan is coming. Obviously Israel cannot remain indifferent to this development in the face of far reaching territorial changes on Israel's Eastern border.[73]

Ben Gurion earlier had stated:

> In my speech of November 2 in the Knesset I stated: We never initiated and we will never initiate war against anybody, and I add, this is the staunch policy of the government and with it we will stand and with it we will fall. ... A pre-emptive war is madness.[74]

The *Davar* newspaper of October 21, merely days before the onset of the Sinai war, published the following statement by the foreign minister, Golda Meir:

> Israel is convinced that moving Iraqi forces to Jordan will constitute a new and grave threat to the security of Israel. It will also change the status quo and will destabilize the armistice agreements between Israel and Jordan. We consider ourselves free to act in accordance to our security needs.[75]

This statement was made while Israeli reserve soldiers were being recalled to active service. The mobilization was generally perceived as proof that a large-scale operation, perhaps war against Jordan, was being planned. The conflict with Egypt was on the back burner. Very few imagined that Israel would get involved in a conflict between Egypt, France, and Britain.[76]

## THE 1956 WAR

An IDF announcement on October 29 stated that:

> IDF forces entered and hit Fedayun units in Rass al-Nakeb and Kountilla. They established positions West of the Nahel junction, in the vicinity of the Suez Canal. This action was a response to Egyptian military operations against Israeli movement on land and sea and is intended to cause damage and prevent peace from the citizens of Israel.[77]

In the Security Council on the next day, October 30, the United States proposed condemning Israel as an aggressor, and demanded no intervention in the conflict by UN members. This was the first time that Britain and France used their veto power against a US proposal. And on November 1, two days after Israel's incursion,

French and British bombers began a massive air attack on Egypt. A ground invasion of the Suez Canal zone was to be the next step.

The Egyptian army retreated and on November 6, Israel completed its conquest of the entire Sinai peninsula and the Gaza Strip. Egypt held the canal, and its allies amongst the oil-producing Arab states blocked the supply of oil to Mediterranean ports.

An Israeli military parade was held in Sharm el Sheikh, whose official name was immediately changed to Solomon's Gulf. Moshe Dayan read the soldiers the following telegram from Ben Gurion:

> To the soldiers of Regiment 9 and its commanders:
> You all enjoyed a unique historic privilege; you completed the most glorious military operation in the history of our people and one of the most amazing operations in the history of the world. In less than seven days the entire Sinai Peninsula and Gaza Strip were cleansed of enemy forces – from the straights of Eilat to Raffah, el-Arish and Kantara, and, from Nitzana to the Red sea in the South ... you extended a hand to King Solomon who developed Eilat as the first Israeli port in the south. The Red Sea straits will now be open to Israeli navigation and Yotvat, also called, Tiran, which was up to 1400 years ago an independent Hebrew State will now become once again part of the Third Kingdom of Israel.
> Honor and glory to the victorious Israel Defense Force.[78]

On November 7 Ben Gurion also addressed the Knesset, where he argued that 1,400 years ago there was an independent Hebrew entity in the island of Yotvat (Tiran). Therefore the entire Sinai peninsula was actually not part of Egypt, and Israel had not really touched any Egyptian territory. He continued, "As I said earlier, our army received strict orders not to cross the Suez Canal and not to touch Egyptian territory and to remain strictly within the boundary of the Sinai Peninsula."[79]

Ben Gurion ended his speech with seven important contentions:

• The Armistice agreement between Israel and Egypt is dead and buried and will never come back to life again.
• Together with the agreement, the armistice boundaries between Israel and Egypt also died.
• There was no conflict between the people of Israel and Egypt. The flight of the Egyptian army from the Sinai testified that they had no interest in fighting Israel in a foreign desert.

- We are prepared to negotiate for stable peace and neighborly relations with Egypt. Direct negotiation must be without pre-condition and compulsion from any side. We hope that all the peace loving nations will support our wish.
- We are ready for such a negotiation with each Arab state. Israel will maintain these agreements for as long as they abide by the armistice agreements, even if they are not ready for permanent peace.
- Israel will never agree under any circumstances that a foreign force be located in its territory or in any of the areas controlled by us.
- Israel will fight no Arab state including Egypt unless attacked by it.[80]

It might be thought ironic that Israel extended a peace offer from the banks of the Suez Canal and declared that it would not fight Egypt unless attacked.

The leader of the opposition, Begin, declared that Yotvat (Tiran) was not the only ancient Hebrew territory. Gaza too was an ancient Hebrew city of the Patriarchs. Another politician claimed that Gaza was a liberated part of the homeland, now returned to Israel.[81] Even the leader of the left-wing Mapam party argued that wars and conquests do not prevent peace. As long as the residents of these conquered areas enjoy equal rights, there is no problem at all.[82]

The festivities of conquest lasted until November 8, past midnight, when the prime minister announced a retreat from Sinai and the Gaza Strip. Ben Gurion talked about the international pressure that forced the retreat. A week later the Knesset convened to discuss the situation. Moshe Sneh of Mapam then said:

> The military attack on Egypt caused Israel unfathomable damage to its international status and security.
>
> This operation presented Israel to the entire world as an aggressor.
>
> It also presented Israel at the forefront of international colonialism in the Middle East.
>
> The attack on Egypt blocked the road to peace with the Arab peoples with insurmountable stumbling blocks. Nobody now will conduct peace negotiations with Israel and no one will take seriously Israeli talk about readiness for peace.[83]

Israel tried to hold on to the Gaza Strip, but on March 14, 1957 the Egyptian governor of Gaza returned to the Strip. Not one inch of Egyptian territory remained in Israeli hands.

The notion that it was possible to continuously expand at the expense of the Arab neighbors and at the same time force the Arabs to accept Israeli peace conditions received a deathly blow.

This adventure ended exactly as described by Israel's foreign minister, Golda Meir: "We have returned more or less to the situation that prevailed on November 29, 1956."[84]

In a recently published article in *Ha'aretz*, investigative reporter Meron Rapaport discovered that the settlement project actually started in 1956. The creation of Jewish settlements on Arab territory is usually related to the aftermath of the 1967 war, but Rapaport argues that Moshe Dayan hatched the idea much earlier. He wanted to build settlements on conquered Egyptian territory to make Israeli control over Gaza permanent. In December 1956, less than two months after the end of the war, the first two Jewish settlements were established in Sharm el Sheikh and in Raffah. This was done while Israel was already evacuating areas because of international pressure.[85]

# 4

# THE LULL IN HOSTILITIES, 1956–67

The third kingdom of Israel in the 20th century lasted four days. The overthrow of Nasser, the expansion of Israel's territory, and the restructuring of political realities in the Middle East were Israel's strategic goals in the 1956 war.[1] None were achieved. What resulted instead were isolation, criticism, and aversion, to a degree that Israel had not experienced since its establishment in 1948. The British–French alliance failed to gain control over the Suez Canal and withdrew, as did Israel, although the departure of Israeli forces from the Sinai peninsula was protracted. The drawn-out process might be attributed to Israel's hope of retaining the Gaza Strip even after relinquishing the Sinai Desert. Maneuvers lasted approximately four months, and Ben Gurion publicly entertained notions of military actions should the Egyptians return to Gaza.[2]

Operationally Israel came out the victor, and Israelis viewed this war a great success, which affirmed Israel's military advantage over its neighbors. The IDF power of deterrence was re-established, and Israel could see itself as the major player in the Middle East. Ben Gurion took credit for this and, at the height of his power, was able to force through any plan or decision he wished. However there was much damage to Israel's international image, particularly among the non-aligned block of nations to which Israel should have belonged. Instead it was viewed by much of the world as an imperialist crony and part of the colonial world that the post-Second World War world was now determined to eliminate.

The real outcome of the Sinai war was to deepen and solidify the animosity and hatred that the Arabs, particularly their leaders, felt towards Israel.[3] But writings by Ben Gurion, Lavon, Dayan, and Alon show that they continued to be more interested in prospects for expansion and domination over the Arabs than in ending the conflict, with the inevitable compromise that such a move would entail.

One lesson Ben Gurion seemed to have learned was the limitation of military power. His earlier expressed ambition of expansion in all directions of the Arabs world was not realistic in a modern world where military might was no longer the single requirement for territorial expansion. A pragmatist, he realized that Israel's best hope was preservation of the status quo established during the signing of the armistice agreements in 1949. He worked to prevent any change in the status quo by augmenting Israel's deterrence power. The IDF was equipped with the best, most advanced weapons available, to ensure that none of Israel's neighbors could contemplate challenging it. The persistent rearming also ensured a growing atmosphere of hostility, and lowered the probability of any peace resolution. The ultimate outgrowth of this line of thinking was the acquisition by Israel of nuclear capability.[4]

Support for Israel's deterrence plans came from Germany. In the early 1950s Israel signed a reparation agreement with Germany, whereby the first significant steps towards Israel's industrial infrastructure were underwritten. In 1957 Israel obtained Germany's agreement to add a military component to the economic package it provided. Ben Gurion at this time spoke of a different Germany which had risen out of the ashes of the defeated Nazi regime.

The eleven years between the Sinai (1956) and the Six Day (1967) wars were relatively peaceful. There were few violent incursions across the Israeli–Egyptian borders and retaliatory operations were rare. There was also a paucity of peace initiatives during this decade. Arab leaders who had previously exhibited interest in exploring peace with Israel launched no more initiatives. The only attempts at peace making during this time were various proposals made to Arab leaders, particularly to Nasser, by outside sources. Any application made to Israel's leadership was met with some interest as long as it posed no threat to the status quo and required no Israeli compromise in territorial or refugee matters.

Israel's recalcitrance was noticed globally. In April 1955, at the Bandung conference of newly independent Asian and African states, which took place in Indonesia, the stated purpose was to promote Afro–Asian economic and cultural cooperation and to oppose colonialism or neocolonialism by the United States, the Soviet Union, or any other imperialistic nations. The conference was an important step toward the crystallization of the Non-Aligned Movement, and declared its support for the rights of the Palestinian Arabs. It called for the implementation of the UN resolutions calling for a peaceful resolution of the conflict.[5] Several subsequent conferences of this bloc of Asian and African nations reaffirmed the resolutions of the Bandung conference: Cairo in December 1957, Addis Ababa in June 1960, and Casablanca in January 1961. The conferences in Cairo and Addis Ababa singled out Israel's non-compliance with UN directives.

## EARLY PEACE INITIATIVES

In 1961 the Israeli newspaper *Ma'ariv* published a story written by Uri Dan, its correspondent in Malta, following a conversation he had with the Maltese labor leader and former prime minister, Dom Mintoff. In 1956, as prime minister, Mintoff had met Nasser on a private visit to Egypt. The two exchanged views on many issues including the Arab–Israeli conflict. Mintoff related that he invited Nasser to Malta and suggested holding a secret meeting with Israeli representatives. The visit was to take place in April 1956. Dan wrote that Mintoff was still excited about the idea five years later. In Egypt he contacted the British ambassador to inform him of the impending visit by Nasser to Malta, and that Nasser had agreed to a secret meeting with Israeli representatives. Mintoff planned to confirm that the appropriate representatives from Israel would come to the meeting.

Apparently this plan was aborted at the behest of the British governor of Malta, who told Mintoff this was not the right time for a visit of any kind by Nasser to Malta. Incredulous, Mintoff insisted on seeing the cable from London, which stated the objections to Nasser's visit. The document, marked "Top Secret," had been sent by the British Foreign Ministry to the British governor of Malta. It stated that London objected to a visit by Nasser to Malta but did not want this objection known. The cable included a reprimand to Mintoff, pointing out that he was not a traveling salesman for peace efforts. In 1958–59 Mintoff sent copies of the cable to both Sharet and Nasser. Mintoff reportedly mentioned that Nasser read the cable and smiled.[6] Nothing further came out of this well-meaning but short-lived initiative.

Another series of episodes on the route towards peace involved Joe Golan. Golan grew up in Cairo and Damascus, and became involved in the activities of the World Jewish Congress under the direction of Nahum Goldman, its president. Golan, who became Goldman's protégé, considered himself an anti-colonialist Zionist, and was appointed in the 1950s to be head of the Arab Desk of the Congress. Goldman hoped Golan would help him establish a semi-independent diplomatic channel of communication with the Arabs that was not bound to official Israeli policies. Golda Meir and Isser Harel, among other Israeli leaders, worked to neutralize any such efforts.[7] Those within Israel who opposed Golan's relationships in Arab countries maintained they were against Israel's interest.

Some of Golan's activities were in Morocco and Algiers. He cultivated a good relationship with the Moroccan king and with the Algerian National Liberation Front (FLN). On one occasion, his contact at the FLN advised urging Algerian Jews to leave the country. When Golan conveyed this message to the chief rabbi of Algiers, the Israelis were enraged and canceled his passport. At one point Golan was invited to meet with the famous Egyptian journalist Hassanein Heikal, a personal friend and adviser to Nasser. Their meeting took place over breakfast in a hotel in Paris. According to Golan, Heikal confirmed Egyptian interest in initiating communication with Israel, but required preliminary meetings to establish the preconditions for any formal contact.[8] Golan reported this to Goldman, who in turn relayed it to Golda Meir. She immediately put a stop to this venture.

Another of Golan's projects was to start a dialogue between Israel and Iraq. Golan established contact with Yussuf al Kabir, an Iraqi Jew who had a friendly relationship with the Iraqi rulers. They wanted to open a dialogue between Israel and Iraq, and al Kabir convinced the Iraqi prime minister, Nuri al Said, to have a meeting at the level of legal experts to assess the value of the assets of Palestinian refugees. These experts were also to assess the assets left behind by Jews who had left Arab countries. Nahum Goldman delivered a detailed report of the plan for such a meeting to the Israeli Foreign Ministry and was promised that the Foreign Ministry would act on it. Yussuf al Kabir later told Golan that nobody ever contacted him.[9]

In May 1956 Colonel Tharwat Okasha, who had assisted Nasser in the Egyptian revolution, contacted Joe Golan and Nahum Goldman. He initially wanted to arrange a Cairo meeting between Goldman and Nasser. Golan believed Nasser himself had initiated Okasha's mission to create a more favorable political climate for Egypt. This was a unique opportunity to pave the road for further contacts with Egypt, according to Golan, who provided a full report to Goldman, who in turn reported to Ben Gurion. Golan later concluded that Ben Gurion and his cabinet trusted neither Goldman nor himself. At that time Shimon Peres, Ben Gurion's right-hand man, advised Ben Gurion to avoid these contacts and approach Egypt through

Marshal Tito, the ruler of Yugoslavia and a close friend of Nasser. Ben Gurion asked Shaike Dan, an Israeli who knew Tito, to explore this route, but attempts to involve Tito angered Colonel Okasha. The colonel reprimanded Golan, because he claimed any meetings between Nasser and Goldman were to have been kept secret and Tito should not have been involved. Nevertheless, Okasha would continue to maintain an open channel of communication with Golan in the hope it might provide some future opportunity.[10]

Ben Gurion acted to position Israel as an undefeatable force and demonstrate Israel's strong adherence to the status quo. In the 1950s and early 1960s Ben Gurion approached Tito and U-Nu, Burma's leader, to arrange a secret meeting with Nasser, but he also wanted to test the pervasiveness of this perception of Israel. In June 1960 a meeting did occur between Nasser and Tito, but the joint statement they issued reflected that they were not cowed by Israel's might: "The problem of Israel must be solved in accordance with the UN Charter and resolution already adopted by the international body in the direction of achieving stable peace."[11]

The conference of Non-Aligned Nations that took place in September 1961 in Belgrade passed another resolution, which essentially reconfirmed the previous joint statement: "The conference participants condemn the imperialist policies prevailing in the Middle East. They declare their support for the full return of the rights of the Palestinian Arab nation in accordance with the Charter and resolution of the United Nations."[12]

In a 1963 interview with Dennis Hamilton, the editor of the London *Sunday Times*, Nasser allegedly said that the problem could be solved if Ben Gurion and he were confined alone in a room for three hours.[13] Hamilton reported this conversation to the Baron Edmund de Rothschild, who relayed it to Ben Gurion. The latter invited Hamilton to Israel, and told him that Nasser was the only Arab leader capable of reaching an agreement with Israel. He asked Hamilton to convey an offer of a secret meeting to Nasser, but it was Nasser who rejected the offer, saying he had no reason to trust Ben Gurion, and reciting a long list of grievances about Israel's actions over the previous 15 years.[14]

## EGYPT, IRAQ, AND SYRIA FORM A CONFEDERATION

In April 1963, Egypt, Iraq, and Syria signed a provisional treaty to form an Arab Federation, the interim constitution of which attached considerable importance to the Palestine issue. This development seems to have caused Ben Gurion a great deal of anxiety, since he sent a series of letters to the leaders of India, the Soviet Union, Britain, France, and most importantly the United States, requesting that the next meeting of the UN General Assembly guarantee the territorial integrity of all the states in the Middle East. Ben Gurion was concerned about a partial encirclement of Israel by the Arab Federation just formed, and that King Hussein of Jordan would be overthrown. He feared Jordan falling under Nasser's sphere of influence, which would complete the encirclement. To avoid this he considered dismantling Jordan by conquering the rest of Mandatory Palestine, or the West Bank of Jordan.[15] In his letter to President Kennedy he elaborated on the need to protect Israel's integrity and borders, but also described the villainy of Nasser and his schemes for destroying Israel, This contradicted his earlier statement that same year to Hamilton about his conviction that Nasser was the only Arab leader capable of bringing about peace.

Throughout Israel's history the Holocaust and its implications for the Jewish people have come up whenever its leadership feels any threat, real or imaginary. This was also the case in Ben Gurion's letter to President Kennedy on April 26, 1963. It expressed his belief that the world had not taken Hitler's threats against the Jews seriously, and his conviction that another similar calamity was imminent, perpetrated now by the Arabs under Nasser's leadership. Kennedy apparently did not share his concerns. The US administration felt that the Tripartite Federation posed no threat to Israel or to the west, and considered the situation in Jordan stable. Israel was strong enough to defeat any attack initiated by a single Arab state, or even by all of them combined. The Arab leaders were certainly aware of this military imbalance. The United States was, however, concerned about Israel's nuclear program, which posed a threat to the interests of the west and the Middle East. Israel's nuclear capability could severely impede any possibility of a peaceful resolution of the Middle Eastern conflict.[16]

## BEN GURION'S FINAL RESIGNATION

On June 16, 1963 Ben Gurion announced his resignation from the government. He was 76 years old, and ended his very long and monumental career pessimistic about the future of the state he had almost single-handedly built. He was replaced by the much paler, less intransigent political figure of Levi Eshkol. There was some hope that following Ben Gurion's departure the prospects for peace would improve, but this was not the case.[17] Eshkol presented his government to the Knesset on June 24. In his inaugural speech he stated that peace could only be achieved through respect for the integrity of all the states in the Middle East. Direct negotiations between Israel and its neighboring Arab states must be held, but only a strong and well-armed Israel could bring about peace. Eshkol's articulated position towards peace with the Arabs marked no significant departure from the views and policies of his predecessor. Although a moderate had replaced the hawkish, biblically inclined prime minister, and a relatively moderate chief of staff took the place of a militarist, a new course towards peace was not charted. Neither the new prime minister nor the new chief of staff seized the opportunity.

Following the assassination of President Kennedy, the new US President, Lyndon Johnson, demonstrated a very pro-Israel stance. In June 1964 he invited Eshkol to the United States for a state visit, an honor that had been consistently denied to Ben Gurion. Eshkol's visit ended with a joint statement calling for an end to violence and aggression, and for the need to preserve the territorial integrity of all the states in the Middle East. Under Johnson the United States abandoned its previous support for changing the 1949 armistice agreements, and instead expressed its support for the status quo.[18]

In 1965 the Tunisian president, Habib Bourguiba surprisingly called on Arabs to abandon their plans to destroy Israel, and instead seek a peace agreement based on the 1947 UN partition plan and the return of the Palestinian refugees. Prime Minister Eshkol responded positively to the Tunisian initiative for the resolution of the Arab–Israeli dispute by peaceful means, but could not support all the details of the actual proposal.[19] Despite Eshkol's ultimate rejection of the proposal, members of a new, hawkish, Ben Gurion-inspired political party, RAFI, attacked the government for giving the plan any consideration and creating delusions of peace. This attack became vitriolic in the run-up to general elections in November 1965. Eshkol's party soundly defeated RAFI and obtained a large number of Knesset seats – 45 versus 10 – but nothing came out of the Bourguiba initiative. The RAFI attack on Eshkol had maneuvered him away from possible negotiation contacts with the Arabs.

Another peace opportunity, initiated by Egypt, was circumvented later in 1965. Meir Amit, then head of Mossad, who shared the convictions of RAFI, Dayan, and Ben Gurion, was invited to a confidential meeting with the deputy commander of the Egyptian armed forces, Abdel Hakim Amer. The secret meeting was to take place in

Cairo. Amit knew this presented a unique opportunity to establish contacts with Nasser, and that Israel must respond to it positively. Seeking economic aid from the United States, the Egyptians apparently wanted to negotiate an offer of free passage for Israeli shipping in the Suez Canal, reduction in the scope of the Arab League boycott on Israeli products, and the toning-down of Arab anti-Israeli propaganda. Initially Eshkol supported the meeting and instructed his deputy defense minister to accompany Amit on the mission, but political differences prevailed and derailed the initiative. Isser Harel, Eshkol's adviser on intelligence, convinced several ministers that Israel had nothing to gain from an initiative that essentially served an improved Egyptian–US relationship. In the end Amit and Eshkol's deputy minister stayed at home.[20]

Eshkol was more successful on the Jordanian front. He established communication with King Hussein to explore the possibilities of future settlement and practical cooperation. Ya'acov Herzog, the director general of the Prime Minister's Office, represented Eshkol in this endeavor. He had already met the king in London in September 1963, and this initial encounter led to a series of subsequent meetings. These led to cooperation between the two countries over water-related issues, primarily water conservation. Israel agreed to support the king's request for American military equipment on condition that this equipment not be deployed west of the Jordan River. Israel also provided information to the Jordanians about subversive activities, and most importantly, plots against the king. The king acknowledged and appreciated this information,[21] but despite the cooperation in a variety of areas, no peace was achieved. A peace agreement with Jordan was only accomplished well after the signing of the treaty between Israel and Egypt.

## CONFLICT OVER WATER

During the 1960s, Israel's borders with Jordan and Egypt were relatively quiet. The reduction in cross-border incidents could be attributed largely to Nasser and Hussein, who were actively involved in discouraging them. However, the conflict over the control of the Jordan River and its northern sources in Syria was a sensitive issue affecting the problematic border between Israel and Syria. In 1964 Israel completed a plan to divert the Jordan River to its southern Negev territory, and Syria, supported by other Arab states, responded by diverting the sources of the Jordan, which were located inside Syrian territory. Although Israel was consistently victorious in the consequent skirmishes between the two countries, Syria was the Arab state most despised by Israel's military leaders. Eshkol's military secretary, Israel Lior, once described this phenomenon as the Syrian syndrome, and accused the chief of staff, Rabin, and the Commander of the Northern Front, Dado Elazar, of being particularly afflicted by it.[22] The Jordan River problem gave rise to belligerent Arab calls for unity, which Rabin took very seriously. He later expressed the view that the dynamics underlying the Six Day War were linked to these Arab pronouncements.[23]

Eshkol and his colleagues vacillated between the perception of Arab belligerence as empty nationalist slogans and the view that it reflected actual preparation for confrontation with Israel.[24] Nevertheless Eshkol asserted that Israel was determined to proceed with its diversion project, regardless of the danger of aggravating the situation on the Syrian border. The Israelis wanted to block Syria's diversion plans but were unclear about strategy. Moshe Dayan argued for war. Others advocated creating a pretext for an Israeli attack to conquer Syrian territory near the sources of the Jordan River. Eshkol preferred to adopt the more moderate proposal of destroying the Syrian heavy machinery that was being used for the water project.[25]

The reason given for attacking Syria during the 1967 war was its frequent attacks on Israeli settlements in the Galilee panhandle. When the Syrians opened fire on an Israeli patrol that crossed the border near Tel Dan, Eshkol approved the deployment of the Israeli air force against Syrian positions. This was the start of a significant escalation of the Israeli response to the Syrian diversion project, which came to be known as the war on tractors. Israel repeatedly fired on equipment used by Syria for work on its diversion project, moving farther and farther away from the border. The message intended by Israel was that Syria had the choice of abandoning the project or risking war.[26] Syria gave in and abandoned the project of diverting the Banias River, a Jordan River tributary.

At this time Israel was also contending with provocations by Palestinian Fatah guerillas, acting independently of the Palestine Liberation Organization (PLO) or of any other Arab authority. Despite attempts by Egypt and Jordan to prevent guerillas from entering Israel across their borders, Fatah units occasionally managed to evade border guards and made their way into Israel. The Fatah squads were supported by Syria, whose attitude could be considered provocative in the context of the ongoing conflict over water and Israeli provocations in the DMZ.

Since Syria was Israel's most obvious source of trouble, Israel's attack against Jordan in mid-November 1966 was shocking to most observers. Even the scale of the operation marked a significant departure from Israel's normal retaliatory practice. The attack on the village of Samu in the southern part of the West Bank was substantial, and involved both infantry and tanks. Close to 100 Jordanian soldiers were killed and about 50 houses demolished. Israel claimed that the operation was a response to the laying of mines by Arab guerillas, although no evidence backed the accusation. The Samu operation was the first step in the countdown to the 1967 war, and its effects were far-reaching. The Israelis, whose aggression belied their assertions of commitment to the integrity and stability of Jordan and to any effort towards peace, let down Jordan's King Hussein.[27]

In the aftermath of the Samu affair Israel's attention focused on Syria. In early 1966 the secular, socialist Ba'ath Party assumed power in Syria and adopted a very pro-Palestinian approach, supporting Palestinian guerilla operations. The Ba'ath strategy intensified the tension between Israel and Syria. Israel's response at the start of 1967 was to resume illegal agricultural activity in the DMZ, and escalate the tension.[28] In April, just two months prior to the onset of the 1967 war, an Israeli tractor plowed land in the DMZ and drew Syrian fire. The cross-border shooting escalated, and led to the deployment of Israel's air force. The Syrians sent MIG fighters to intercept the Israelis, and in the ensuing air battle six Syrian fighters were shot down. This was the first time in the history of the conflict that Israeli jet fighters penetrated Syrian air space all the way to the capital, Damascus, where some Syrian jets were shot down. According to Avi Shlaim, the escalation on the Syrian front "was probably the single most important factor in dragging the Middle East to war in June 1967."[29]

At that time most Israelis, including the authors, believed that Israel went to war against Syria on the Golan Heights to suppress aggression against Israeli settlements in the border region. Moshe Dayan himself refuted this pervasive conviction. In 1997, 16 years after Dayan's death a young reporter, Rami Tal, published a series of interviews he had conducted with him. He published them with the permission of Dayan's daughter, Yael Dayan. This is what Dayan had to say about the conquest of the Golan Heights:

I know how at least 80 percent of the clashes there started. In my opinion, more than 80 percent, but let's talk about 80 percent. It went this way: we would send a tractor to plow someplace where it wasn't possible to do anything consequential in the demilitarized area, and knew in advance that the Syrians would start to shoot. If they didn't shoot, we would tell the tractor to advance further, until in the end the Syrians would get annoyed and shoot. And then we would use artillery and later the air force also, and that's how it was. I did that, and Laskov and Tchara [Zvi Tsur, Rabin's predecessor as chief of staff] did that, and Yitzhak did that, but it seems to me that the person who most enjoyed these games was Dado [David Elazar, OC Northern Command, 1964–69].[30]

After Israel shot down six Syrian MIG fighter jets, there was an intensification of Palestinian guerilla penetrations into Israel. Israel threatened Syria with massive retaliation, and chief of staff Rabin wildly contemplated the occupation of Damascus. Some Israeli cabinet ministers reacted to Rabin's idea with dismay, and the prime minister actually reprimanded his chief of staff.[31]

The escalation of tension with Jordan and with Syria placed mounting pressure on Nasser to show support for both. Nasser did not rush into the fray, although his reluctance to get involved threatened his position as the leader of the Arab world. His attitude might be attributed to his recognition of Israel's military superiority. But Egypt had a defense agreement with Syria, requiring it to come to Syria's aid in the event of an attack by Israel.[32] Nasser requested the UN emergency forces to leave Egyptian territory, and sent Egyptian forces into the Sinai peninsula. He once again blocked the Straits of Tiran, the entrance to the Gulf of Aqaba, to Israeli shipping.

Despite these steps and despite the growing hysteria in the Israeli public and media, a significant number of Israeli leaders, among them Ben Gurion, were convinced that Nasser was not planning to go to war. Ben Gurion made this point to Rabin, and claimed that Nasser's hand was forced by Israel's military actions, commencing with the Samu operation. Ben Gurion concluded his discussion with Rabin by saying that the mobilization of the Israel military reservists was a grave mistake and Israel must not go to war.[33]

Israel's military leadership was determined to commence military operations against Egypt immediately, but Eshkol first wanted to establish the position of the Americans, who had made a commitment of support to Israel in 1957. President Johnson confirmed Ben Gurion's opinion that Egypt was not planning a war against Israel. In a meeting with Israel's foreign minister, Abba Eban, Johnson reassured him that Israel would not be alone unless it decided to go it alone, and it need not worry about the blockade of the Gulf of Aqaba.[34]

On May 28, 1967, Eshkol met with the military leadership, and the generals did not hide their lack of confidence in the politicians. They suggested sending the former head of military intelligence, Meir Amit, to the United States to reexamine the American position. In the interval between the Eban and the Amit US visits, a major shift did occur. Now the United States gave Israel the green light to attack Egypt,[35] which Israel decided to do on June 4, 1967.

The entire Middle East was about to undergo a radical and perhaps permanent change.

# 5

# THE AFTERMATH OF THE JUNE 1967 WAR

During the Six Day War Israel assumed control of territories conquered from its neighbors Egypt, Syria, and Jordan. Israel gained control of the entire area west of the Jordan River, which was all of Mandatory Palestine. It also conquered the entire Sinai peninsula from Egypt and the Golan Heights from Syria. This June war permanently changed the Middle East and the Arab–Israeli conflict. It gave Israel territorial conquests that would not be easy to relinquish.

Shortly after the war, the contention that it had been a defensive war was disputed. A significant number of Israel's leaders eventually admitted that Egypt had posed no real military threat, and the 1967 war had been expansionist.[1] Avi Shlaim commented that the war aims had emerged only in the course of the fighting, in a confused and contradictory fashion.[2] Israel's newly appointed defense minister, Moshe Dayan, categorically stated that Israel had no conquest intentions and was interested in exchanging territory for peace. He claimed that he had waited for a telephone call from the Arab leadership, particularly from the Jordanian king – but it never came. The altered map of the Middle East left only one issue apparently open for debate: how much of the land acquired would remain in Israeli hands.

Several years later, it became clear that the Arab–Israeli conflict now became the Israeli–Palestinian conflict. Egypt, Jordan, Syria, and Lebanon were no longer the primary opponents.[3]

Ben Gurion's dream came true, as territory for which he had claimed biblical entitlement was now under the control of the State of Israel. The Israel leadership, civilian and military, were wittingly or unwittingly intoxicated by this achievement of messianic

70

dimensions.[4] Between June 1967 and October 1973 there was a paucity of peace initiatives. A percolating expansionist-messianic spirit accompanied the attractive new geopolitical landscape of the Middle East, and Israel was reluctant to initiate change. The few initiatives that did occur offered no significant modifications.

The Israelis continued to celebrate their victory in what could be described as a drunken euphoria, while the Egyptians, Jordanians, and Syrians focused on steps to recapture their lost territory. Nasser initially intended to resign, then changed his mind under grassroots pressure. Israeli leaders produced competing schemes to hold on to the conquered territory. Even Abba Eban, a self-proclaimed dove, now referred to the armistice boundaries as the Auschwitz lines, while nationalists like Menachem Begin demanded the outright annexation of both the West Bank and Gaza.[5] Thoughts of transfer that had been articulated in the Ben Gurion era resurfaced. When the war dust settled, close to 400,000 new refugees had been driven out of their homes in Palestine.[6]

Israel wanted peace on terms that would reflect its victory. Less than two months after the war, on July 26, Yigal Alon presented a plan to cabinet, which most of the leadership and the Israeli public considered very generous. He proposed that the West Bank be divided between Israel and Jordan. Israel would retain the Jordan valley, an 8–10 km security strip along the western bank of the Jordan River, and the Latrun Enclave. Jordan would annex the rest of the West Bank area. This proposal was never formally approved, but nevertheless remained the unofficial platform of all Labor Party governments until 1977.[7] After the Alon Plan was presented, the Eshkol government decided to establish Israel's boundaries strictly in accordance with its security needs. Therefore it effectively made the decision not to return to the pre-war borders and keep control over the Gaza Strip and Sharm el-Sheikh, as well as a land corridor along the Red Sea from Sharm to Israel's Eilat.[8] This amounted to an unofficial rejection of any attempt to negotiate.

## SETTLEMENTS

The move to plan and build settlements in the West Bank and the Golan Heights began within days of the war. On June 14 the Mugraby neighborhood adjacent to the Wailing Wall was evacuated, and in a proposal to cabinet on the same day Alon recommended the immediate rebuilding and settlement of the Jewish quarter in

East Jerusalem. He suggested surrounding Jerusalem with Jewish neighborhoods so that Jerusalem could never be separated from Israel. Alon's proposal was backed by Dayan and approved by cabinet. Within days of the cabinet approval of Alon's plan, several hundred Palestinian families residing in the Jewish quarter were evicted.[9] One month after the war and in defiance of statements made about negotiating for peace, the center of old Jerusalem was cleared of its Arab residents and Israel's settlement movement commenced. Having conquered East Jerusalem and the West Bank, Israel formally annexed East Jerusalem and areas of the West Bank adjacent to it on June 25.[10]

Sixty-two years after the State of Israel was established there is still no resolution of the Israeli–Palestinian conflict largely because of this settler movement. Without a master plan and without formal cabinet approval, the building of settlements in the conquered territories was gathering momentum, encouraged by the surge of messianic-expansionistic sentiments. The Israeli military and an array of politicians initiated the pattern of creating facts on the ground, and military support was noticeably given to new settlements in both the Golan Heights and the West Bank.[11]

In the summer of 1967 the cabinet approved several temporary work camps in the Syrian DMZ and then permitted agricultural activity in the Golan. These decisions were followed by the establishment of military Nahal outposts, which were settlements manned by soldiers. At the end of the soldiers' compulsory military service it was expected they would remain as residents of the area. The Golan settlements coincided with the establishment of the first settlements in the West Bank. In September the National Religious Party initiative to settle the Gush Etzion block, a group of Jewish settlements established prior to 1948, was approved, and the first settlements there were established.[12]

The early settlements were mostly built in areas that were not heavily populated by Palestinians. This may have been due to the caution of those leaders who still entertained thoughts of trading land for peace, although this notion was in conflict with the prevalent desire to retain tracts of land that were deemed biblically significant. But in January 1968 Alon proposed the first settlement in a populated area just outside the city of Hebron. A group of Gush Emunim (Block of the Faithful) members, an extremist settler organization that grew out of the religious Zionist youth movement Bnei Akiva, were led by Rabbi Moshe Levinger. Initially they were given permission to celebrate the passover *seder* in a hotel outside

Hebron. The permit was issued for one day but they never left. Yigal Alon supported the settlers since the National Religious Party was a critical coalition partner. The Jewish presence in Hebron has expanded ever since.[13]

One revealing government strategy was its land policy. This policy allowed the government to take over lands that had belonged to Jews prior to 1948, regardless of the legal heirs of the original landowners. It also permitted appropriation of state land in conquered and occupied areas, in blatant contravention of the Geneva Conventions. This amounted to over 50 percent of the entire West Bank. The government also took over land privately owned by Arabs, when it deemed this necessary for security. Often the land was handed over to settlers. The relationship between official Israel, who supported the settlers, and the Palestinians was inescapably defined by the acrimony this created.

The occupation soon became everyday reality, but there were many ministerial differences about future measures. Moshe Dayan proposed that the border of Israel in the east run along the Jordan River, and that the West Bank be economically integrated with Israel. He expected that within five years the West Bank would be an autonomous region. He said, "We will give them self-rule; economic independence and we will undertake to protect them." Alon proposed giving the West Bank the status of a state and supporting its membership in the United Nations. He wanted to build twelve settlements in the Jordan valley, but Eshkol was not convinced about the wisdom of settlements built at the hub of the Palestinian population. He did not want to develop Arab cantons, and was concerned about Israel's ability to integrate one and a half million Arabs.[14]

Alon's autonomous region idea was supported by a group of local Palestinian elders,[15] but Dayan, along with most of the Labor Party ministers, opposed the idea of Palestinian statehood as this presented a possible existential threat to Israel's sovereignty. Dayan appeared a pragmatist but he also claimed that the annexation of the West Bank and Gaza were inevitable. He effectively tied the economies of the West Bank and Gaza to Israel, and ultimately removed close to 400,000 Palestinians who became refugees.[16] Dayan and many of his military contemporaries favored the carrot and stick method of encouraging Palestinian emigration. General Uzi Narkiss suggested paying people money as an incentive to their departure, and others preferred making their lives uncomfortable. Such measures as limiting land and water availability or restricting industrial development would mean the Palestinians would want to leave. This policy was partially successful, and contributed to the creation of a large Palestinian diaspora, particularly in the oil-rich Gulf states.[17]

## ANOTHER ROUND OF INITIATIVES

One peace initiative at this time was spearheaded by Aziz Shehadeh, a West Bank lawyer, who met with a group of Palestinian dignitaries in Jericho in 1967 to launch a program for Palestinian independence that would be acceptable to the Israelis. The group considered interim solutions such as self-rule and regional autonomy leading to full independence.[18] Reserve officers in the IDF named Kimchi and Bavli, who were initially appointed to contact Arab leaders and elders to assess prevailing attitudes, met Shehadeh, and once convinced of his sincerity, recommended negotiations to the Israeli authorities. But these did not occur.[19]

A parallel initiative known as the Mayors' Initiative was led by Sheikh Ja'abri, who in 1969 organized a committee of notables, religious leaders, and mayors in the Hebron area. Ja'abri was willing to consider a limited level of autonomy for the Palestinian community, leading to the possible establishment of an autonomous region within a Greater Israel. Ja'abri tried to include other areas in his committee, but Israel would not permit him to extend his activities beyond the Hebron region. Apparently one of the tasks of the intended expanded committee would be to negotiate with Israel on solutions for the Palestinian problem.[20] The Ja'abri initiative was supported by the mayors of Bethlehem, Beit Sahor, and Beit Jallah, but ended under pressure from all sides: Israel, Jordan, and the Palestine Liberation Organization (PLO).[21]

The notion of a Palestinian autonomous region within a Greater Israel was popular in the late 1960s with many civilian Israeli leaders, including Prime Minister Eshkol. The main opposition to this concept came from the military, who were opposed to the idea of autonomy leading to statehood. Since the Palestinian public and PLO supporters also rejected this concept, its demise was predictable.[22]

A subsequent initiative based on the support of local leaders and their clans was the village leagues concept. This was developed and financed by Israelis in the early 1970s, and gained the support of some Arab leaders, who seemed willing to accept life under permanent Israeli rule. The Palestinian public, however, rejected it and considered the leaders of the village leagues quislings. This attempt was not successful.[23]

One clear direction in Israel's policies was its preference for striking a deal with Jordan. Shortly after the June war, King Hussein found himself vulnerable to PLO plans and local Palestinian activity for independence. His response was an announcement that residents of the Occupied Territories could maintain their Jordanian citizen ship, and all public-sector employees would continue to receive salaries from Jordan. But he also stated that the West Bank was in the Jordanian homeland and would remain so. The Alon Plan was singularly unacceptable to the King since it implied that Israel would not relinquish its control of the West Bank of the Jordan River or East Jerusalem. The plans drawn up by Alon and Dayan reflected no intention by Israel to return territories it had conquered during the war.[24]

## ISRAEL'S TERMS OF NEGOTIATION

At a cabinet meeting shortly after the war, on June 19, 1967, Eshkol expressed his intention to meet Arab leaders to negotiate a permanent peace agreement on terms prepared by the Defense Committee. To summarize the main points in the proposal:

- An agreement with Egypt would be based on the security needs of Israel and established at the international border that prevailed prior to the founding of Israel in 1948. That would leave the Gaza Strip under Israeli control. Free passage in the Straits of Tiran and through the Suez Canal would be guaranteed. The Sinai peninsula would be demilitarized and Israel would continue to hold all the conquered territories until the agreement was signed.
- The agreement with Syria would also be based on the security needs of Israel, and established at the international border. The Golan Heights would be demilitarized and Syria would guarantee the free flow of water from the Jordan River. Israel would continue to hold on to the Syrian conquered territories until the agreement was signed.
- An outline of the terms for peace with Jordan was postponed.
- The Palestinians were not mentioned.[25]

This plan of the Defense Committee was never disclosed to the Israeli public. Outside the members of the cabinet nobody knew anything about it. Abba Eban in New York communicated it to US Secretary of State Dean Rusk. According to Eban, the Americans considered the proposal generous, particularly since it came just days after a stunning victory. However Syria and Egypt strongly rejected it. Their position was that Israel's withdrawal from the conquered territories had to be unconditional.[26]

Meanwhile under the influence of the generals, primarily David Elazar, Eshkol's Defense Committee concluded that a return to the international border would be a mistake and Israel must retain security-sensitive territories, especially in the Golan Heights.[27] The government issued permits for settlements in the Golan Heights, and the "generous" plan was formally abandoned in October.

## THE KHARTOUM SUMMIT

At the August 1967 Arab League summit meeting in Khartoum, the Arab leaders took a hard-line position and agreed that there would be no peace with Israel, no recognition of Israel, and no agreement to negotiate with Israel.[28] Israel used this triple refusal as an example of Arab hard-line intransigence, and responded with a policy of negotiation on defensible borders for Israel, which meant no return to the 1949 armistice boundaries.[29] The Khartoum summit was actually a victory for the moderates of the Arab world, led by Nasser and Hussein. They convinced the Arabs that the use of force was not the only way to solve the conflict. Officially the summit refused to recognize Israel *de jure*, but left the road open to a *de facto* recognition. Although no direct negotiation was allowed, negotiations via a third party were not prohibited.

Hussein expressed his belief that the decisions made at the summit were a joint achievement with Nasser, moving towards a settlement with Israel.[30] Israel, apparently unaware of the moderating efforts of Nasser and Hussein, reacted as though the path to any negotiation was now closed. On October 30, 1967 the Knesset cancelled its June 19 proposal and decided to abandon any attempt to seek peace based on international borders with Syria or Egypt. Egypt and Syria would now have to accommodate the security needs of Israel.[31]

## UN RESOLUTION 242

UN Security Council Resolution 242 was possibly the most significant event to occur in the international arena after the June war. The resolution prohibited forceful acquisition of territory, and emphasized the necessity for a just and lasting peace, based on Israel's withdrawal from territories occupied in the war. All states in the region had the right to live in peace within secure and recognized borders.[32] The resolution was ambiguous, but acceptable to the United States, the USSR, Jordan, Egypt, and Syria. Israel's interpretation of the resolution was that the phrase "to withdraw from territories" did not linguistically specify from *all* territories. The other signatories and the United States, however, interpreted it as a requirement to withdraw from all territories, and return to international borders. Israel did not officially accept the resolution until August 1970, although in 1968 Eban informed the United Nations that Israel unofficially accepted it, albeit with its own interpretation.

Gunnar Jarring, Sweden's ambassador to Moscow, was appointed by the United Nations to implement Resolution 242. Most of the confrontation states enthusiastically supported Jarring's mission. Israel and Syria were not interested. Abba Eban was assigned the job of negotiating with Jarring and the United Nations, and did so with endless memos, documents, and briefs. The mission failed but Resolution 242 was, and still is, a pivotal and fundamental document underlying the efforts to resolve the Middle East conflict. Not for the first or last time, Israel rejected UN-determined boundaries and territories.

### FROM ESHKOL TO GOLDA

During his final years in office, Eshkol tried to convince the Jordanian king to accept some version of the Alon or Dayan plans, but the king's representative, Zaid al-Rifai, responded that this was unacceptable since the plans infringed on Jordan's sovereignty.[33] Eshkol died in 1969, and Golda Meir replaced him as leader of the Labor Party. She had been called back from retirement as a compromise choice to avoid a bitter and potentially destructive confrontation between two younger candidates, Alon and Dayan, and she became Israel's fourth prime minister.

Golda Meir was known to be strong, and possibly overbearing. She demonstrated little sympathy for the Arabs, rejecting the notion that they were victims of a great injustice.[34] She accepted the accusation of intransigence when it concerned Israel's security, and claimed that this was much preferable to a fine, liberal, anti-militaristic, dead Jewish state.[35] With regard to the West Bank, her position did not differ much from Eshkol's. Both opposed the annexation of the West Bank and leaned towards some form of agreement with Jordan that would maximize Israel's territorial gain and minimize its exposure to a Palestinian population. Meir's first speech to the Knesset as prime minister presented the principles that would guide her approach to the conflict: no return to the pre-1967 borders, and direct negotiations leading to peace treaties with the Arabs. Although this seemed a reasonable approach to peace, her resolve about the pre-1967 borders precluded the possibility of making any progress. She did not specify what would constitute secure borders for Israel.[36]

An interview with Victor Shem-Tov, the minister of health in Meir's government, was published in *Ma'ariv* on the 25th anniversary of the 1973 war. Shem-Tov described the government rejection of Gunnar Jarring's 1971 initiative as catastrophic and unforgivable. Since it had been supported by both the United States and the USSR, that initiative had been an enormous opportunity for peace which was terribly squandered by the government. Shem Tov strongly condemned this rejectionism, saying that history would not forgive Israel.[37]

Although the majority of Meir's ministers were moderates, she supported proposals brought forth by the government's more hawkish members. The IDF leadership had always influenced government policy, but Meir seemed intimidated by the generals, or uncomfortable with military-security issues, and therefore tended to accept their suggestions. She rarely resisted military advice, and military policy increasingly prevailed.[38]

## THE WAR OF ATTRITION

The War of Attrition broke out in 1969, and led to another peace initiative, named after US Secretary of State William Rogers. The Rogers Plan, officially announced on December 9, 1970, required Israel to withdraw to the pre-1967 borders and Egypt to agree to a binding and specific commitment to peace. Israel considered the plan an attempt to appease the Arabs at Israel's expense; Egypt and the USSR both rejected the proposal, characterizing it as pro-Israeli. The Egyptian rejection of the Rogers Plan could also be attributed to separate demands placed upon it to demilitarize the Sinai peninsula and guarantee shipping rights to Israeli ships. However, it is likely that another reason was Israel's unrelenting control of Sharm el Sheikh.[39]

Assuming that the American plan was intended to bring the fighting to a halt, Abba Eban proposed that cabinet accept a limited ceasefire as part of a peace endeavor. Golda Meir strongly objected, and he withdrew his proposal.[40] Meir's rigidity was coming under increasing pressure, and on April 28,1970 she received the first of what later became a series of letters from senior high school students questioning their own ability to carry out their duty in the army into which they would soon be inducted. This letter was provoked by a formal invitation issued a few days earlier by Nasser to Nahum Goldman, the head of the World Jewish Congress, to visit him in Cairo. Meir's government refused to authorize the visit, and the trip was never implemented. The students' letter was sparked by a concern that Israel's government was not actively seeking peace and triggered a heated internal debate about who was responsible for the continued state of war.[41]

The War of Attrition continued unabated, and its escalation threatened a confrontation between the United States and the USSR. On June 19, the US secretary of state, Rogers, introduced Rogers Plan B, which included the following elements:

• restatement of support for UNSC 242
• three months ceasefire
• withdrawal from occupied territories
• immediate negotiations under the supervision of Gunnar Jarring.

In a letter to Meir, US President Nixon urged her to accept Rogers Plan B, and although some of her colleagues bolted from the coalition, she did. A ceasefire with Egypt began on August 7.

## PALESTINIANS INTENSIFY THE STRUGGLE

Meanwhile the Palestinians intensified guerilla operations against Israel, but the odds were heavily stacked against them. Palestinian hopes of a popular rebellion did not materialize. Instead Palestinian networks across the West Bank were significantly damaged. The Palestinian response was to launch guerilla operations from bases in Jordan across the Jordan River. In one incident an Israeli school bus hit a mine 20 km north of Eilat. Two adults were killed and ten school children were wounded.[42] Israel's retaliation became known as the Karameh operation. Israeli intelligence in this instance was inadequate, and the assumption that the Jordanian Legion, Jordan's regular army, would not get involved proved wrong. The Jordanian Legion was well prepared and waiting for the Israeli onslaught. Hundreds of well-armed guerillas took on the Israeli forces, which withdrew without accomplishing the total destruction of the Fatah bases in and around Karameh. Israel suffered major losses: nearly 40 soldiers died and over 150 were wounded. About 30 Israeli tanks were damaged. But the PLO and the Jordanian Legion suffered a much higher rate of casualties. The Israeli forces destroyed about 200 of the buildings in Karameh. The Arabs nevertheless hailed this operation as a great victory. It became a symbol of Arab and Palestinian heroism and of Israel's vulnerability. Karameh was a strong morale incentive for later resistance efforts.[43]

On May 26, 1970 Moshe Karmel, a member of the Achdut Ha'avoda Party and a former general, a former government minister, and a confirmed hawk, made the following declaration in the Knesset during the debate on the prime minister's statement on foreign policy and defense:

[I don't agree] with the view that we have taken all possible initiatives concerning peace. I am sure that the fundamental stand of the government is correct. That it is the road to peace, and that the government wholeheartedly strives towards peace. But I do not agree that every initiative which might have been taken, was indeed taken. I shall relate two examples which I think indicate misjudged passivity in the political sphere. Although we should beware of deluding ourselves, it is important to convince the world and the people in this country that no opportunities were missed in our efforts to achieve peace.

The first case: In an interview published last week in *Die Welt*, Nasser said that he favoured a peace treaty with Israel, in line with the Security Council resolution of November 1967 [i.e. UNSC 242], and that he would recognize Israel's pre-Six Day war borders and its shipping rights in the Gulf of Aqaba in exchange for evacuation of all the conquered territories and a solution of the Palestine problem either through new settlements for refugees or compensation payments for those wishing it.

The second case: A few days ago, King Hussein of Jordan told a correspondent of *Der Stern* that he would agree to conduct talks with Israel on condition that Jerusalem would be one of the subjects of those talks. Nobody would suggest that Hussein is independent of Nasser in the matter of negotiations with us. However, I would like to ask why no authoritative reaction was heard affirming our readiness to negotiate with Jordan without prior conditions ...[44]

This complaint about the position of a government in which his own party was a coalition member raises questions about Israel's pronouncements of peace. Peace, on Israel's terms, could be achieved easily if the Arabs would accept Israel's demands and its refusal to negotiate the refugee problem. No Arab leader would accept these opening preconditions, and Israel refused Nasser's and Hussein's proposals because both undercut Israel's precondition that the status quo must be maintained.

## NASSER DIES

Nasser died of a heart attack at the age of 52 on September 28, 1970. His successor, Anwar el Sadat, was not expected to last in power for very long.

A few months later the Nixon administration urged Israel to engage in peace talks under the supervision of Gunnar Jarring. The document containing his proposals for the resolution of the conflict, which was submitted to the Egyptians and the Israelis, demanded that Israel withdraw to the international border. It demanded that Egypt immediately begin peace talks with Israel. Egypt informed Jarring that it would enter negotiation provided that the agreement would include all undertakings provided for in the UNSC Resolution 242. Israel would have to withdraw from the Sinai peninsula and from Gaza, and commit to settle the refugee problem. Finally Egypt proposed the establishment of a peacekeeping UN force. This was the first time that an Arab government had announced its willingness to sign a peace treaty with Israel, and both the United States and the United Nations welcomed the Egyptian response. Israel expressed satisfaction, but at the same time unequivocally rejected a return to the pre-war boundaries.[45]

Sadat, Egypt's new leader, launched a new initiative on February 4, 1971, which involved the reopening of the Suez Canal and the partial withdrawal of Israeli forces to an approximate distance of 40 km from the canal. Yitzhak Rabin was then Israel's ambassador to the United States, and said that Israel should accept the proposal. But Rabin was not the prime minister yet. Golda Meir expressed her misgivings about it in an interview with an American TV network. Her main fear was that a partial withdrawal would lead Israel back to the international border, but with further encouragement by the US administration, Meir conceded that she might accept Sadat's proposal with restrictive conditions. Since Dayan argued in favor of the Egyptian proposal, the cabinet finally accepted an interim agreement based on the Egyptian proposal, although this did not result in its implementation.[46]

In a speech to the UN General Assembly, Secretary Rogers urged implementation of the interim agreement as a first step towards UNSC Resolution 242. This followed discussions between the United States and the USSR in which the two superpowers agreed upon a proposal which was communicated to the Israelis by the President's advisor Henry Kissinger on November 5, 1971. Israel's rejection of the proposal led to further discussions between Kissinger and Rabin, and finally the president invited Meir to visit the United States. In December 1971 Meir met President Nixon, and convinced him to abandon the Rogers Plan and to renew the shipment of arms from the United States to Israel.[47] In exchange for these concessions Meir would be more flexible in the interpretation of the interim agreement. She remained adamantly opposed, however, to Israeli withdrawal from the Sinai peninsula and to any return to the pre June war borders.

The upcoming interim agreement was regarded by Abba Eban as the beginning of a new era in the Middle East. Dayan, however, was setting up settlements in the Gaza Strip, contradicting Israel's intention to relinquish any control over this area by establishing new facts on the ground. In the two years leading to the 1973 war Israel's main preoccupation was preserving the status quo by a strategy Abba Eban described as attritional, which implied that the Arabs would eventually concede that they could not defeat Israel by force, and also that pressure from the great powers would not retrieve their lands. Then the Arabs would come to the negotiation table willing to satisfy Israel's territorial demands. Eban suggested that Israel did not consider the possibility that the Arabs would choose the option of war.[48]

Henry Kissinger was the Nixon administration's man in charge of the Middle East. Under his supervision, Israel and the United States became strategic allies to all practical purposes. Both the United States and Israel regarded Jordan as non-threatening, and the attritional strategy was directed primarily at Egypt. Throughout Meir's leadership Israel maintained direct contact with King Hussein and his representatives, reminiscent of the pre-state contacts between Meir and the king's grandfather, King Abdullah. In 1947 Meir had signed an agreement with King Abdullah to divide Palestine between what was to become Israel and TransJordan. That early agreement had been engineered at the expense of the majority of the population in Mandatory Palestine, the Palestinians. Meir viewed the Palestinians as Israel's staunchest enemy, with whom it would be impossible to reach agreement. She refused to consider the Palestinians as a nation or even as a people and clearly stated, "It is not as though there was a Palestinian people and we came and threw them out and took their country away from them. They did not exist."[49] She considered them a threat to Israel and to Jordan, and she preferred to reach an agreement with King Hussein that would divide Palestine between Israel and Jordan as had been suggested on numerous occasions in the past.

She was eager to pursue the Alon Plan but the king was uninterested. Any proposal based on the Alon Plan would maintain a role for Israel in governing the West Bank, and this could not be acceptable to the king.[50] In 1972 he launched his own plan, that of a United Arab Kingdom which consisted of a two-part federation: the region of Jordan, extending over the east bank of the river, and Palestine comprising the West Bank and the Gaza Strip. The king envisaged Amman as the capital of the east bank region and Jerusalem as the capital of the West Bank. The introduction of this plan affirmed his intention to maintain the role of ruler and representative of the West Bank and its people. Egypt and Israel, and more importantly the PLO, all rejected this proposal.[51]

In July 1972, Sadat unexpectedly announced the evacuation of all Soviet military personnel from Egypt. This move was believed to mark the end of Egypt's military stance, and was seen as a victory for the attritional approach to the conflict. Gideon Rafael, the director general of the Israeli Foreign Ministry, thought otherwise. He warned that this might actually be a prelude to war. His opinion was largely discounted.[52] But in 1972 Sadat was in fact making preparations for war. He did however make one last effort to negotiate. He sent his national security adviser, Hafez Ismail, to convince the United States to pressure Israel to accept Sadat's political solution. Another series of meetings between Kissinger and Ismail, King Hussein and Golda Meir followed, but failed to produce any positive result.

Against the background of this flurry of inactivity, Moshe Dayan became the spearhead of the settlement movement. He saw the expansion of settlements in the West Bank as a way of redrawing the map of Israel. Standing at the ancient fortress of Masada in the spring of 1973, he announced that the jurisdiction of the government of Israel would now extend from the Jordan River to the Suez Canal. On July 30, 1973, in an interview with *Time* magazine he was more emphatic: "There is no more Palestine, finished."[53]

The doves in the government, led by Eban, tried to change the course of this endeavor. Eban warned that if the Arabs felt there was no hope of any political and territorial gain, war would become inevitable. Pinhas Sapir, less outspoken than Eban, also spoke of the damage that the occupation and the settlements would cause to Israel's moral fiber. In an attempt to resolve this internal conflict between the doves and the hawks, Meir's confidant Israel Galilee was assigned the task of proposing a compromise. The result was the Galilee Document, which completely supported Dayan's vision of expanding existing settlements and building new ones. The Galilee Document restated the expansionist positions of Meir, Dayan, and Alon. It was no conciliatory step towards peace, and reinforced the Egyptian and Syrian inclination to go to war.

As predicted by Labor Party doves, the Arabs initiated military operations.[54] Early in the afternoon of October 6, 1973 Egypt and Syria launched a combined military offensive against Israel.

# 6
# FROM YOM KIPPUR TO LEBANON

Radical change is often the product of war. The scars formed by a war that just ended are revealed, and new opportunities for conflict resolution are presented. This was not the case in the aftermath of the 1967 and the 1973 wars. To the victorious Israelis the 1967 war generated a feeling of invincibility, and the 1973 war left a collective post-war trauma. Although Israel had the upper hand in 1973, the sensation of invincibility was lost. The prevailing mood was a somber sadness mixed with outright fear. Israelis realized that at a certain point Israel almost lost that war. On the other hand, the Egyptians and the other Arab nations involved in the conflict were jubilant, having successfully salvaged Arab pride and overcome the humiliation suffered by the Arabs after Israel's 1967 victory.

Both wars ended with tremendous opportunities for resolution of the conflict, but Israel did not take any advantage of them, with some leaders regarding them as a competing opportunity to expand Israel's territory between the Jordan River and the Mediterranean Sea. Rather than peace, the emerging militant settlement movement in Israel and the Palestinian resistance movement became two major antagonistic players in the conflict.

However, the 1973 war produced a growing awareness among Israelis that the Middle East conflict could not be solved by military means, and a peace agreement achieved by political means became crucial. The war led to the Israeli–Egyptian peace agreement, but the rest of the Arab world did not join the peace process. Israel's refusal to give up territories acquired by war and to recognize the national aspirations of the Palestinian people, now almost exclusively ruled by Israel, continues to be responsible for the fact that the peace process is still far from being complete even more than 30 years after this war.

The October 1973 war caught Israel by surprise. It was unprepared despite repeated admonitions by doves such as Abba Eban and Pinhas Sapir that failure to resolve the conflict would inevitably lead to another war. Any suggestions that Sadat and Assad were preparing for war were ignored. Zvi Zamir, the head of Mossad explained, "We simply did not believe that they could do it .... We scorned them."[1]

Many leaders, even Moshe Dayan, believed that eventually the Arabs would have to go to war. Dayan claimed that the Arabs did not have to win a war. A credible performance by the Arab armies would be sufficient to erase the humiliation of previous defeats and restore Arab honor.[2]

On October 6, 1973 Syria and Egypt launched a coordinated attack against Israel. Sadat and Assad were not necessarily convinced they would be able to defeat Israel. Although Israel reached deep into Syrian and Egyptian territory, the Arabs fully achieved their more limited goals. Israeli military self-confidence was severely shaken when Egypt destroyed the Bar Lev fortifications along the Suez Canal and took control over  two significant strips of land extending into the Sinai peninsula.

Following a resolution by the UNSC and under pressure from the superpowers a ceasefire was imposed at the end of October. A series of subsequent mini agreements paved the road to the Egyptian–Israeli Peace Treaty. On November 11, 1973 Israel and Egypt signed a formal cease fire. On January 18, 1974 the first Israeli–Egyptian disengagement agreement, and on April 31, 1974 the Israeli–Syrian disengagement agreements were signed.[3]

Indirect negotiations in 1974–75 were intended by Egypt primarily to liberate the captured Sinai peninsula. Israel's position was more complex. Israel stated its desire to end the continued belligerence, but at the same time to retain all or most of the territories it had acquired during the 1967 war. Kissinger, the mastermind of the post-1973 war negotiations, declared the Israeli position inflexible and suspended the talks. At this point the US Administration declared a reassessment of its relationship with Israel. On September 4, 1975 the sides finally signed the Sinai II Agreement.[4]

The intimate and decisive involvement of the United States in those negotiations had a significant effect on future negotiations for peace. There were to be no more secret initiatives whereby one leader would whisper their willingness to enter peace negotiations into the ear of a go-between. Contacts for the purpose of peace negotiations were now done in the open, and almost always through the involvement of a third party: in most cases, the United States.

## YATZHAK RABIN, FIFTH PRIME MINISTER

Yitzhak Rabin, Israel's fifth prime minister, took office on June 3, 1974 after Golda Meir's resignation. Rabin was a very different leader from all his predecessors, and became prime minister from outside the usual political party mechanism. He was born in Palestine and spent most of his adult life in the Israeli military. He also spent about five years as Israel's ambassador to the United States, which greatly influenced his views on Israel's global position. As an ex-general, Rabin was concerned about security issues, and as an ex-ambassador he recognized the vital importance of Israel's relationship with the United States.[5]

Rabin's attitudes to the prospect of peace and the preservation of the status quo also differed from those of his predecessors. In his early speeches to the Knesset he expressed the view that the quest for peace would involve considerable risks, which he was prepared to take. He proposed a course of indirect negotiations with a third-part involvement, and declared a willingness to trade land for peace.[6] Rabin was the first Israeli leader to openly adopt a limited strategy of land for peace. He was less clear about the specifics of the strategy, but was convinced that Israel would have to give up most of the territories it had conquered during the 1967 war, and that the primary partner for peace would be Jordan. The peace deal that Israel would offer Jordan was essentially a slightly modified version of the Alon Plan. Rabin did not think Israel could negotiate effectively after the October war, so he believed it must gain time. Once Israel could re-establish its deterrence power, its ability to negotiate effectively would improve.[7] He considered the growing settlement movement a potential stumbling block to future peace with Jordan, but could take little action on this issue. His coalition was narrow, and he could not risk losing the main supporter of the settlers, the National Religious Party.

Although the PLO did not participate in the October war, its leaders took significant steps to moderate their militant pre-war positions. The change was an acceptance of a multi-stage approach to peace. The first stage they were willing to consider was the status of an independent national authority for the Palestinians, or a government with limited powers operating alongside Israel.[8] This concept preceded the Oslo Accords by two decades, and was similar to what was put in place at Oslo.

Neither Rabin nor his ministers considered the PLO a potential partner for peace. Aharon Yariv and Victor Shem-Tov, two of Rabin's more moderate ministers, proposed a formula for negotiations with the PLO, but none of their colleagues were willing to consider it. The main objection Rabin and his colleagues had was the PLO determination to end up as a sovereign, independent state. Territorial compromise was abhorrent to Rabin and others, and although they supported the Jordanian option, they were equally unwilling to offer much to King Hussein of Jordan. Rabin could not be persuaded by the United States to improve upon the Alon Plan deal he was willing to offer Jordan.[9]

Rabin did approve, however, of another plan for the resolution of the Palestinian problem presented by Shimon Peres to King Hussein. This involved a joint Jordanian and Israeli administration of a Palestinian entity, which would be a demilitarized body politic with no unified sovereignty. Some residents of this entity would carry Jordanian passports while others carried Israeli passports. Jordan, Israel, and the Palestinian entity together would form a united economic unit. King Hussein shrugged off this proposal, and was equally unenthusiastic when another of the participants, Yigal Alon, proposed the enticement of turning the town of Jericho over to the kingdom for the Jordanian administration of the West Bank.[10]

Although a genuinely moderate prime minister, Rabin did not produce a proposal that was acceptable to the Jordanians or to the Palestinians, whose rights of self-determination he rejected. This impasse underlies almost all Israeli peace negotiations: Time and again Israel insisted on maintaining the post-1967 status quo while simultaneously demanding a peace treaty. Many moderate Israeli leaders were taken aback that no Arab leader ever agreed to a solution based on the status quo. The post-1967 borders violated UNSC Resolution 242, which underpinned any acceptable peace solution for the Arabs, the United Nations and most of the western world. Nevertheless, Rabin, Peres, Dayan, Alon, and others actually presented themselves as true peace seekers.

The Seventh Arab League Summit in Rabat, Morocco in October 1974 brought an end to the Jordanian option. The PLO was resolute about being the only representative of the Palestinian people, who were determined to be granted the right for a fully independent state in all of the West Bank and Gaza, or any part that would be liberated. King Hussein had to accept the resolution of the Rabat meeting.[11]

Within weeks the leader of the PLO, Yasser Arafat, was invited to address the General Assembly of the United Nations, which then passed a resolution recognizing the right of the Palestinian people to self-determination. Rabin's response was an announcement that he would only negotiate with the king. Despite the Rabat decision and the UN General Assembly resolutions, the meetings between the Israelis and King Hussein continued up to 1976, and with the same absence of results.[12]

On the Egyptian front, President Sadat was trying to move towards a global settlement. Since 1976 was an election year in the United States, Sadat's efforts were not given much enthusiastic support. Rabin was more interested in a separate agreement with Egypt than in any global arrangement. He even involved the Moroccan King Hassan to back his quest for direct talks with Sadat, but the Egyptians showed no keen interest.[13]

However, in 1977 Egypt's vice-president, Hassan Tuhami, requested Austria's Chancellor Bruno Kreisky to arrange a meeting for him with Shimon Peres, which Rabin vetoed. Rabin was possibly concerned that he could do nothing Sadat would want without risking his coalition majority. At this time Rabin's leadership was troubled by scandals involving some key figures in his political party.[14]

Jimmy Carter's victory in the US elections delivered some surprises for Rabin. Carter wanted to move beyond the permanent-interim agreements towards a global settlement of the conflict. He was the first US president who considered new solutions. When Rabin visited the White House in March 1977, the president had already determined that a complete Israeli withdrawal to the pre-June boundaries and the reconvening of the Geneva Conference were essential. Carter also concluded that the United States and Israel should support the rights of the Palestinians to national self-determination under the leadership of the PLO. Carter's views contradicted the prevailing Israeli approach of interim agreements leading to separate agreements with individual Arab states. They clearly defied Israel's hope to avoid recognition of the rights of the Palestinians for an independent state of their own.[15]

## THE *MAHAPACH*

A foreign bank account indiscretion by Rabin's wife led to his resignation in April 1977. The Labor Party Alignment appointed Peres as the head of a caretaker government. An election on May 17 resulted in the dramatic *mahapach* (turnabout), which brought the opposition to power under the leadership of Menachem Begin. Things were never the same again. There were two relatively short periods where the Labor Party Alignment returned to power, but Begin's right-wing Likud has since maintained political control.

Seven years earlier Begin had resigned his position as minister without portfolio to protest against the government's acceptance of UN Resolution 242 and the land for peace concept. With Begin now leading the government of Israel, Carter's approach to resolving the conflict was not likely to be implemented. The Labor governments had occasionally expressed some support for territorial compromise and a land for peace strategy. Begin's opposition had always been intractable. Undeterred, Carter still hoped for a multilateral conference to achieve a global solution. His administration understood that the conflict could not be resolved unless the rights and aspirations of the Palestinians were recognized.[16]

## CARTER'S INITIATIVE

Unpredictably in his first meeting with Carter on July 19, 1977, Begin agreed to accept UNSC Resolution 242 as a basis for future peace talks. He also vaguely agreed to freeze the building of new settlements in the occupied territories. He even told Cyrus Vance, the US secretary of state, that he planned to meet Sadat.[17] But upon his return to Israel, Begin immediately legalized several settlements that had been set up by the previous government.

Vance visited the Middle East in August, and Sadat presented him with a peace plan and a willingness to meet with Begin.[18] Vance now found an uncompromising Begin who declared he had no intention of evacuating the occupied territories but might consider granting the residents cultural autonomy. Moshe Dayan, Begin's new foreign minister, wrote Vance on September 2 that Israel planned to retain the Gaza Strip, Sharm el Sheikh and the strip of land connecting it to Eilat. Dayan implied that Israel would retain the West Bank, and the only offer it might make was part of the Golan Heights.[19]

These were the declared starting positions, and yet on a trip to Morocco Dayan requested the king's help in arranging a meeting with the Egyptians. Several days later he did, in fact, meet Egypt's deputy prime minister, Hassan Tuhami, who told him that President Sadat was very serious about achieving peace.[20] Egypt's non-negotiable conditions for peace, however, included a complete withdrawal from all occupied territories including East Jerusalem.

Success in such negotiations would bring Syria and Jordan into the peace process too. Sadat was adamant about not signing a separate peace agreement with Israel, and would meet Begin only if Israel accepted these preconditions. Dayan apparently responded that Israel would consider withdrawing from the Sinai peninsula in order to achieve peace. He seemed to believe that despite Sadat's position, it would be possible to negotiate a separate peace deal between Israel and Egypt.[21]

On October 1, 1977 the USSR and the United States jointly asserted the necessity for an Israeli withdrawal from the occupied territories and for a resolution of the Palestinian issue that would guarantee the rights of the Palestinian people. Due to Israeli and American Jewish pressure, the US administration retreated even from this position, which fell short even of Sadat's conditions. In a speech to the UN General Assembly, Carter proclaimed that the United States would not impose a solution to the Middle East conflict. This left Sadat with the option of an unprecedented step aimed directly at Israel. If the fundamental obstacle to peace was a psychological barrier of mistrust, only breaking the psychological logjam could permit progress. Sadat's astounding visit to Jerusalem was the first step.[22]

This visit reflected his belief that time was running out, and that if no imminent progress were made there would inevitably be another war, which the Arabs were unlikely to win. Sadat's two heart attacks probably reinforced the urgency.[23] In October Carter had sent a handwritten letter to Sadat requesting his help in removing the difficulties on the road to a peace conference in Geneva. Sadat responded in a handwritten note promising Carter a bold step.[24] Sadat deliberated about a visit to Jerusalem with several of his closest advisers, among them his foreign minister, Ismail Fahmi. Fahmi was opposed, and warned Sadat that this would be a disaster that would cause irreparable damage to Egypt's position in the Arab world.

On November 5 Sadat told the Egyptian Security Council that he was ready to go to Jerusalem and give a speech in the Knesset if this would save the blood of his sons.[25] Four days later in a speech to the Egyptian Parliament he announced his plan in public. Other Egyptian leaders were stunned. Syria declared a day of mourning. Although Sadat informed Carter of his intentions before making the speech, his announcement caught both the United States and Israel by surprise. Israelis by and large thought this announcement should not be taken too seriously. Begin even suggested Sadat was unhinged.[26] Defense minister Weizman and other military experts

believed that this was a scam or an Egyptian deception. Only Begin
and Dayan knew about the Tuhami talks in Morocco, and considered Sadat's plans sincere, despite their outrageousness. One day
prior to Sadat's visit, Begin shared this information with his advisors
but the Israeli military intelligence still considered Sadat's proposal
a well-designed trap.[27] In any event Begin announced that if Sadat
would come, he would be greeted with all the respect due a president.[28] Begin's position was that Israel would be willing to evacuate
the entire Sinai in exchange for peace.

## SADAT IN JERUSALEM

Despite the protest resignations of foreign minister Fahmi and his
deputy, and the problems in his own government, Sadat was undeterred.[29] His plane landed at Ben Gurion airport on November
19. After the official pomp and ceremony he met with Begin for a
private conversation. Sadat communicated that the goal of the visit
was to address the Knesset and convey the importance of a solution
to the Palestinian problem. He was not interested in reaching a
separate peace deal with Israel.[30] At the Knesset in the afternoon of
November 20, he reiterated the Arab position, and pointed out that
his visit was not intended to abandon the Arab cause or negotiate
a separate peace between Israel and Egypt. He wanted an overall
peace based on a total withdrawal of Israeli forces from occupied
territories, and at the same time a just resolution of the Palestinian
case.[31] Despite the momentous historical overtone of this visit,
Begin reacted to the Sadat speech with his standard inflexibility,
promising nothing. He called attention to the fact that the Egyptian
president had come to Israel knowing the differences between Israel
and Egypt's views on boundaries and resolutions. Begin made no
mention of the Palestinians.

The two leaders came to a general agreement about not going to
war, and agreed that Egypt would resume its sovereignty over the
entire Sinai and that most of it would be demilitarized.[32]

Sadat's visit to Jerusalem broke the psychological barrier. Up to
this time, Israeli governments had kept silent about any Arab leaders
who were willing to make peace, and even pay a considerable price
to achieve it. After Sadat's speech in Jerusalem the conciliatory
intention of this Arab leader was no longer secret.[33] The Israeli
leadership now needed to produce a counter-offer to offset the
impact created by Sadat's visit to Jerusalem; to demonstrate that
Israel was also interested in peace and willing to make concessions.

But Begin also had to take into consideration Sadat's clear support for Palestinian self-determination. The opportunity to present the Israeli plan for peace occurred in mid-December during Begin's visit to Washington.

Prior to his trip, Begin conducted extensive discussions with Israel politicians, military people, and even jurists. A two-tier plan evolved: a peace treaty with Egypt, and a concept for Palestinian autonomy in the West Bank and Gaza. The autonomy conceived was non-territorial and would apply only to the people living in these areas but not to the territories themselves.[34] This allowed the rejection or postponement of the issues of sovereignty and self-determination for the Palestinians, and was consistent with Israeli policy. Any genuine Israeli desire for peace was compromised by a determination to hold on to territory acquired in war. The plan also addressed another nagging problem for Israel: preventing the influx of Palestinian refugees into Israel and capping the number of Arabs who would become citizens of the State of Israel.

Two weeks after Sadat's visit to Jerusalem, King Hassan of Morocco hosted a meeting between Dayan and Tuhami which demonstrated the difference between Sadat's attempts to achieve a global peace involving the entire Arab world, and the single-minded Israeli desire for an exclusive agreement between Egypt and Israel. Israel wanted an agreement that would leave the Palestinians out of the equation. After Begin's trip to Washington, Dayan and Tuhami met again in Morocco to sound out the new Israeli plan. Tuhami rejected the plan, which ignored Sadat's intention of a comprehensive peace.[35] Another meeting, this time in Egypt, between Weizman and several Egyptian leaders, made little more progress. This stalemate continued until the next summit meeting at the end of December. Sadat probably expected some reciprocity to his own grand gesture, but Begin gave very little. The unavoidable conclusion was that unless the Americans became more deeply involved in the peace process, nothing would develop.

Carter met Sadat in Aswan, Egypt on January 4, 1978, and the two issued the joint Aswan Declaration. They concluded that peace must be accompanied by the normalization of relationships, by the total withdrawal of Israel forces from occupied territories, and by the recognition of the legitimate rights of the Palestinians.[36] Israel immediately announced the construction of four new settlements in the Sinai, reinforcing Carter's doubts about Begin's intentions and reliability.[37]

The PLO, in the months following Sadat's visit to Israel, increased its guerilla campaign against the spurious peace process. They attacked both Egyptian and Israeli targets, leading to two distinct developments. Angered at the PLO for the murder of the editor of *Al Ahram* newspaper and other hostile actions, Sadat gradually moved towards acceptance of a separate peace treaty with Israel. After the PLO hijacked an Israeli bus on a coastal highway, Israel's position hardened further. Dayan and Sharon wanted to renew settlement construction, and Weizman had to threaten resignation from the cabinet to block this attempt. Whereas Sadat had moved closer to the Israeli position in his quest for a resolution, Israel remained recalcitrant.[38] Both Sadat and Begin were faced with growing domestic pressure. Sadat's came mostly from Arab rejectionists who insisted that Egypt quit the peace process. Begin's came from Israelis who felt that Begin's rigidity and intransigence were preventing a historic opportunity to achieve peace.

An Israeli peace movement started with a letter signed by several hundred Israeli reserve soldiers and officers, among them senior officers, protesting that the government was resistant to peace. At the end of March this new movement, Peace Now, assembled more than 40,000 people to demonstrate at Begin's official residence. After only a few weeks, 100,000 people signed a petition urging the government to stop impeding the peace process.[39] Begin and his government dismissed these protests as insignificant, but they understood that they expressed the views of a significant portion of the Israeli public. The official Israeli position remained unchanged despite increasing domestic and American pressure.

## CAMP DAVID I

In July 1978 Sadat told Weizman that if no progress were made by October, he would resign.[40] Since he could not convince Begin to make any gesture that would resuscitate Sadat's enthusiasm, Weizman publicly declared that "I am not sure the government wants peace."[41] Sadat also told President Carter of his intentions to withdraw from the peace process since he saw no point in further talks with the Israelis. Soon after, on July 30, Carter convened a three-way summit meeting at Camp David, which Begin had to attend.[42] The Israeli government prepared for the Camp David summit by agreeing that Israeli air bases and settlements in the Sinai would remain in Israeli hands. There would be no withdrawal from the West Bank and Gaza, and no acceptance of Palestinian self-determination. Sadat was adamant that Israel must withdraw totally from Sinai but less insistent about the Palestinian issue.

The Camp David summit was initially intended to be a three-day affair. It took two weeks of bargaining and negotiating to reach a compromise agreement. Israel agreed to evacuate all of the Sinai and remove its bases and settlements. Egypt agreed to postpone the resolution of the Palestinian issue to a further date and leave the West Bank and Gaza under Israeli occupation. The Palestinians got nothing but a vague document entitled *Framework for Peace*.

## THE EGYPT–ISRAEL PEACE TREATY

It would seem that Begin woke up suddenly after Camp David horrified at his concessions, because immediately upon his return to Israel he tried to undo some of them. President Carter observed this, and commented that Begin was trying to dilute as much of the commitment he had made at Camp David as possible.[43] Despite the difficulties and setbacks, agreement was reached and on March 26, 1979 the peace treaty between Israel and Egypt was signed in a lavish ceremony on the lawn of the White House.[44]

The implementation of the peace treaty with Egypt was basically successful, but this was not true of the issue of Palestinian autonomy. Begin appointed Yosef Burg, the minister of the interior, to head the autonomy negotiations. Burg was the leader of the National Religious Party (NRP), the political base of the Gush Emunim settlers' movement. He was clearly not the right person to bring the Palestinian autonomy talks to a successful conclusion. His appointment was perceived as an overt snub to Moshe Dayan, the foreign minister, who actually wanted a successful conclusion. Begin also introduced changes to the wording of the autonomy plan, stating that Israel would maintain sovereignty over the West Bank and Gaza even after the five-year duration of the talks.[45]

When the government began to expropriate private Palestinian land for new settlements, Dayan resigned from the Cabinet on October 2, 1979. Gradually, in the course of the negotiations, Dayan changed his hawkish position to support peace. Yitzhak Shamir, as uncompromising as Begin himself, replaced him as foreign minister. He shared a deep commitment with Begin to the revisionist notion of the homeland, which was more extensive than Ben Gurion's. The government's message was that the era of pragmatic flexibility was over. Now the struggle was to prevent the success of the Palestinian autonomy talks and any possibility of an independent sovereign Palestinian state.

The hardening of Israel's position in the best tradition of revisionist Zionism marked the departure from the government of another central figure, the defense minister Ezer Weizman. Weizman wanted to fulfill the agreement on autonomy as defined in the Egyptian–Israeli treaty, and was interested in making further efforts towards peace. When Palestinians from the occupied territories organized to advance their struggle for a complete Israeli evacuation from the territories and the establishment of a Palestinian state, Weizman was prepared to engage in talks with them and convince them to join the ongoing talks between Israel and Egypt. In May 1980, Weizman resigned. On the way to hand in his resignation, outside the prime minister's office he shouted, "No one here wants peace."[46] Weizman later wrote, "Alarmed by the peace treaty they had just concluded, Begin and his supporters withdrew into their mental ghetto and into their pipe dreams."[47] Begin took over the defense portfolio, and kept it until he formed his second government.

The autonomy talks ended in 1982. Sadat first broke them off in May 1980, and then again when Israel annexed East Jerusalem and imposed Israeli law. There were several meetings in 1980 and 1981 but no progress was achieved.[48]

The most powerful Israeli ammunition to circumvent their agreement for Palestinian autonomy leading to sovereignty was the settlements. While the autonomy talks were ongoing, during the period from 1979 to 1982, the government was supporting the settlements and the settlers in full view of the Americans and the Egyptians. When Begin's Likud initially took control there were about 4,000 settlers living in the occupied territories. The government's plan was that by 1983, the number of settlers would rise to 100,000 and the number of settlements to over 100. Many of the intended settlements were in Palestinian population centers. With Ariel Sharon as minister of defense and Yitzhak Shamir as foreign minister, Begin's government was not likely to commit to the autonomy talks or to any other provision of the peace treaty.[49]

## SADAT ASSASSINATED

Sadat was murdered on October 6, 1981 while inspecting a military parade. Vice-president Hosni Mubarak was sworn in as the new president of Egypt, and all political circles involved with the Middle East wondered whether the new president would undertake the commitments of his predecessor.[50] At Sadat's funeral, Mubarak assured both the Israelis and the Americans that all the provisions of the treaty would be met.

Israel's withdrawal from Egyptian territory was completed by April 1981. In a demonstrative final act, Sharon, the new minister of defense, razed the Sinai town of Yamit to the ground despite Egypt's offer of US$50 million to keep it untouched. One issue still lingered: Israel's insistence that Taba, a tiny area south of Eilat, belonged to Israel. After one decade and international arbitration, it was determined that Taba actually belonged to Egypt.[51]

The Egyptian–Israeli peace treaty endured assassinations and wars but failed to deliver the resolution of the Palestinian right to national self-determination, which should have been its most important component.

# 7

# FROM LEBANON TO OSLO

From the establishment of the State of Israel in 1948 to the signing of the Israeli–Egyptian peace treaty, Egypt had been Israel's enemy and perceived primary threat. The assassination of Anwar Sadat and the installation of Husni Mubarak as the new Egyptian president changed this. Egypt was no longer Israel's enemy. The Palestinians and the PLO now became the core of the conflict and primary enemy. What had been the Arab–Israeli conflict up to 1981 turned into the Israeli–Palestinian conflict. This transformation has lasted until today, with no sign of imminent change. One characteristic of the period between 1981 and the outbreak of the First Lebanon War is the downgrading of the remaining hostile Arab states to a secondary role.

Since the issue fueling the hostilities had always been the struggle for control over Palestine, this shift was merely the unmasking of the true nature of this conflict. Early in its evolution, the neighboring Arab states realized that there could be no resolution without an appropriate solution to the Palestinian problem. Although some of the Arab states, primarily Jordan and Egypt, tried to benefit territorially at the expense of the Palestinians, their ambitions were consistently thwarted. Israel always believed that a permanent solution could be reached in one of two ways: by breaking the will of the Palestinians, or by negotiating with neighboring Arab states over the territories occupied by Israel at the expense of their Palestinian residents. Over the years Israel reluctantly began to realize that the solution would have to come through direct – either hostile or peaceful – confrontation with the Palestinians alone. But its commitment to maintaining the status quo never wavered: Israel totally rejected the concept of an independent Palestinian state in any area west of the Jordan River.

The focus of the Palestinian struggle to regain their homeland changed with the global circumstances. Sometimes it centered on the Gaza Strip while at other times it moved to the Jordanian border on the West Bank. After the Black September confrontation between the PLO and Jordan, the PLO was no longer welcome in Jordan, and in the early 1980s the flashpoint of the conflict moved to Israel's weakest neighbor, Lebanon. Most of the PLO leadership and fighters, including Yasser Arafat, moved to Lebanon, where they were able to recruit fighters from the many Palestinian refugee camps established there after the 1948 war. Most of the PLO forces were located in southern Lebanon, as close to the Israeli border as possible. In the early 1980s the PLO essentially controlled south Lebanon. The establishment of the PLO headquarters in Lebanon paralleled the rise of Ariel Sharon to power in Israel, and marked the beginning of the countdown to the First Lebanon War.

## THE BEGIN DOCTRINE AND THE BOMBING OF IRAQ'S NUCLEAR PLANT

On June 7, 1981 Israel surprised the entire world by attacking and destroying the Iraqi nuclear plant at Osirak. This operation destroyed the nuclear reactor without losing a single fighter plane, and guaranteed the Likud Party a victory in the general election held 21 days later. The proximity of the operation to the Israeli election raised a howl of protest from the opposition, who described it as an election stunt. But the reality was more complicated, and is best described in terms of the Begin doctrine.[1] In Begin's words, anything that could or might pose an existential threat to Israel or of another Holocaust on the Jewish people must be defeated. Whether Begin actually considered the Iraqi reactor a direct existential threat or was cynically trying to win another election is immaterial. Within the cabinet and in the face of opposition, Begin adhered to the doctrine bearing his name, insisting that the unfinished Iraqi nuclear reactor did pose an existential threat to Israel.[2] The attack risked a hostile reaction by the United States and Egypt. It may have been intended to test Egypt's commitment to the peace treaty it had recently signed or to provoke a reaction. Begin appeared willing to face an outraged Egypt or a cancellation of the newly signed treaty.[3] One suspicion that is impossible to prove is that Begin actually hoped to provoke the cancellation of the Egyptian–Israeli peace treaty. His negative reaction after the Camp David agreements, and the impression he gave of wanting to back out of the deal, suggests that a deliberate provocation of Egypt cannot be totally dismissed.

The Israeli raid triggered numerous protests globally. The Reagan Administration immediately cancelled the delivery of aircraft promised to Israel. Since the attack took place only three days after a summit meeting between Begin and Sadat in Sharm el Sheikh, the Egyptian president was made to look like an Israeli accomplice. The anticipated fury in Egypt did not abate even after Begin sent a personal letter to President Sadat, but the peace treaty survived. Sadat clearly understood Israel's attitude and stated, "Once again, we face the same Israel that is completely oblivious to what happens in the Arab world and to what the Arab world thinks of it."[4]

The election results seem to confirm the opposition's claim. In opinion polls conducted prior to the raid the Likud lagged the Labor Alignment by 20 percent. After the bombing, the Likud pushed ahead by a margin of one seat. When Begin presented his new government to the Knesset in August 1981 he reasserted his government's platform, which reaffirmed the right of the Jewish people to the entire land of Israel.[5] His statement was a direct rejection of his own undertaking at Camp David, where he accepted the rights of self-determination of the Palestinian people and undertook to grant them full autonomy eventually.

Begin made another surprise decision on December 14, 1981: to annex the Golan Heights. Unlike the attack on the Iraqi nuclear reactor, this move was actually supported by a large number of members from the Alignment Party. Eight Knesset members of the Alignment voted with Likud. Begin had apparently just realized that although the colonial powers had changed the status of the Golan Heights after the First World War they had always been part of Palestine. According to Begin, therefore, the Golan Heights were actually part of the land of Israel and reclamation was justified.[6] However, by annexing the Golan Heights Israel was violating agreements it signed as well as international law. Although Israeli policy had been to avoid confrontations with Syria, in his speech to the Knesset Begin declared that reclaiming the Golan Heights would not be an obstacle, should Syria be serious about negotiating peace.

After Israel's withdrawal from the Sinai, one intention of the annexation of the Golan Heights may have been to deliver a message that it would offer no further territorial concessions. In effect, Israel was reflecting its lack of interest in a global peace agreement with the Arab world.[7] Begin and his supporters persisted, oblivious to the decision of the UN Security Council about the illegality of forceful territorial acquisition and its request that Israel revoke its annexation decision.

## SHARON WAGES WAR

In 1982, while the Golan Heights turmoil was still brewing, the war in Lebanon erupted.[8] The architect of Israel's attack on Lebanon was Ariel Sharon, the newly appointed minister of defense. His plan was two tiered. He wanted to destroy the PLO infrastructure in South Lebanon and its political organization, and at the same time he hoped to restructure the Middle East by forming an alliance with the Christian Lebanese Meronites. By supporting the Meronite efforts to gain control over Lebanon, Israel could establish its own hegemony. His rationale was that to eliminate the Palestinian claims on the West Bank, he had to destroy the PLO and Palestinian nationalism. And in order to enable the Lebanese Christians to prevail in Lebanon, the Syrians had to be greatly weakened.

Sharon had completed his plans but needed a pretext to launch the operation in such a way that it would be supported by the majority of the government and would not incur the wrath of the United States. Initially Sharon and his chief of staff, General Eitan, tried to encourage PLO rockets on Israel's settlements by launching a few minor attacks on PLO targets.[9] The PLO did not take Sharon's bait and the Lebanese border remained quiet at this time. However on June 3, 1982 Shlomo Argov, the Israeli ambassador to London, was shot and seriously wounded by Palestinians. Members of the Abu Nidal group, sworn enemies of the PLO, against whose leader the PLO had issued a death sentence, carried out this operation. But this provided a sufficient pretext for retaliation against the PLO. When informed that the Israeli ambassador had been attacked by arch enemies of the PLO, Begin said, "They are all PLO."[10] The response of the Israeli chief of staff, Refael Eitan, was, "Abu Nidal, Abu Shmidal, we must strike at the PLO."

On June 6, 1982 Israeli forces crossed the international border and invaded Lebanon. The leader of the Christian Phalange was told that the Israeli forces would soon link up with his forces, and therefore he should commence his attack on Beirut and prepare to form a new government in Lebanon, controlled by the Christians.[11]

In Israel initially there was widespread support for the operation. Begin apparently believed that Israel could go to war in Lebanon without having a confrontation with Syria. He addressed the Syrian president in his speech to the Knesset on June 8, appealing to Assad not to get involved and thus avoid harm to his forces. But Assad considered the war against the weaker Lebanon as a deliberate and provocative act against Syria,[12] and despite Begin's Knesset speech, the First Lebanon War turned into a war between Israel and Syria. It also involved the siege of a major Arab capital, Beirut.

One consequence of this war was the predictable rage of the Reagan Administration. Begin sent a very strange personal letter to the US president, which raised suspicion among many people – including Israelis – that the Israeli prime minister was unbalanced:

> Now may I tell you, dear Mr. President, how I feel these days when I turn to the creator of my soul in deep gratitude. I feel as a Prime Minister empowered to instruct a valiant army facing "Berlin" where amongst innocent civilians, Hitler and his henchmen hide in a bunker deep beneath the surface. My generation, dear Ron, swore on the altar of God that whoever proclaims his intention to destroy the Jewish State or the Jewish people, or both, seals his fate, so that which happened once instructions from Berlin with or without inverted commas, will never happen again.[13]

Alexander Haig, the US secretary of state, who was suspected of secretly supporting Israel's war against Lebanon, retained his trust in Begin. But George Shultz, soon replaced him, and appointed Philip Habib to end this war. The main problem was the fate of the besieged PLO forces. Sharon had a grand plan: he proposed that the PLO forces be transferred to Jordan. Jordan would become a *de facto* Palestinian state and end the rule of King Hussein. This would eliminate the need for a Palestinian state west of the Jordan River. Using an intermediary Sharon suggested this to Arafat, who refused. An exasperated Sharon was reported to have vented great rhetorical rage.[14] Philip Habib eventually convinced Tunisia to accept the PLO forces, and in late August all the PLO fighting units were evacuated there by sea.

Begin described the operation called Peace for the Galilee as a great success that achieved most of its objectives.[15] Since the PLO was no longer in Lebanon, Sharon focused on plans to set up his Christian-Phalange collaborators as rulers and thus make Lebanon Israel's vassal state. Initially the plan seemed successful. Bashir Gemayel, the Meronite leader, was elected president to the great jubilation of the Meronites and the deep satisfaction of Israel. With the PLO gone and the influence of Syria much diminished, Israel was confident about the signing of a full peace treaty between Lebanon and Israel. Gemayel, however, had other ideas. His main objective was to re-establish Lebanon as a legitimate member of the Arab world, and he called for the evacuation of all foreign troops from

Lebanese territories.[16] Since Gemayel did not act as expected by his Israeli protectors, he was invited to a meeting with Begin and Sharon to discuss Israel's expectations. However, the meeting ended with no resolution.

## THE SABRA AND SHATILA MASSACRE

Bashir Gemayel was not president of Lebanon for long. Three weeks after his election he was assassinated by perpetrators rumored to be Syrian intelligence agents. Sharon, ignoring the chain of command, gave a direct order to IDF forces to enter West Beirut, and gave the Phalangists permission to enter the Palestinian refugee camps of Sabra and Shatila. Sharon's conviction that thousands of PLO fighters remained hiding in Palestinian refugee camps was the reason given for the order. But it resulted in the massacre of unarmed civilian Palestinian refugees committed by the Phalangists. The exact number of those murdered is unknown, but it is estimated at around 2,000.[17]

The Sabra and Shatila massacres of September 16 and 18, 1982 were devastating, and had far reaching consequences. The impact of these events was probably more significant than any other aspect of this otherwise disastrous war in Lebanon. After the atrocity, Sharon was removed from the position of minister of defense and Begin did not remain Israel's prime minister for much longer. More than 500 Israeli soldiers and thousands of Lebanese had lost their lives serving Sharon's dream of a new Middle East with an alliance between Israel and a Christian-led Lebanon. But it did galvanize the Israeli peace movement, which organized what is still considered the largest political protest rally ever held in Israel. The emergence of a block of pro-peace groups in Israel may have been a major factor determining the peace talks and accords that occurred later.

Bashir Gemayel's brother Amin replaced him as president of Lebanon, but was not interested in maintaining his brother's contact with Israel. Moshe Arens replaced Sharon as Israel's minister of defense, and unlike his predecessor, knew that Israel could not maintain its presence in Lebanon indefinitely. With the active involvement of the United States, Israel and Lebanon reached an agreement to end the war. Israel undertook to remove its forces from most of Lebanon to a security zone about 40 km along the international border. One assumption underlying this agreement was that Syria would also remove its forces from Lebanon, but Syria did not. Late in 1983 Israel began its withdrawal without waiting for the

Syrians, and this unilateral retreat vastly weakened the agreement signed between Lebanon and Israel.[18] The Egyptian–Israeli peace treaty survived under the leadership of Hosni Mubarak, Sadat's successor, despite the strain placed on it by Israel's actions.

## SUPER HAWK PRIME MINISTER

Yitzhak Shamir replaced Begin as prime minister in 1983. More intransigent than Begin, he considered the only acceptable position for Israel to be no retreat at all, and peace was not particularly high on his agenda. It made little difference to him whether the territory in question was one to which Israel had any historic or emotional ties. Earlier as foreign minister he had opposed the withdrawal from the Sinai and voted for the annexation of the Golan Heights.[19] Early in his premiership, the Americans gave up on convincing Syria to withdraw from Lebanon. Shamir was delighted by this, and agreed with George Shultz that Israel would remain in Lebanon as long as the US Marines were there. He did this despite the fact that the IDF leadership almost unanimously felt that Israel ought to withdraw unilaterally from Lebanon. The United States and Israel agreed to maintain constant pressure on Syria to withdraw from Lebanon, but Syria ordered Amin Gemayel to abandon the non-belligerence agreement between Israel and Lebanon. The combination of Shamir and Schulz made the prospects of peace between Israel and Lebanon more remote.[20]

The elections in Israel of July 1984 provided no party with results solid enough to form a coalition, and a national unity government was unavoidable. It resulted in a rotation arrangement of the hard-line Shamir with the moderate Peres. Peres was to act as prime minister for the first two years and then Shamir was to take over for the remainder of the four-year term. This National Unity Government adopted a long list of guidelines, among them a commitment to withdraw from Lebanon while ensuring the security of Israel's border settlements. The government also committed to solidifying the peace treaty with Egypt while pursuing the peace process in a renewed negotiation with Jordan. Both partners in this odd political leadership were strongly opposed to a Palestinian state and to negotiation with the PLO. They also established several new settlements in the West Bank within the first year of its tenure, with more planned for later in the government's term.[21]

Peres was interested in resolving the Palestinian problem but not willing to begin negotiations with the PLO. He wanted to reintroduce Jordan as the ruler of the West Bank. With the support of defense minister Rabin, Peres set up a task force to determine implementation procedures for the newly revived Jordanian option. The task force recommended a Camp David model of direct negotiations between Israel and Jordan, with the active involvement from the United States and Egypt.[22] King Hussein seemed interested in reopening negotiations but he had to overcome two stumbling blocks. The first was the Arab League decision at the 1974 Rabat summit that the PLO was the only representative of the Palestinians. The second was another Arab League decision at the 1982 Fez summit that negotiation was viable only by means of an international conference. This did not provide for exclusive, direct talks between Israel and Jordan. King Hussein proposed an international conference with the participation of the permanent members of the Security Council, all the parties to the conflict, and the Palestinians. Israel did not approve of this proposal.

For Israel, the key issue was the exclusion of the PLO from any negotiations. But Hussein was adamant that the PLO would participate in the proposed international conference. Peres suggested including non-PLO Palestinians in the Jordanian team, which Hussein refused. The United States supported Israel's anti-PLO position, and Jordanian efforts to convince Richard Murphy, the US negotiator, failed. The Reagan Administration objected to any contact with the PLO. This was an unborn peace initiative, thwarted by procedure.[23]

At the end of 1985 the king seemed to be moving towards the American position that the PLO could not yet be considered a legitimate participant in the peace talks. To Peres, this shift implied the revival of the Jordanian option. He now needed to convince his own government of the merits of an international conference without the PLO.[24] While contacts and meetings between Israeli leaders and Hussein continued, the relationship between Jordan and the PLO deteriorated. In the spring of 1986, Hussein ordered the closure of the PLO offices in Amman and the expulsion of Arafat's deputy from Jordan. Both the United States and Israel were pleased with these developments, and in an interview Rabin clearly stated, "The policy of Israel is to strengthen the position of Jordan in Judea and Samaria and to strike at the PLO."[25]

However all efforts to negotiate and confer came to a halt on October 20, 1986 when Shamir became prime minister according to the rotation agreement. Peres moved to the Foreign Ministry. The new prime minister wanted nothing to do with any peace proposal or initiative, whether through Jordan or directly with the Palestinians, through bilateral negotiations or the disputed international conference.[26] Shamir's goal to maintain the status quo was flawlessly achieved and he curtailed all peace initiatives brought forth by Peres and Rabin.[27] There was a growing realization that Israel was blocking any hope for peace while building more settlements on Palestinian land, and a growing sense of anger and tension. Shlaim described the atmosphere in the occupied territories at the end of 1987 as a tinderbox waiting for a spark.[28]

## THE FIRST *INTIFADA*

That spark came soon afterwards, although it is not entirely clear exactly what produced it. The *Intifada* was triggered, according to one version, by a glider attack on an IDF command post in Lebanon sent by the Popular Front for the Liberation of Palestine (PFLP).[29] Another version claimed it was a traffic accident in which an Israeli driver killed four Palestinian residents of the Gaza Strip.[30] Rumors circulated afterwards that the driver had killed the Palestinians deliberately and caused turmoil in the Strip. Demonstrations followed by general strikes and other unplanned popular protests against the hated occupiers were attended by thousands of Gaza Strip residents. Israel's military efforts failed to quell the protests and actually provoked further protests. Within a few days the First *Intifada* had erupted. Whatever triggered it, most agree that it was spontaneous and grassroots in nature.[31]

Israel nevertheless accused the PLO of planning and organizing it. Arafat himself was unprepared for the rebellion, but willingly adopted it and intimated that the PLO was behind it.[32] The Palestinians had been living under Israeli occupation for over 20 years of humiliation. Arbitrary detentions, curfews, and closures were aspects of their reality. Palestinians were arrested, many in administrative detention, with no trial and often without being told why.[33] The economic and social hardships of the occupation, and growing suspicions that Israel planned to stay and build more settlements in the West Bank and Gaza, certainly contributed to the uprising.[34]

The development of the Shi'ite Lebanese militia, the Hezbollah, in Lebanon and the relative success of their guerilla warfare against Israel encouraged the Palestinians, raising their confidence.[35] The unplanned *Intifada* became a political struggle for self-determination and independence.[36]

Unprepared for the *Intifada*, Israel initially thought it would last no longer than a month. A few weeks later it became clear it was not going to fade away, and Israel had no apparent plan to deal with it. Every short lull convinced the Israeli leadership that the *Intifada* was about to end, but another minor incident would then occur to reignite the confrontation.[37] Arrests, deportations, beatings, and even targeted assassinations all proved ineffective. And Israel's mantra had long been: If force doesn't work, try more force. Not a few Israelis were becoming convinced that the *Intifada* and the conflict could not be resolved by force. The solution had to be the emergence of a political solution acceptable to both sides. Deep disagreements among the political parties still prevailed. Peres in the Labor Party leaned towards a political solution but Rabin still considered force the only method of ending the *Intifada*. The differences among members of the Likud coalition were more intense. Shamir blamed the Labor Party for the entire outbreak, accusing Peres's concept of Gaza First of wetting the Arab appetite for: Gaza today, Judea and Samaria tomorrow, and the Golan Heights after that.[38]

The *Intifada* lasted several years, and there is some debate about when it actually ended. Some say it continued until the first peace accord between Israel and the PLO was signed in Oslo at the end of 1993.[39] Others contend it ended in October 1991 with the Madrid peace conference.[40]

A significant outcome of the *Intifada* was the recognition by the United States of the PLO as the true representative of the Palestinians and thus as a potential participant in future negotiations. After several visits to the Middle East, George Shultz came up with a fresh US proposal for Palestinian autonomy, which recognized Israel's tendency to drag things out. He wanted a shorter timetable and attempted to lock together the interim phase of Palestinian self-rule with negotiations for the final status. Foreign minister Peres supported the initiative, as did Egyptian President Mubarak. King Hussein more guardedly supported the proposal, and asked the other Arab leaders not to reject it. The response of the Palestinians may have been disappointing to the Americans, but accurately reflected the tensions between the PLO leadership in Tunis and the local leadership that emerged in the *Intifada*. Most of the Arab states supported the PLO in Tunis as the only legitimate representative of the Palestinians.

Shamir initially showed some interest in the proposal but soon reverted to his traditional rejection of a peace conference. He certainly opposed the concept of locking together the transitional phase with the final solution. Shamir wanted to replace the principle of land for peace that appeared in several UN resolutions, with that of "peace for peace." Shamir's rejection placed the Shultz initiative among the long list of stalled peace proposals.[41]

In the summer of 1988, King Hussein announced that Jordan was pulling out of its long-standing role as a negotiating representative of the Palestinian people. Shultz's concept had involved a joint Jordanian–Palestinian delegation, and this may have been the final nail in the coffin of this initiative.[42] It also put an end to an old concept popular among some Israeli leaders: the Jordanian option was now clearly dead.

At the end of 1988, Israelis and the Palestinians were facing each other alone for the first time. Neither Egypt nor Jordan was acting as an intermediary. The political picture was bleak for both. Israel's National Unity Government was paralyzed by the fundamental disagreements between Likud and Labor. The Palestinians were split between the increasingly radicalized Islamic Hamas Movement, the secular PLO leadership in Tunis, and the more moderate local Palestinian leadership. This background did not bode well for a breakthrough on the peace front.[43]

Feisal Husseini, Hanan Ashrawi, and many other local Palestinians who had first-hand experience of living under Israeli occupation were consistently more moderate than their PLO Tunis counterparties. This pushed the PLO Tunis leaders to re-examine their position. At a November 1988 meeting of the Palestinian National Council (PNC) in Algiers, the moderates prevailed. The statement issued by the PNC addressed the need for a political settlement of the conflict through direct negotiations with Israel. It called for an international conference based on UN Resolutions 242 and 338, thus agreeing in principle to a two-state solution. In an interview shortly later, Arafat stated that the future was of two states, Jewish and Arab, living peacefully side by side."[44]

## POST-*INTIFADA* INTRANSIGENCE

Shamir, however, wanted nothing to do with the PLO at any level of moderation. The moderate Peres also criticized the PNC, describing their announcement as more extreme than previous statements.[45] In a press conference held during a UN General Assembly meeting in Geneva, Arafat announced that the PLO would now renounce any kind of terrorism and fully accept UN Resolutions 242 and 338 as a basis for negotiations with Israel in the framework of an international conference.[46] Apparently satisfied, the Americans immediately engaged in a series of discussions with the PLO. But Shamir criticized this, characterizing the American move as a blunder. Regardless of anything Arafat did or said, the West Bank and Gaza would remain part of Israeli sovereignty. A sequence of opinion polls revealed that Israeli public opinion was closer to the American position than to their own government's.[47] Most of this government's ministers, supporting Shamir and Shimon Peres, described the US–PLO talks as a sad day for all of us.[48]

The new US president, George H. Bush, and his secretary of state, James Baker, had little patience with Shamir and his inflexibility. The Israeli leadership began to realize that the status quo could not be maintained indefinitely. Some ministers concluded that Israel would have to launch its own peace initiative. The first to state this was Peres, but in 1989 Rabin was the first to present a plan, which focused on ending the *Intifada* in exchange for an expanded Palestinian autonomy and Palestinian elections. Combined pressure from the United States and from his own ministers pressured Shamir to come up with his own plan. On May 14, 1989 he presented a plan that ignored a changed perception of the legitimacy of the PLO. It called for elections in the West Bank and Gaza for a non-PLO representative body with which Israel would negotiate some form of autonomy. The Palestinian negotiating team had to be exclusively non-PLO and a Palestinian state was not to be contemplated. After a fierce debate the cabinet voted to support Shamir's plan.[49] The US position articulated by James Baker was that Shamir's plan was unrealistic, and the Israeli leadership was concerned that the Bush administration would reshape it into something that might be accepted by the Palestinians.[50]

Ironically, members of Shamir's government such as Sharon, Levi, and Modai, from the far right, rebelled against Shamir's plan. The modifications they proposed included no contact with the PLO, that no part of the land west of the Jordan River could be divided, and that Palestinians residing in East Jerusalem would not be allowed to participate in the proposed elections. Shamir made no effort to salvage his plan, and allowed the rebels to destroy his own plan at a meeting of the Likud Central Committee.[51] The American reaction was predictably angry, and Baker said that when Israel was more serious about negotiations, they know how to reach him.

In 1989 Egyptian President Mubarak proposed his own plan, which involved land for peace but did not openly support PLO participation in negotiations. Israel's Labor Party ministers ended up supporting the Mubarak plan over the plan of their own prime minister. The Americans suggested peace talks between Israel and the Palestinians to be held in Cairo, but the constant bickering in Shamir's government precluded the possibility of such talks, and the government approached the brink of collapse. The Israeli president asked Peres to form a new government in March 1990 after a no-confidence motion in the Knesset, but Peres was unsuccessful.[52] Shamir formed a narrow coalition composed entirely of right-wing parties, creating the most right-wing government in the history of Israel. In presenting this government to the Knesset, Shamir declared there would be no Palestinian state and there would be no negotiations with the PLO. East Jerusalem would remain under Israeli sovereignty and new settlements would be built.[53]

The events that dominated the 1990s were the invasion of Kuwait by Saddam Hussein, the ongoing *Intifada,* and the collapse of the Soviet Union. Days after the defeat of Saddam Hussein's Iraq, US President Bush informed the US Congress on March 6, 1991, that the time had come to put an end to the Arab–Israeli conflict.[54] He consulted with the countries involved in the conflict about a possible international conference on peace. Mubarak, Hussein, and Assad responded positively. Since the Arab leaders responded favorably it was difficult for Shamir to refuse. In August he gave the United States a conditional acceptance.[55] Several non-PLO-affiliated Palestinians were recruited to participate in the conference as part of a Jordanian–Palestinian delegation. This became the first time in their political history that Palestinians were officially participating as an almost independent delegation in a peace conference related to their future.[56]

## MADRID, ANOTHER FAILURE

The Madrid conference in October was co-chaired by President Bush and President Gorbachev. The plenary sessions lasted three days, and were followed by bilateral meetings between the delegations.[57] The greatest achievement of the conference may well have been the agreement to continue to meet. Bilateral and multilateral meetings took place in Washington, then in Moscow, and later in several other European capitals. The Israeli–Jordanian talks made some progress, but those between the Israelis and Palestinians were mired in "paralysis and inertia," according to Hanan Ashrawi. The Israeli delegation was involved in a pretence participation, since Shamir never intended to achieve any progress. His intention was to drag out the negotiations for at least ten years.[58]

Dr. Abd el Shafi, the leader of the Palestinian delegation, on the other hand gave a speech that addressed the Israelis directly, and declared the willingness of the Palestinians to live side by side on the basis of equality and reciprocity.[59] He made it abundantly clear, though, that the occupation must end.

In all the talks that followed the Madrid conference, Israel was essentially interested only in implementing some form of Shamir's concept of peace for peace. The Israelis would grant the Palestinians some form of self-rule wholly supervised and managed by the Israelis. Yitzhak Rabin claimed that the talks deliberately were merely grinding water.[60]

On June 23, 1992, after 15 years in power, Likud was defeated. Yitzhak Rabin, leading the Labor Party, cobbled together a very narrow coalition with the left-leaning Meretz Party, and with the non-participatory support of the Israeli Arab parties. Not much changed in the immediate aftermath of the return of Labor to power. All the Middle Eastern participants in the conflict were waiting for the results of the US elections. But even during this quiet period, the Syrian leadership expressed interest in negotiating peace. The terms they offered included full normalization of relationships in exchange for a full withdrawal from the Golan Heights to the international border. Although a left of center coalition now led Israel, Israel was watching the US elections.[61]

# 8

# THE PLO AS A PEACE PARTNER?

A growing recognition that the Palestinians in the occupied territories were a political entity onto themselves made the Jordanian option, and others like it, no longer viable. Israel had to come to terms with the reality of the PLO as the only legitimate force representing the Palestinians for the foreseeable future.

In 1992 after Yitzhak Rabin became Israel's prime minister, the unquestioned assertion that Arabs understand only the language of force, and if the principle of force does not work, you should use more force, was becoming suspect in Israel. More Israelis had come around to the view that the resolution of this lingering conflict must be political, by means of a negotiated solution with the Palestinians and the PLO. Although many in the Israeli leadership found the prospect of talking directly to the PLO distasteful, they could no longer avoid it. In January 1993 the Knesset repealed the law forbidding contact between Israeli citizens and members of the PLO, which had been enacted by a Labor government and was in effect for six years prior to its repeal. One peace activist, Abie Nathan, actually sat in jail for violating this law.

The recognition of the PLO as an inescapable negotiating partner paved the initial path to the negotiations between Israelis and Palestinians that led to the Oslo Accords a few months later. But it also became clear that any political solution attained through negotiation would have to involve compromise. The Palestinian compromise had already been made clear well before Oslo. After 1967 the best hope for the Palestinians was a state on 22 percent of Mandatory Palestine, according to the boundary known as the Green Line. The nature of the Israeli compromise for peace was not at all apparent.

Yossi Beilin, a Labor Party leader and the driving force behind the initial Oslo negotiations, stated in an interview on Israeli radio that everybody knows what is required from Israel to provide the minimum acceptable to the Palestinians: a return to the pre-1967 borders, the dismantling of the settlements, and the establishment of East Jerusalem as the capital of the Palestinian state. The question is whether we Israelis are willing to pay that price. No serious Israeli leader has ever publicly denied wanting peace, but peace meant many different things to them. Seventeen years have passed since the Oslo Accords, the first formal peace agreement between Israel and its Palestinian neighbors. Since then Israel has had six prime ministers, each with a unique version of peace and of Israel's possible compromises for peace. And over the years there have been many confrontations, many deaths, and much bloodshed. The Israeli leadership must not have understood, or not wanted to offer, the minimally acceptable solution to the Palestinians.

## OSLO

The First *Intifada* which began in 1987 persisted for six years despite Israel's immense efforts to end it.[1] The failure to stop this uprising led many Israelis, including several Labor Party leaders, to the conclusion that the conflict could not be resolved militarily. The Palestinians were losing the support of a disintegrating Soviet Union, and of several Arab countries, mainly Saudi Arabia and the Gulf Emirates, unhappy about their support of Iraq's invasion of Kuwait. This Palestinian vulnerability suggested that the Israelis had a unique opportunity to extract an agreement from a weak opponent.[2] Despite the law forbidding contact with the PLO, talks aimed at achieving a peace agreement did occur.[3]

In December 1992 an Israeli academic, Yair Hirschfeld, encouraged and supported by Yossi Beilin, met with Ahmed Kurei, a senior member of the PLO leadership also known as Abu Ala.[4] Hirschfeld was apparently authorized by Beilin to initiate talks about a peace agreement between Israel and the PLO. On January 20, 1993, one day after the Knesset law banning contact with the PLO was repealed, he met with Abu Ala again, along with another Israeli academic, Ron Pundak. Their talks led to agreement in some areas and to further meetings which took place between January and May 1993. The result was a Declaration of Principles (DOP).[5]

The main issue agreed upon in the DOP was the establishment of Palestinian autonomy in disconnected parts of the occupied territories, first in Gaza and then in Jericho. The autonomy would be followed by Palestinian elections, eventually moving to negotiations and a final settlement. Israel would initially withdraw its forces from the Gaza Strip, and the area would come under direct but limited Palestinian rule. While Israel agreed to Palestinian autonomy in the Gaza Strip, it refused to dismantle any Jewish settlement in the area. Some settlers were willing to leave Gaza for alternative housing inside Israel, but Prime Minister Rabin refused their demands for compensation.[6] A Palestinian National Council (PNC) resolution, which accepted the principle of the partition of Palestine for the first time, preceded their pragmatic acceptance of a restricted autonomy.[7] The Labor Party victory in the 1992 Israeli election mirrored some of this pragmatism, with a government that considered giving up some of the occupied territories. On September 13, 1993 the DOP was signed in a ceremony on the lawn of the US White House.[8]

But it was an interim agreement, outlining several critical issues to be dealt with after its implementation. The status of Jerusalem, Palestinian refugees, and the fate of the Jewish settlements were to be negotiated at some point in the future.[9]

## RABIN'S DELIBERATE AMBIGUITY

One month later, in Taba, Israel revealed its intention to maintain control of more of the Gaza territory than just the settlements. Israel demanded that the Jewish settlements in Gaza be grouped into three settlement blocks, with the land between them also under full Israeli control. Nabil Sha'at, the PLO chief negotiator, furiously referred to the Israeli demand as a Swiss cheese plan for the cantonization of Gaza.[10] Nevertheless, in Cairo a mere two weeks later the Palestinians capitulated to the Israeli demands. Tanya Reinhart described this succinctly: Arafat protested, cried, and signed.[11] The Palestinians also agreed to link the negotiations on the final status to Israeli satisfaction with the implementation of the interim agreement.

The Israelis postponed negotiations over the status of the settlements to a future date linked to the final settlement negotiations, and tied them to a successful and peaceful implementation of the interim agreement. Effectively this gave control over this phase to the Israelis, and placed judgment on the terms of the agreement in the hands of Israel's captains of security.[12] The agreement explicitly stated that neither side should initiate or take any step that would change the status of the West Bank and Gaza Strip pending the outcome of the permanent status negotiations. But immediately after signing the interim agreements Israel commenced construction of new settlements and expansion of existing ones, for which land had to be confiscated. The expansions continued throughout the four years of Labor rule following the signing of the Oslo agreement. Between 1993 and 1996 the Labor government invested more than its Likud predecessors in settlement activity, and the settler population in the West Bank and Gaza increased dramatically: by 48 percent in the West Bank and by 62 percent in the Gaza Strip.[13]

The Palestinians may have agreed to these concessions because they sought official Israeli and international recognition of the Palestinian Authority in areas evacuated by Israel. Perhaps more importantly, article 5, clause 3 of the DOP allowed both parties to bring any subject into the final status talks, and they wanted to introduce the subject of full Palestinian sovereignty.[14] Neither the DOP nor the Oslo Accords mentioned the right of the Palestinians for self-determination or the establishment of an independent Palestinian state.

During the negotiations that preceded the signing of the DOP, Rabin appeared resigned to a possible Israeli withdrawal from all the area occupied by Israel since 1967. Much of Israeli and international public opinion largely supported this possibility. But it is difficult to reconcile Rabin's apparent resignation with his refusal to remove the Gaza settlements and his expansion of the area Israel controlled in Gaza.

The ongoing increase in settler population in the occupied territories made their future evacuation all the more difficult, and suggests that the Israeli leadership were not concerned about a future independent Palestinian state in those areas built to house Jewish settlers. Israel's expansion efforts included construction designed to protect the settlers and facilitate their daily life: an entire network of bypass road and tunnels was built. Even in Palestinian areas, the settlers could move about freely under the ground. For the sake of these roads, fences, and tunnels, hundreds of Palestinian homes and agricultural areas had to be demolished. And the roads had to be protected and monitored by means of a network of military checkpoints maintained throughout the occupied territories by Israeli soldiers. This contradicted agreements stipulating that Israel guarantee safe passage of Palestinians between the West Bank and Gaza and within the West Bank itself.[15]

Despite the incongruity between the Oslo agreements and their interpretation on the ground, the Oslo process prevailed for quite some time. It continued after Rabin's assassination, throughout the short period Shimon Peres served as prime minister, and for several years after the election victory of the Likud headed by Binyamin Netanyahu in 1996. Oslo survived because the Israelis and much of the international community supported it, and believed that it was leading the region towards peace.

## THE ATROCITY OF DR. GOLDSTEIN

The process suffered a dramatic setback on February 25, 1994 when an American-born Jewish physician who was a militant settler, Dr. Baruch Goldstein, entered the Tomb of the Patriarchs in Hebron, opened fire on Muslim worshippers, and killed 29 unarmed people. Shocked and angry reactions came from the PLO, Hamas, and even the Israeli public at large. The PLO suspended peace talks and demanded that Israel remove the militant settlers from Hebron. Many Israeli cabinet ministers and much of the Israeli public realized that the settlers were a major obstacle to peace, and supported their removal from Hebron. But the architect of Oslo, Rabin, refused to remove any of them on the grounds that the Oslo Accord did not require such measures during the interim period.

Rabin's position was incomprehensible. If the Oslo process was intended to lead towards a permanent resolution of the conflict through Israeli territorial compromise. and towards the establishment of an independent Palestinian state, his obduracy about the Hebron settlers was inexplicable. It leads one to question his concept of the outcome of the Oslo Accord, and of the possibility of a truly independent Palestinian state side by side with Israel.[16]

## OSLO ON THE WANE

The rigidity displayed by Rabin and the IDF and the violent Palestinian reactions did not totally derail the Oslo process. Oslo II was signed on September 28, 1995 in Washington. It provided for the withdrawal of the IDF from the main Palestinian towns and cities; for elections to the Palestinian Council; and for the transfer of authority from Israel to the Palestinian Council. Its most important achievement was the division of the entire West Bank into three separate areas, conveniently named A, B, and C. Area A extended over approximately 6 percent of the West Bank, and included most of the large Palestinian towns. It would now come under full Palestinian control. The Palestinians would exercise administrative jurisdiction over Area B, which comprised approximately 25 percent of the West Bank, while Israel would maintain its military-security control. Israel retained full and undivided control over Area C, which was approximately 60 percent of the West Bank. In the Gaza Strip Israel retained control over about a third of the area, and the rest came under the administrative authority of the PLO. This division of the occupied territories and the distribution of control remain largely intact to this very day.[17] The protracted negotiations allowed Israel to impose its version of a settlement without addressing issues critical to the Palestinians, such as refugees and the status of Jerusalem.[18]

Rabin outlined his vision of the future permanent settlement in a much-interrupted speech to the Knesset: an undivided Jerusalem under Israeli control; annexation of all the large settlement blocks along the 1967 boundary; and military control, with no formal annexation, of the Jordan valley. The Palestinian body politic would be less than a full sovereign state and its territory would be completely demilitarized. The Knesset approved Oslo II by a very slim majority.

## RABIN ASSASSINATED

The assassination of Yitzhak Rabin by Yigal Amir, a member of the far-right settler movement, occurred when the differences between the Labor and Likud were essentially narrowing. On November 4, 1995, following a peace rally with more than 100,000 participants, Yitzhak Rabin was shot. His assassin confessed that his purpose was to derail the peace process and prevent any transfer of territories. Amir and his colleagues dreaded that Rabin might agree to a major territorial compromise with the Palestinians, but he was more likely to dismantle a few small and isolated settlements than to risk a full-fledged confrontation with the settlement movement. The Labor-Likud election platforms for the 1996 elections revealed considerable similarities. Both parties objected to the dismantling of any settlements in the occupied territories and intended that most would come under full Israeli sovereignty. They agreed that a Palestinian state, looking much like a South African bantustan, would be established on whatever was left of the territories after Israel implemented a permanent settlement.[19] This was a far cry from Yossi Beilin's earlier description of the minimum required by the Palestinians to achieve peace.

The initial Palestinian support of the Oslo agreement had gradually waned, and with no obvious progress, it died completely. Suicide missions that the Hezbollah in south Lebanon had initiated earlier now occurred in the West Bank during 1994. They accelerated in

1996 after Labor's defeat by Netanyahu's Likud, and especially after the new prime minister provocatively opened a tunnel under the Haram Al Sharif, widely considered the third holiest site in Islam. The violence simmered until 2000, when the new Camp David talks were heading towards failure and Ariel Sharon, with the approval of Ehud Barak, made a confrontational visit to the Haram Al-Sharif. The Second *Intifada* erupted.

Among the many attempts to achieve peace, one succeeded before Rabin's murder: the October 1994 peace agreement between Israel and Jordan, the best of enemies. King Hussein, and before him his grandfather King Abdullah, had tried to broker a peace deal with Israel for many years prior to 1994. The two countries had ongoing contacts and cooperated unofficially on various projects for decades. They shared western concepts of the Middle East and the same set of enemies. One issue prevented an earlier resolution, and it took about 15 years after the Egyptian–Israeli peace treaty to achieve peace between them. Both King Abdullah and King Hussein wanted to annex the West Bank and East Jerusalem to Jordan. The Likud government rule during the previous two decades made the transfer of any part of their concept of the biblical homeland to Jordanian sovereignty exceedingly implausible.[20] During this period Jordan abandoned its hope of annexing the West Bank. The emergence of a legitimate Palestinian nationalist movement and pressure from other Arab states and the Arab League forced King Hussein to officially relinquish any claims over this territory at the Rabat conference. The Israeli–Palestinian DOP ended an era in the relationship between Israel and Jordan by supposedly removing the West Bank from consideration.[21]

On October 26, 1994 Israel and Jordan signed a treaty in a large tent in the Arava, a ceremony witnessed by King Hussein, President Clinton, and the Russian foreign minister. Unlike the treaty with Egypt where Israel fought over every inch of disputed land, this treaty reflected a positive attitude towards Jordan. Israel agreed to return an area of 300 sq km that had been taken from Jordan in the 1960s and 1970s. It permitted Jordan to pump water from the ceded area that came from an aquifer shared with Israel.[22] Once the PLO became the representative of the Palestinian people, Israel had no further territorial claims to Jordanian land.

There was much agitation in the political right wing during the period between the signing of the DOP and Rabin's assassination. The campaign against Rabin and his colleagues was vicious and unruly. Rabin was compared to Eichmann, and both Rabin and Peres were described as Nazis, quislings, traitors, and *Judenrat*.[23] This irresponsible campaign was mounted against a relatively prudent and cautious leader who had demonstrated no intention of giving anything away towards the creation of an independent, sovereign Palestinian state alongside Israel. The moderate views Rabin expressed not long before his death were formed reluctantly and hesitantly. Despite the vitriolic campaign against him, many Israelis supported Rabin. They appreciated his straightforward approach and his *Realpolitik*. More than any of his predecessors, he began to recognize the need to support the establishment of a fully independent Palestinian state. Rabin's assassination may have eliminated the only chance for a true peace between Israel and the Palestinians that had ever existed.[24]

## PERES BRIEFLY PM

Shimon Peres was supported by 112 of the 120 members of the Israeli Knesset to replace Rabin. Seven months remained until the next general election. His short tenure as prime minister was eclipsed by a multitude of factors: the upcoming elections, the implementation of Oslo II with the IDF pullback from Palestinian centers of population, and the intensification of Muslim extremists' activities designed to derail the peace process. It was also affected by a fierce personal campaign against Peres by the political right. Although polls taken at the beginning of 1996 consistently predicted a Labor victory, they did not factor in the impact of suicide bombings generated by the Hamas and Islamic Jihad. Not did they consider the impact of Israeli assassinations of Hamas leaders on the sequence of events. When the Lebanese Hezbollah launched a rocket offensive on northern Galilee, the election results were effectively redefined.[25]

During the seven months of his tenure Shimon Peres tried to make some progress towards peace. His first initiative was a proposal to renew the peace talks with Syria. Aside from regional political considerations, progress on the Syrian front was bound to help with his election campaign. But Assad was unlikely to strike any deal before the election scheduled for October. Then Peres opted for an earlier election in May, which may have hastened the end of his term. Probably the most important contribution to the cause of peace made during the seven months was the Beilin–Abu Mazen document, the result of meetings that took place in October 1995 shortly before the Rabin assassination.[26] It was later considered such a far-reaching agreement that no prime minister was willing to accept its terms until Ehud Barak took the helm.

A few years later, Beilin presented the details of the Beilin–Abu Mazen understandings to his cabinet colleagues. He was then the minister of justice in Barak's government.[27] Israel would withdraw from 90–95 percent of the West Bank, but approximately 130 settlements would remain under Israeli sovereignty. Fifty settlements would remain but under Palestinian sovereignty. The Jordan valley would be in Palestinian sovereignty, but Israel would maintain a military presence there. The Palestinian Authority would recognize West Jerusalem as the capital of Israel and Israel would recognize the area defined as Al-Quds prior to the 1967 war, and which exceeds the area annexed to Israel in 1967, as the capital of the Palestinian state. The Haram Al Sharif would be placed under Palestinian control.

The document suggests significant Israeli concessions, primarily the withdrawal from 90–95 percent of the West Bank. But the area under Palestinian control would include 50 Jewish settlements, and the Israeli army would maintain its presence and forces in the Jordan valley. Al-Quds, which is mentioned as the area to become the Palestinian capital, is actually the village of Abu Dis.

In a March 1996 interview, Yossi Beilin said:

> As an outcome of my negotiations, I can say with certainty that we can reach a permanent agreement not under the overt conditions presented by the Palestinians, but under a significant compromise [on their side] …. I discovered on their side a substantial gap between their slogans and their actual understanding of reality – a much bigger gap than on our side. They are willing to accept an agreement which gives up much land, without the dismantling of settlements, with no return to the 67 border and with an arrangement in Jerusalem which is less than municipality level.[28]

The Palestinian agreement to accept 50 Jewish settlements in a sovereign Palestine is perplexing. Reinhart suggests that the authors hoped a fully independent Palestinian state would be able to tolerate a peaceful presence of Jewish settlers whose presence would be limited to the land they already owned – much like the presence of the Arab citizens of Israel. It is inconceivable, however, that Israel would agree to abandon the settlers and forgo its commitment to their defense.[29] The Israeli press hailed the understandings as a major milestone towards resolving the Israeli–Palestinian conflict.[30] Nevertheless the Israeli public and the media considered the Beilin–Abu Mazen understanding as the beginning of a period of

Israeli concessions. But the concessions proffered were significantly less than Beilin himself had considered earlier to be the minimum acceptable to the Palestinians.

## NETANYAHU IN POWER

Netanyahu defeated Peres on May 29, 1996 in direct elections for the post of prime minister. With 50.4 percent of the vote, Netanyahu won by a margin of 30,000 out of 3 million who cast their votes, and put together a stable coalition with a comfortable majority of 67 seats.

A few weeks after his election victory, Netanyahu presented his government's basic guidelines. He declared a deepening in the scope of peace with the neighbors, and the reopening of negotiations with the Syrians and the Palestinian Authority. The basic guidelines included preconditions. The Golan Heights were crucial to Israel's security and therefore would remain under Israeli sovereignty. The new government would oppose the establishment of an independent Palestinian state, but consider the possibility of autonomy and self-rule. Netanyahu's government opposed the right of return but would focus on developing the settlement project. A united Jerusalem would be the capital of Israel and would remain forever under Israeli sovereignty. Peace, according to the new government, was blatantly a hollow concept.[31]

Months went by with no progress in negotiation or in the implementation of Oslo II. The Middle East was a powder keg waiting for a spark, which the new prime minister provided. On September 24, 1996, in an effort to Judaicize the entire city of Jerusalem, he extended an archeological tunnel along the Western Wall, creating an exit into the Muslim quarter of the Old City. The Israeli move triggered massive demonstrations, which spread to other Palestinian cities and continued for several days. More than 70 Palestinians and fifteen Israeli soldiers were killed. Hundreds were injured.[32]

In an attempt to defuse the situation, President Clinton insisted that Netanyahu and Arafat both come to Washington, where he pressured Netanyahu to agree to a renewal of the Hebron talks started by the previous government. The Israeli prime minister agreed to withdraw Israeli forces from most of the city of Hebron. Clinton wanted Netanyahu's commitment to close the tunnel's exit, but the prime minister refused to commit himself to a date for the Israeli withdrawal from Hebron and simply refused to close the tunnel.[33]

## LIKUD'S FIRST CONCESSIONS

Very reluctantly and under much pressure, an agreement was signed on January 14, 1997. Israel made substantial paper commitments. It agreed to the withdrawal of the IDF from 80 percent of the city of Hebron, remaining only where the settlers lived. Netanyahu agreed to release a number of Palestinian prisoners, to open Palestinian air and seaports, and to open a safe passage between the Gaza Strip and the West Bank. Finally Netanyahu agreed to troop withdrawal from other areas of the West Bank by mid-1998. Arafat agreed to dismantle whatever was left of the Palestinian terrorist infrastructure. He agreed to eliminate all references in the Palestinian Covenant to the destruction of the State of Israel. Despite serious objection, including the resignation of one cabinet minister, Netanyahu pushed the agreement through the cabinet.

In January the Israeli forces left most of Hebron and transferred the Arab sectors to the control of Palestinian police.[34] This was the first time that a Likud government, ideologically committed to Greater Israel, had relinquished a slice of the homeland and transferred it to Palestinian control. No further progress towards the implementation of the agreement was achieved in 1997. The US administration brought the two sides together, but the Netanyahu government was ideologically reluctant to implement Oslo II and Hebron agreements. Suicide missions undertaken by extremists provided the government with additional excuses not to proceed with the peace process. There was no second-stage withdrawal, the Palestinian air and seaports were not opened, the Palestinian prisoners were not released, and the Gaza–West Bank safe passage was not created. Netanyahu nevertheless insisted that the Palestinians reciprocate by implementing their own undertakings as part of Oslo II and the Hebron talks.

US Secretary of State Madeleine Albright urged Netanyahu in 1998 to execute a further withdrawal of Israeli troops from about 13 percent of the West Bank, as agreed in Oslo II and Hebron. Netanyahu refused. The Palestinians had initially demanded a 50 percent withdrawal from the West Bank, but under US pressure, agreed to the 13 percent denied by Israel.

Under combined pressure from the Americans and members of his own government, Netanyahu eventually agreed to implement the 13 percent withdrawal. He demanded that it be carried out in three stages, each tied to a distinct reciprocal step by the Palestinians. Pressure also came from Jordan and Egypt, who threatened to lower the level of their diplomatic representation in Israel if progress was not made. Arafat finally announced that in accordance with the Oslo Accords, he would declare Palestinian statehood at the beginning of May 1999.[35]

## THE RIVER WYE PLANTATION

Arafat and Netanyahu began another session of negotiations at the River Wye Plantation in the fall of 1998. Netanyahu was as reluctant as ever to concede even an inch of territory, but agreement was finally reached on October 23. Netanyahu surprised Clinton by requiring the release from prison of Jonathan Pollard, an American Jew who had spied for Israel. Clinton dismissed this demand, and Netanyahu was forced to back down.[36]

Under the terms of the River Wye memorandum, Israel agreed to withdraw from 13 percent of Area C. Three percent of this area was to be designated a nature preserve, preventing the Palestinians from building or changing its topography. One percent of the area would be transferred to Area A and 12 percent to Area B. An additional 14 percent would be transferred from Area B to Area A. Israel undertook to complete these withdrawals within twelve weeks of the signing of the memorandum. Following the completion of this withdrawal there would be another withdrawal of unspecified size. Netanyahu promised the Israeli public that this final withdrawal would not exceed 1 percent of the West Bank.

Arafat agreed to a meeting of the Palestinian leadership which would be addressed by President Clinton and which would reaffirm Palestinian support for the peace process. It would also reaffirm previous Palestinian resolutions to eliminate all offensive sections of the Palestinian Charter. Both sides agreed to start final status negotiations immediately, with the goal of concluding them before May 4, 1999.[37]

Netanyahu's coalition partners were shocked by the agreement, and suspicious that he might actually hand over 13 percent or perhaps more of the West Bank to the Palestinians. The parties on the left and some of Netanyahu's more moderate coalition partners suspected that Netanyahu would find excuses to justify not implementing the transfer of territory.

Netanyahu asserted that his withdrawal commitments were contingent on the Palestinians fulfilling their undertakings, which he believed would never happen. Therefore there was nothing to worry about. To the moderates he explained that he had been elected on a platform of peace with security, and that was what he had accomplished in the River Wye agreement. Netanyahu's word was given little credence on either side of the Israeli political spectrum.

On November 20, 1998, Israel handed over 2 percent of the West Bank hitherto included in Area C. It now became Area B. About 7 percent of area B was handed over to the Palestinians and became part of Area A. A few days later, Israel allowed the official opening of the Gaza International Airport and the release of approximately 250 Palestinian prisoners. The Palestinians reaffirmed the elimination of all the clauses in the Palestinian Charter that called on the destruction of Israel on December 14.

Netanyahu's coalition partners threatened to bring down the government if he proceeded with the rest of the withdrawal. The withdrawals scheduled to take place in January and February 1999 did not occur. The pretext used was that the Palestinians had not lived up to all their commitments. Netanyahu found himself in an impossible squeeze.[38]

## NETANYAHU CALLS FOR NEW ELECTIONS, AND BARAK WINS

Netanyahu decided to dissolve the Knesset and called for an early election in May 1999. The candidates for prime minister were Netanyahu for Likud and Ehud Barak for Labor. But the electoral confrontation was complicated by the emergence of a Center Party. Yitzhak Mordechai, who had been fired from the cabinet by Netanyahu, joined this grouping and became the Center Party's candidate. The election commotion stopped any implementation of withdrawals. The River Wye agreements now joined a very long list of peace initiatives that died prematurely.

On May 17, 1999 Barak defeated Netanyahu with the support of 56 percent of voters against 44 percent. Barak's victory was celebrated by Israelis who gathered in the early hours of the night in Rabin Square, the site of Rabin's assassination. Barak claimed Rabin as his mentor and promised the huge crowd that he would carry out Rabin's peace legacy.

The electoral system in Israel prevented Barak, despite his stunning victory, from forming a Knesset majority. He had to form a center-left coalition that would rely on the support of the Arab Knesset members, or move to the right and form a coalition with the religious parties. One of the religious parties, Shas, emerged from the elections with 17 seats, and Barak took the second option.

Barak's coalition decreed that his government would be significantly restricted in any effort to bring about peace. But he was spared the abuse previously heaped on Rabin's government, which had been based on a narrow center-left coalition.

It appeared that after several years of stagnation, the Middle East was entering a new period that held some promise for peace, despite serious difficulties.

# 9

# BARAK LEAVES NO STONE UNTURNED

From the time Ehud Barak formed his government in 1999 to Operation Cast Lead, or the Gaza war, at the very end of 2008, there were nine years of frequent but ineffective efforts to achieve peace. Despite the obvious need and the global clamor, bringing an end to the Palestinian–Israeli conflict through a fair and equitable solution continued to elude the negotiators. This was a period that began with great hopes for a permanent solution.

The expectation of peace in the Middle East and the rude awakening that followed were linked to the newly elected and presumed left-wing leader of the Labor Party, Ehud Barak. He decisively defeated the incumbent, Binyamin Netanyahu, coming into politics straight out of a dazzling military career in which he had become the most decorated soldier in the history of the IDF. Barak's security credentials were worth their weight in gold, and he seemed to be just the right person to end the war that had begun before the establishment of the State of Israel in 1948. He ran the election campaign on an unambiguous peace platform, presenting himself as the disciple of the assassinated Yitzhak Rabin. He claimed commitment to the legacy of the slain leader in the spirit of the Oslo Accords, and expressed confidence in achieving the goal of peace in a period of months rather than years on three fronts: Syria, Lebanon, and the Palestinians.

Barak may have believed in his ability to reach agreements on all fronts, but it soon became clear that his concept of achieving peace was disappointingly futile. He set out to present the negotiating parties with offers he argued they could not refuse, and seemed to believe they would not have the audacity to oppose. He embarked on this presumptuous project with very little consultation and little inclination to listen to expert advice. His negotiations failed despite the sincere efforts of many others involved in the process, who thought success might have been possible had Barak listened to advice and prepared the ground appropriately.[1]

The Syrian negotiations were probably doomed by the intransigence of both sides, the Israelis and the Syrians. This was not the case for the Palestinians. Arafat initially resisted participation in Camp David II, but relented to pressure from US President Clinton. Using the Beilin minimum criteria, Barak's offer did not come close, although he successfully portrayed the failure of Camp David II as a function of Arafat's intransigence. He repeated the phrase "We made them an offer that could not be improved," and then came to the conclusion that "There is no Palestinian partner for peace." This phrase became the mantra for all the prime ministers, equally reluctant to achieve peace, who followed Barak, and contributed perhaps more than anything else to the destruction of the peace camp. The expression was actually coined well before the start of Camp David by Moshe Gaon and Tal Zilberstein, Israel public relations promoters and Barak advisers. They suggested that any failure of the talks be blamed on Arafat, and that it was important to demonstrate that it was Arafat who did not want to reach an agreement.[2]

## A GENEROUS OFFER SHATTERS THE PEACE CAMP

Barak's most palpable success was convincing people to believe in a false mantra. His version of the reasons for the negotiation failures dealt a blow to the peace camp and to the entire left wing in Israel. In February 2001 he was defeated in the elections by the extremely hawkish Ariel Sharon, and Barak unabashedly joined the globe-trotting speech-making circuit. A significant clue to Barak's intended generosity towards the Palestinians is that the number of settlements almost doubled rather than decreased during his term of office. The Israeli left continued to self-destruct after Barak resumed power within the Labor Party. Today, and for the foreseeable future, there is no effective left and no significant united peace camp in Israel. The two political representatives of the left, the Labor Party and Meretz, hardly matter anymore in the political scheme of things.

In the period immediately following Barak's election all eyes were focused on the negotiations between Israel and the Palestinians. On September 4, 1999, under the direction of President Clinton the two sides met in Sharm el Sheikh to sign a revised Wye Plantation agreement, to set the parameters for implementation of the original River Wye agreement signed by Netanyahu. This revision became necessary since Netanyahu had not fully implemented the terms concerning the withdrawal of Israeli forces.

## TALKS WITH SYRIANS RATHER THAN PALESTINIANS

Suddenly and surprisingly the focus shifted from negotiations with the Palestinians to talks with Syria. In December 1999 President Clinton announced his intention to relaunch peace talks between Israel and Syria. The Israeli response to the American initiative was very positive. Polls conducted by the Institute of Strategic Studies at Tel Aviv University showed a 60 percent majority of Israelis supporting a complete Israeli withdrawal from the Golan Heights in exchange for peace with Syria.[3] The Israeli public generally believed that in return for peace, Israel would dismantle all the settlements on the Golan Heights and withdraw from the entire area. This was the view presented by the Israeli media. There was a great deal of optimism about these talks, which commenced in December in West Virginia. Just as quickly they ended. The last meeting was on January 9, 2000, and nothing further happened. President Clinton invited Syrian President Assad in March to a summit meeting in Geneva in an unsuccessful attempt to revive the talks, but they were formally declared a failure. The official explanation given by Israel was Assad's insistence on retaining a strip of land on the shore of the Sea of Galilee that did not belong to Syria according to the international border.[4]

Contrasting media releases provided to the Israeli public can illustrate the obfuscation of intention. The headline of *Yediot Aharonot*, Israel's daily newspaper with the highest circulation, on December 10, 1999 quoted Barak saying, "The Golan Settlers will leave their homes after completing their historic mission." On another page in the same issue Barak is quoted without a word about the settlers leaving:

> They built a home, vineyard and village, and if it weren't for their work, determination and moral stature it wouldn't have been possible to begin negotiations with Syria, and we would have been now without security and without the Golan. We are all deeply connected to the Golan's landscape, to the settlement mission on the Golan, which was mostly done by people who

were sent by our party. I say to the people of the Golan; we take your hand in appreciation for what you did.[5]

Barak's ambiguity was consistent. On his way to the Shepherdstown West Virginia talks he gave a speech on the tarmac alluding to their historical importance. He pointed out that he was departing from the same spot where Sadat of Egypt had first landed in Israel, and from where Menachim Begin embarked to make peace with Egypt. He spoke of the difficult compromise required in the Golan, and that Israel would not sign a peace treaty at any price. Israel would sign nothing that compromised its security. He kept his promise and signed nothing.[6]

## FROM A SYRIAN TO A PALESTINIAN FAILURE

Unlike many other negotiations, the Shepherdstown talks produced a written document, carefully prepared by the Americans. Different versions of the leaked document appeared in the Syrian and Israeli press. According to *Yediot Aharonot* on January 13, 2000, the Syrians were unwilling to give up the disputed strip of land because of its importance for the control of water sources. The Syrian position as reported in *Al Hayat* on January 9 was that Syria would be willing to cooperate in drawing the actual permanent lines. If that strip of land were the only reason for the failure of the talks, even some Israeli observers felt that Syria's position indicated willingness to compromise.[7]

Israel often explained the failures in reaching agreements as threats to its security. But in the section about security arrangements, section C, of the Shepherdstown document, Syria agreed to the presence of an international force under American command. Syria undertook to prevent Hezbollah acting against civilians along Israel's northern border with Lebanon. The summary of the document that appeared in *Al Hayat* on January 9, 2000 strongly suggested that Syria was serious about negotiating peace with Israel. The full version published in *Yediot Aharonot* on January 13 revealed how far apart the two sides actually were. The Israeli report demonstrated Barak's reluctance to commit Israel to a clear borderline. He wanted the issue of borders to be left to the end of the negotiations. The document itself stated that the shape of the borders would be decided later in accordance with security and other considerations.[8]

In Shepherdstown the Israelis consistently refused to use the

word "withdrawal" and insisted on "redeployment." The difference
between the two terms is not merely semantic but, as in the Oslo
negotiations, indicates Israel's refusal to withdraw its forces and
dismantle its settlements. The Syrians talked about the withdrawal
of military and civilian Israeli presence, while the Israelis discussed
the redeployment of military forces exclusively. Israel was unwilling
to commit to the dismantling and evacuation of settlements, and
construction on the Golan Heights continued throughout the
negotiations.[9]

The fact that Syria suddenly walked away from the talks was
used to put the blame of the failure of the talks on Syria. According
to Dennis Ross, a US representative who was supportive of Israel,
the Syrians left when Israel published the full text of the document,
which was supposed to be highly confidential. That, said Ross,
killed everything.[10]

When President Clinton invited Assad to a meeting in Geneva in
March 2000, the Israeli media suggested that another meeting was
necessary because of Assad's stubbornness. In an article in *Yediot
Aharonot* written by senior reporter Shimon Shiffer on March 23,
the headline claimed this was an opportunity for Clinton to insist
on Syrian flexibility. The article itself focused on US complaints
about Barak's ambiguity over withdrawal to the 1967 borders, as
demanded by Assad.

In Israel, the summit's failure was again attributed to Assad's
unwillingness to compromise over a strip of land of less than 500
meters along the shore of the Sea of Galilee. Israel was portrayed as
both flexible and generous, but it was Israel's last attempt to reach
a peace agreement with the Syrians.

## THE FOCUS BACK ON THE PALESTINIANS: CAMP DAVID II

The focus shifted back to the Palestinians. On July 11, 2000,
following a series of preparatory contacts, President Clinton
convened another meeting, the Camp David II summit. Barak
presented himself as a grand master of compromise who was about
to make concessions of such magnitude that no Israeli leader before
him would have considered. Israelis believed him, and thought that
such offers were unlikely to be made again in the future. According
to the Israeli press, Barak offered the Palestinians 90 percent of the
West Bank and all of the Gaza Strip. The remaining 10 percent of
the West Bank, which contained most of the large settlement blocks,
would be annexed to Israel. More importantly, Barak offered to

divide the city of Jerusalem, allowing the Palestinians to establish their capital in part of the holy city.

The prevailing view in Israel was that the Palestinians rejected this generous offer and made no counter-offer, demonstrating their refusal to reach agreement. The United States and most of the western world accepted this view, and it was repeatedly employed by much of the global media. In a series of *New York Times* articles one year later, Robert Malley, Clinton's special advisor for Arab–Israeli affairs, published his version of what actually happened at Camp David.

Israel repeatedly argued, and many came to believe, that the Palestinian rejection of Barak's offer reflected the Arab rejection of Israel's right to exist. But an examination of the Palestinian position since Oslo shows a different reality. They accepted the June 4, 1967 borders for their state. They accepted Israel's annexation of territories in the West Bank to ensure that the large settlement blocks remain in Israeli sovereignty. The Palestinians accepted Israeli sovereignty over Jewish areas built in East Jerusalem after the 1967 war. Although the Palestinians insist on the right of their refugees to return, Malley argues, they agreed that the implementation of this should not be threatening to the security of the State of Israel. Malley contended that no other Arab interlocutor ever came close to such compromises.[11]

What Barak really offered at Camp David is difficult to assess since no documentation was ever presented to support his claim of generosity. Akiva Eldar, a veteran reporter for *Ha'aretz*, wrote, "Hardly anyone has any idea what these understandings are. No one has seen a paper stipulating these understandings, because no such paper exists."[12]

Robert Malley confirmed that Israelis thought Barak's offer to the Palestinians broke every conceivable taboo and went much further than any previous prime minister had ever gone. But the reality was that Barak's actual offer was very difficult to figure out. The prime minister's strategy was not to reveal Israel's true and final positions, even to the Americans. The US participants at the talks would not be able to describe Israel's real position. Malley said that, strictly speaking, there never was an Israeli offer. At Camp David proposals were never presented in writing but as spoken ideas. Yet the Americans were putting a lot of pressure on Arafat to accept these vague ideas as a basis for negotiations before the start of more rigorous negotiations.[13]

Despite the smoke screens, bits of information gradually found their way to the media, and a more accurate examination of Israel's actual offer became possible.

Barak's proposals at the Camp David II talks were essentially based on the Beilin–Abu Mazen accord of 1995.[14]

### The Beilin–Abu Mazen understanding: a summary

Israel would withdraw from 90–95 percent of the West Bank, *but*:

- 130 settlements would remain under Israeli sovereignty
- an additional 50 settlements would remain within the Palestinian state
- the Jordan valley would revert to Palestinian sovereignty but Israeli military forces would remain there
- the Palestinian state would recognize West Jerusalem as Israel's capital
- Israel would recognize the area defined as Al Quds (prior to the June war), which is the village of Abu Dis, as the capital of the Palestinian state
- the Temple Mount (Haram el Sharif) would revert to Palestinian sovereignty.

The exceptions to the 90–95 percent concessions establish that the area to revert to Palestinian rule would in fact be much smaller than 90–95 percent of the West Bank.

### Barak's Camp David II offer

Although a partial replica of the Beilin–Abu Mazen offer, Barak's offer was less generous. Barak insisted that the large settlement blocks be annexed to Israel. In the Beilin–Abu Mazen talks the settlements to be annexed to Israel did not include the land connecting these settlements to one another. Barak's proposal simplified the map, and annexed the settlements *and* the land connecting them to one another. In an article in *Ha'aretz*, the political columnist Danny Rubinstein estimated that this would leave about 120,000 Palestinians stranded, and they would have to become residents of Israel rather than Palestine.[15] To avoid giving Israeli citizenship to these 120,000 Palestinians, Barak suggested they should participate in elections in the Palestinian state rather than in the state under whose sovereignty they would actually live.[16]

A key controversy in the public debate about Camp David was that despite Barak's election promises to keep Jerusalem united and the eternal capital of the state of Israel, he agreed to divide it. This was believed to be true by many on all sides of the political spectrum, in large measure because of the terminological confusion surrounding the proposal. When dividing Jerusalem is discussed, it is usually assumed that East Jerusalem would be separated from West Jerusalem: East Jerusalem and its mostly Arab neighborhoods would be separated from Jewish West Jerusalem and become the capital of the Palestinian state. But at Camp David Israel did not offer East Jerusalem to the Palestinians as their future capital. It offered three villages located next to East Jerusalem, the largest being Abu Dis.

The concept of an Abu Dis solution was not new, and had been accepted by previous Israeli governments, with Palestinian state institutions moved from Jerusalem to Abu Dis. Palestinians received permits to build a parliament house and government offices, which were almost completed in Abu Dis when Camp David was convened. Several years before Camp David, *Ha'aretz* correspondent Akiva Eldar reported on a meeting with the Foreign Affairs Council in New York, where Arafat was asked about a solution based on Abu Dis. His response was, "Certainly, it is possible to accept the idea of Abu Dis which belonged to Al Quds already under Jordanian rule."[17]

Before Camp David, Israel was supposed to transfer Abu Dis and two other villages to the Palestinian Authority as part of the second deployment agreed upon in the Sharm el Sheikh meeting in 1999. Both Palestinians and Israelis operated on the assumption that Barak would agree to this transfer before the summit. Barak reneged. Robert Malley and Hussein Agha refer to this development in their article in the *New York Review of Books*. When Clinton, who had been previously requested to convey the transfer to Arafat, learned of Barak's change of heart, the US president was not amused.[18]

The Israeli public was led by the press to believe that Barak was going to offer East Jerusalem to the Palestinians, with headlines such as the one reading "Barak was ready to divide Jerusalem" in the *Jerusalem Post* of July 27. Later in the article it stated, "Ehud Barak, at the end of the Camp David summit has been willing to consider the possibility of creating a Palestinian Al Quds besides the Jewish capital, effectively dividing Jerusalem." According to one member of the negotiating team quoted in the *Jerusalem Post*, the proposals included allowing several neighborhoods outside Jerusalem's Eastern boundary to be annexed to the future Palestinian state. It would seem that Barak did not really offer anything that had not been offered before.

A central issue forcing Arafat's hand was Barak's insistence that the sides sign an "end of conflict" declaration, as part of the final agreement document. Barak's insistence could be considered threatening, since it meant that if the Palestinians wanted to have a state of their own they had first to agree that the Palestinian–Israeli conflict had come to an end. Barak concluded with, "The alternative is a bloody confrontation that would bring no gain."[19] Such an end of conflict declaration would have meant the abolition of several critical UN resolutions (UN 242 and 194) that were essential to the resolution of the conflict.

In a book about Camp David called *BeMerchak Negiya* (Within Reach), Gilad Sher said that Barak wanted to force a reinterpretation of UN Resolution 242. Another participant in Camp David, Shlomo Ben Ami, suggested converting the Clinton parameters into a UN Security Council resolution to replace Resolution 242. In a review of books about Camp David in *Le Monde Diplomatique*, the Israeli journalist Amnon Kapeliouk contended that Yossi Beilin, who was Israel's minister of justice at the time, was the only one who did not attempt obfuscation, which he felt served only to increase the distrust during the talks.[20] Beilin maintained that Barak's plan at Camp David was inferior to the Beilin–Abu Mazen understanding, which did not include any reference to an end of conflict.

Clinton had considered using the Abu Mazen–Beilin understandings as the basis for the Camp David summit. Barak was not interested, and insisted that an explicit end of conflict statement be included in the opening statement. Barak must have known that Arafat could not agree to this, and would not be able to persuade the Palestinians to agree. Therefore it is tempting to conclude that he participated in the Camp David summit in the hope that it would fail.[21] And fail it did.

Another significant contribution to the failure was the fate of the settlements designated to remain within Palestinian sovereignty. Barak's senior assistant, Gilad Sher, suggested that these settlements would be evacuated unless the settlers decide to remain and live under Palestinian rule. The wording is important here because it leaves the final decision in the hands of the settlers.[22] When less idealistic settlers in Gaza wanted to leave their settlements and relocate inside Israel with appropriate compensation, the government refused. Under such circumstances the settlers would stay, because the State of Israel leaves them no choice. The state's attitude to the relocation of settlers strengthens the suspicion that Israel never intended to dismantle settlements in the process of making peace with the Palestinians. Further calculation also reveals that the area of these settlements, their lands, roads, and defensive areas, leaves the balance of the West Bank under the Palestinian Authority at about 40–45 percent of the total. The Palestinian leadership could not accept a solution based on 40–50 percent of the West Bank, and Barak's only concession was that the fate of the settlements inside the future Palestinian state and of the militarily controlled Jordan valley would be decided later, perhaps 10 to 15 years later. Aluf Benn, writing in *Ha'aretz* on January 15, 2001, supported this assessment of the intentions of the Barak government.[23]

## THE RIGHT OF RETURN

Any discussion of the Palestinian refugees and their Right of Return was and continues to be inflammatory. The Israeli consensus is that the Right of Return demonstrates that the Palestinians do not really accept Israel's right to exist in peace and security as a Jewish homeland. The Palestinians want to carve out part of the ancient Jewish homeland to build a Palestinian state, and then flood Israel with millions of refugees, thereby destroying the Jewish character of the state. This would lead *de facto* to two Palestinian states. This issue has always been so hot a topic that no Israeli government was willing to address it, let alone consider its implementation. This is despite the fact that UN Resolution 194 of December 11, 1948 established the right of the Palestinian refugees to return to their homes, if they so wish.[24]

No one really knows how many Palestinian refugees would choose to use their Right of Return to what is now a foreign country in which their homes and properties no longer exist. Dr. Shikaki, the head of the Palestinian Institute of Social Research, conducted a poll of Palestinian refugees in several countries to assess how many of the refugees would actually wish to return. The poll found that less than 10 percent of the participants expressed an unambiguous desire to return.[25] Among many other proposals, the Saudi peace plan adopted by the Arab League on March 28, 2002 refers to various solutions that would be agreed upon, such as possible compensation or relocation into the future Palestinian state. Most Arab proposals include an element of return for some Palestinian refugees into Israel proper, with the actual number to be determined through negotiations.[26]

The Right of Return was the component of all agreements least acceptable to Israel. The Israeli public was convinced that any discussion of this issue constitutes a threat to the existence of the Jewish state. In Oslo the Palestinians had accepted the concept that their refugees who choose to return would become citizens of a Palestinian state. They were, however, seeing the number of Israeli settlers in their midst constantly increasing, and the amount of land available to them decreasing. This intensified the importance of the issue and of their right.[27]

Barak apparently wanted a declaration ending the conflict which would mean that the Palestinians waived the right to return to their homeland. Indeed, he went as far as to suggest that this be left to the sole discretion of Israel. Israel never even agreed to accept as few as 10,000 refugees, although Beilin, Abu Mazen, and Barak calculated that around 150,000 Jewish settlers in the large settlement blocks would remain in Palestine.[28] As part of the reconciliation process, there was no acknowledgement by Barak of Israel's role in creating the refugee problem. He made a vague statement about Palestinian suffering, leaving the impression that his generous offer was heading towards neither reconciliation nor conflict resolution.

## THE SECOND *INTIFADA*

In October 2000 the Second *Intifada* (the Al Aksa *Intifada*) broke out. An armed insurrection of an occupied population, it was very different from the First *Intifada*. The frustration over the failure of the Camp David II negotiations is generally held to have triggered the rebellion against the Israeli occupation. The provocative visit by Ariel Sharon, then the leader of the opposition, to the Haram El Sharif, guarded by hundreds of policemen and security people, may have been the spark. But the prime minister gave his blessing for this visit, indicating Barak's frustration at the failure of his "generous" offer. The protests against Sharon's visit were met by thousands of armed Israeli soldiers using massive amounts of live ammunition to quell the Palestinian protests. Shaul Mofaz, the chief of staff, immediately launched operation Field of Thorns, which had been planned years earlier.[29] Despite the armed nature of the rebellion, the Israeli reaction to the confrontation was disproportionate. In the first month of the *Intifada*, when the Israelis were not even prepared, the death toll amounted to 115 Palestinians compared with 12 Israelis.[30] In the Second *Intifada* the Israelis employed a policy of relative autonomy of local commanders of military units. This approach, initiated by General Shaul Mofaz, practically encouraged disproportionate reaction by ensuring that commanding officers of brigades and battalions had no fear of the consequences of their decisions. When General Ya'alon later assumed command of the Central Command he went further by placing the entire blame for the conflagration on the Palestinians, and wanted to brand into the Palestinian conscience the realization that they would achieve nothing through violence.[31]

Before leaving office following his electoral defeat by Ariel Sharon, Barak was involved in one other peace initiative. After several months of violent confrontation, many Israelis began expressing the desperate hope that perhaps one more round of peace negotiations would bring about a solution. On January 21, 2001, peace talks were held in Taba, Egypt, just across the border from Eilat. The talks were initiated by US President Clinton and were based on the Clinton parameters. Both Clinton and Barak were close to the end of their terms in office, but there seemed to be widespread conviction that the sides were as close to an agreement as they had ever been. The eventual failure of the Taba talks was blamed on the fact that they occurred too late.[32]

## WHAT ACTUALLY HAPPENED AT TABA?

The first major stumbling block was the sudden and inexplicable resignation of Prime Minister Barak, leading to a new election campaign where Barak now ran against Sharon. At the Taba talks Barak was merely a caretaker prime minister, and this did not auger well for a successful completion to the talks. The talks could have been a final effort to appease Barak's traditional base of support among the Israeli left. Many in that camp were furious at his conduct in the earlier negotiations with the Palestinians and his handling of the *Intifada*. Clearly, Barak was going into an election and may have wanted to neutralize these negative feelings through another set of talks.[33]

The senior members of Barak's negotiating team were Beilin, Ben Ami, and Sarid, all leftists. This choice was expedient. The three convinced the Palestinian chief negotiator to sign a document confirming that: the two sides had never been closer to reaching an agreement.[34] It is unlikely the Israeli delegation could have achieved a substantive agreement. In the middle of the negotiations, Barak's man Gilad Sher told the two delegations that no decision can be made without his presence and approval. Barak wanted to ensure that no real decision was made while, at the same time, gaining an electoral advantage. Even Yossi Beilin, the politician most committed to the peace effort among the Labor members, mused that the Taba talks could achieve no more than set a framework or reference points for the government that would assume power after the elections. Every member of the Taba team knew that decisions reached at the talks would not be binding.

The Taba talks were not based on any written document despite the fact that the promoter was the US president. To judge by reports in the Israeli media, Clinton's parameters were again quite similar to the Beilin–Abu Mazen understandings. Barak's position at Camp David was also rather similar to these understandings. This time the Palestinians agreed to the proposals, perhaps as a result of pressure by President Clinton, who was quoted in Palestinian sources telling Arafat, "If you don't answer affirmatively to this proposal, it will serve as proof that you are not interested in peace. In such a situation, Barak will declare war on you and we will support him."[35]

The Taba talks also produced no written documentation, and what is known about them is based on extensive notes taken by ambassador Miguel Moratinos, the EU representative to the Middle East. Both sides agreed that Moratinos's report was fair and accurate, and *Ha'aretz* published it on February 15, 2002. According to Moratinos's report the Israelis offered the Palestinians 92 percent of the West Bank, but wanted to annex 6 percent of the area and place another 2 percent under a lease agreement. Subject to a land swap, the Palestinians agreed to Israeli annexation of 3.1 percent of the area. This was a serious concession for the Palestinians since the land was located at the very center of the West Bank and would leave all major settlements under Israeli sovereignty inside Palestine. The land swap offered by Israel referred to areas of sand dunes near Halutza that were not contiguous to the West Bank or to Gaza.[36] Israel presented maps showing areas for future settlement expansion in the center of the Palestinian territory, to which the Palestinians vehemently objected.[37]

The Israelis insisted that Jerusalem be the capital of both states: that is, Jerusalem would be the capital of Israel and Al Quds, or Abu Dis, the capital of the Palestinian state. The Palestinian concern was that their capital should be East Jerusalem rather than the village of Abu Dis, and this issue had to be left for a future date.[38] There was some willingness on the Israeli side to consider the evacuation of settlements in the Jordan valley as long as an Israeli military presence remained. The Jordan valley, or approximately 10 percent of the West Bank would always be sovereign Palestinian territory but it would be full of Israeli soldiers.[39]

The Palestinians wanted full control over their future borders, while the Israelis insisted on some form of Israeli oversight. This applied to the border with Jordan, where Israel wanted to control the influx of refugees into the newly established state, and it contradicted Israel's agreement to give the Palestinians freedom to allow in as many refugees as they saw fit. Despite its optimistic vocabulary, the Moratinos report acknowledged this very basic difference between the positions of both sides.[40]

The Taba talks did not offer the Palestinians anything substantially different from past negotiations. Perhaps as a result of pressure from left-leaning Israelis participating in the negotiating team, Barak relented on his demand for an end of conflict document. The Israelis agreed to forgo this demand and revert back to the two critical UN resolutions, 242 and 194, as the basis for future negotiations. As Shlomo Ben Ami said of these talks, "We almost did it, however almost is a long way from actually doing it."

The Taba failure was the beginning of a relatively long period with no direct negotiations. There were several attempted mediations, mostly by Americans, but the Israelis and Palestinians faced one another across their respective gun sights.

Despite its declarations, Israel has never changed its position and never bettered its offer since the early Alon plan. All Israeli proposals, official and unofficial, offered since have been restatements with insignificant modifications of the Alon Plan. Yossi Beilin's plan could well be described as "Alon Plus," and Barak's as "Alon Minus," but the resemblances are undeniable.

With very few exceptions, the majority of Israelis want to live in peace. Most of the polls continue to show a majority of Israelis supporting the evacuation of settlements. But this was never reflected by the political leadership or the security establishment. The Taba talks that marked the end of Barak's career as prime minister also marked the high point in the attempts to resolve the conflict. Since then the process has been going downhill.[41]

# 10

# PEACE ON A DOWNHILL SLOPE

In February 2001 Ariel Sharon soundly defeated the incumbent prime minister, Barak, with 62 percent of the votes. Sharon had waited a long time to become Israel's prime minister, and was 71 years old. Although Sharon grew up in Kfar Malal, a cooperative agricultural village, in a deeply Labor environment, his political career was very right wing. Initially he opposed the Oslo Accords and any agreement with the Palestinians, and considered Arafat just a terrorist. As Sharon matured politically, he learned that despite many contradictions, the Israeli public wanted to hope. Denying the possibility of negotiation with the Palestinians was not what they wanted, so he presented himself as more conciliatory, and perfected the ability to let talks stagnate or continue indefinitely.[1]

Sharon had held a large array of positions, mostly in the military, although the position of chief of staff of the IDF had eluded him. He had served in various ministerial capacities, including minister of agriculture and minister of housing and infrastructure. The most important post he had held previously was that of minister of defense, a position later denied to him because of his involvement in the Sabra and Shatila massacre during the first Lebanon War. He was arguably the most well-known officer in the history of the Israeli Army, from his early command of Unit 101 (a commando paratroop unit notorious for bloody cross-border operations) followed by his command of the paratroop forces. After leaving the army Sharon quickly became involved in politics and merged the centrist General Zionists and the right-wing Herut party to form Ga'hal, the first substantial alliance of the right.

Throughout his long career Sharon was nicknamed "the bulldozer." Impatient and irreverent, he was powerful and controlling, displaying little concern for the consequences of his actions. He flamboyantly disobeyed orders, particularly when these came from leaders he did not respect. When Sharon was still a junior officer, Ben Gurion commented that he would go far if only he learned not to lie so often. Yet, in later years, when most considered him a spent force, Uri Dan, his biographer, predicted that Israelis who did not want Sharon as minister of defense would have to accept him as prime minister. This prediction came true despite the fact that Sharon did not learn to tell the truth more frequently.

## SHARON PRESENTS HIS GOVERNMENT

On March 7, 2001 Sharon presented his government to the Knesset. During his Knesset speech, the police and the army were on high alert. All major Palestinian cities were under closure, although Arafat had sent him a congratulatory telegram on the occasion of his presentation. Sharon's speech was masterful: on the one hand he declared that his government was ready to extend a hand of peace towards the Palestinians, recognizing that both sides would have to make painful compromises. On the other hand, in the same speech he stated that despite great concessions made by several Israeli governments they still had not encountered, from the other side, a will towards reconciliation and real peace. Sharon declared his commitment to the pursuit of peace, but not under pressure from terrorism and violence, and expressed his understanding of the suffering of the Palestinian people.[2] Arafat was not overly impressed by this speech, which came soon after two other statements made by Sharon at that time. "The government will raise the flag of Zionism in education, in the integration of immigrants, and in the settlements," was one. The other was a reconfirmation of his government's eternal commitment to Jerusalem.[3]

Arafat soon convened the Palestinian legislative council, where he did not officially call for an end to the *Intifada*. Instead he confirmed the Palestinian commitment to move towards peace, and appealed to the Israelis to restart the negotiations from the point they had ended at the Taba talks one month earlier. He also asked for the deployment of an international force to protect the Palestinians from Israeli repression.[4] Both leaders knew full well that their proposals would be unacceptable to the other side.

On the occasion of Sharon's first visit as prime minister to Washington on March 19, 2001, the *New York Times* columnist Thomas Friedman commented that this was the most favorable period towards the Jewish state in Washington, whereas Arafat's ratings could not have been any lower. According to Friedman, President

Bush's administration agreed with Sharon's analysis of the Middle East situation.[5] The conceptual similarities between the US administration and the Sharon government were not likely to advance the cause of peace, and the process did deteriorate.

Sharon missed no opportunity to blame the ongoing violence on Arafat. George Tenet, the head of the CIA, and the Mitchell Committee (a committee headed by Senator Mitchell) were charged by President Bush to investigate the ongoing violence and make recommendations to end it. Sharon wanted all participants in this venture to establish that all responsibility for the violence was Arafat's. There was no evidence found by the Israeli intelligence community or by the US authorities that could substantiate the accusations against Arafat. But Sharon and his cabinet members persisted in their accusations because the collapse of the Israeli peace camp after the failures of the Camp David and Taba talks left a vacuum in the opposition. There was no political force in Israel to oppose Sharon's aggressiveness.

The strongest voice of opposition was that of Yossi Sarid, the leader of the left-wing Meretz Party. And yet in a Knesset speech he had this to say to Arafat: "It is time for you to stop your grotesque and pathetic participation in summits. Stay in Gaza and Ramallah and start to put things in order there .... Do not lead us to believe that you prefer the violence of armed struggle to the creation of a Palestinian state."[6] If this was the voice of a moderate and a peace leader, it is not surprising that a poll conducted in March found almost 60 percent of the Israeli public had a negative view of the Palestinian people. Over 60 percent considered it was no longer possible to reach a peace agreement, and over 70 percent supported a proposal to seal off all the Palestinian cities and towns. The same poll, predictably, found that a majority of Palestinians now supported the *Intifada*.[7]

In an interview that Ari Shavit of *Ha'aretz* conducted with Sharon on April 12, 2001 Sharon said that he might agree to a Palestinian state on approximately 42 percent of the West Bank. But this would have to be tied to a non-belligerency agreement extending over an indefinite period, and conditional on the Palestinian undertaking of preventive action against terrorism, ending all incitement and conducting a formal education program for peace. This concession of 42 percent of the West Bank was offered a few months after the Taba discussion of about 92 percent of the West Bank. The article was published under the heading "Sharon is Sharon." It included Sharon's stipulation that while the Palestinians must maintain the non-belligerency undertaking, Israel would be free to expand its settlements, and that no concessions would be made in Jerusalem or Hebron. Nor would concessions be made in the Jordan valley or the Golan Heights.

## EGYPT PROPOSES PEACE VIA JORDAN

The next effort at peace making came from Egypt, but was presented to Israel by the Jordanian foreign minister. The proposal outlined three steps: the imposition of a ceasefire on the Israelis; the implementation of the previously agreed interim agreements; and finally, the resumption of talks on the status of the Palestinian territory. The negotiations were to be completed in a specified period of time. Sharon found no merit in the proposal, but Shimon Peres, his foreign minister, announced that Israel accepted the Egyptian proposal in principle provided that modifications be made. The main requirement was that Israel would continue to build in the settlements according to the prime minister's policy of natural growth.[8] After meeting with the Jordanian king, Peres met with Egyptian president, Hosni Mubarak, at the end of April. The Egyptian president was convinced that a ceasefire between Israel and the Palestinians was in the making, and announced this conviction on television. When Peres returned to Israel he changed his position. He stated that no deal about a ceasefire had been made with the Palestinians and Mubarak was mistaken. The Egyptian president responded with the claim that Peres had misled him.[9]

## THE MITCHELL COMMITTEE REPORT

The Mitchell Committee issued its report on May 21, 2001. It established that the Israeli accusation that the PLO had planned the *Intifada* and deliberately made it bloody to turn public opinion against Israel was incorrect. The committee found no evidence that Israel planned to respond to the Palestinian demonstrations with lethal force. It found no evidence that the Palestinian Authority (PA) had made serious efforts to contain the demonstrations once they started, but could not find any evidence either that Israel had attempted to control the protests through non-lethal means. The committee contended that although Sharon's visit to the Haram el Sharif did not in itself trigger the *Intifada*, its poor timing and provocative nature had contributed greatly to the tension. The use of lethal force on the second day of demonstrations and the large number of Palestinians killed did contribute to an escalation in the violence.[10]

The committee endeavored to be even-handed, and advised the Palestinians to tighten control of demonstrations and of the violence, and clearly establish that violence was unacceptable and would be punished. It demanded that Israel stop all settlement activities, even those related to the internal growth of the settlers' population.

The US administration sent William Burns, the former US ambassador to Jordan, to the area to assist the implementation of the Mitchell recommendations. While Burns was shuttling between the PA and the government of Israel, the Palestinian violence continued. The PA was apparently unable to stop the violence, and Israel made it clear that there would be no freeze on settlement construction.

In the first half of 2001, European envoys such as the German and Russian foreign ministers came to Israel, which might have encouraged President Bush to get more involved. He sent George Tenet to the region in June 2001. Tenet convinced the sides to restart security meetings, the first of which took place the next day. Tenet provided a timetable for the implementation of the Mitchell report, and requested a response the very next day. Israel's standard response was that the Palestinians must stop all forms of terrorism and violence, and apprehend dozens of Hamas and Islamic Jihad leaders, named on a list they would willingly provide. The Palestinians explained that the violence was inextricable from the political situation, and that the Palestinian public would agree to a cessation of violence if they were convinced an agreement was imminent. According to Ilan Paz, an Israeli general, Israel was largely responsible for the fact that the Palestinians were incapable of stopping the violence, because of Israel's systematic destruction of the Palestinian security system.[11]

In two days the Tenet mission reached an impasse. The Israelis demanded an absolute cessation of violence, the apprehension of Hamas and Jihad leaders, and a buffer zone within Area A of the West Bank. The Palestinians rejected the proposal, particularly the notion of a buffer zone. Tenet threatened to lay the responsibility for the failure of his mission on the Palestinians.[12] The Palestinians then held intense discussions at Arafat's headquarters, which were bugged by the Israelis who could hear everything. Arafat told Tenet that he would accept everything but the creation of a buffer zone.[13]

The Tenet ceasefire, largely following the Mitchell Committee proposals, was announced on June 13. Sharon's office then issued a statement ostensibly supporting the Tenet plan, but warning the Palestinians that there would be harsh responses to any violation of the peace. That night a Palestinian man was killed just outside Ramallah. The next day a senior Israeli officer was killed at a meeting with a Palestinian informer. There were several incidents, and then a delegation of settlement officials and Likud members demanded an end to the ceasefire and a return to military operations. The violence escalated, with Israel employing tanks, missiles, and aircraft. Sharon insisted that the Palestinians perfectly execute their part, but simultaneously Israel seemed to demolish any Palestinian capacity to stop the violence or neutralize its own extremists. Police stations were destroyed and police commanders killed. Al'Ali, the head of the local Security Council in Gaza, described the situation to *Ha'aretz*: "Israel is actually stopping us from operating against terrorists ... one of my officers was killed by Israelis while trying to stop a group of terrorists." He wondered how Arafat's people could be effective without any control over the territory in which they are supposed to operate.[14]

## TARGETED ASSASSINATIONS INTENSIFY

In August a missile shot from a helicopter killed Abu Ali Mustafa, the political leader of the Popular Front for the Liberation of Palestine (PFLP), who had taken over from the legendary George Habash.[15] This was an unprecedented act of killing the head of a Palestinian organization not involved in operations. Several military intelligence officers opposed targeted assassinations, saying they would raise the level of violence rather than stop it. Matti Steinberg, a senior Shabak analyst, commented that by killing Abu Ali Mustafa, Israel had crossed a line, creating a desire for revenge by the Palestinians.[16]

Another journalist, Offer Shelah, writing on the *Yediot Aharonot* website, commented that such operations were not designed to reduce the level of violence but rather to appease the Israeli public. Frustrated, tired, and angered by the fact that there are Israeli victims of the violence, the Israelis generally support such military operations, knowing that they will not stop the activities of the PFLP. The government understands the public sentiment.[17]

Addressing congressional leaders at the White House on October 2, 2001, President Bush stated that the idea of a Palestinian state had always been part of a vision, so long as the right of Israel to exist was respected.[18] This was the first clear expression by an

American president in support of Palestinian statehood. Secretary of state Colin Powell articulated the US expectation that this would be the outcome of direct negotiations between the two sides. Although there was nothing particularly exceptional in the concept presented, they triggered a state of emergency at the Israeli prime minister's office. Suspicious of American intentions, Sharon became convinced that the United States was about to impose a new peace plan on Israel.

Sharon's advisers recommended that he wait until a clearer picture of the American plans and intentions emerged. But Sharon instructed his generals to proceed with operations in the Palestinian autonomous area in Gaza. Several confrontations took place. There were rumors about Saudi pressure on the United States to solve the Palestinian problem as part of the struggle against al Qaeda. Sharon took this to mean that Israel would be made to pay the price of the battle with al Qaeda. He called upon the world, particularly the United States, to avoid using Israel as the scapegoat by turning it into a 1938-style Czechoslovakia. The US ambassador to Israel demanded an immediate retraction, which Sharon gave unenthusiastically. Colin Powell told Sharon that his retraction was unacceptable, and that comparing the US president to Neville Chamberlain was offensive.[19]

Secretary Powell presented another peace initiative in October. This one mentioned not just a Palestinian state but also a viable one. That implied territorial contiguity and rejection of the official offer of a mere 40 percent of the West Bank. Powell's plan saw Jerusalem as the capital of both states, and concluded that the refugee problem would have to be solved outside Israel. Bush's ally, Tony Blair, supported this American peace plan, and the Palestinian response was enthusiastic.

Meanwhile, Israel's targeted assassinations of Hamas leaders continued, with several media sources contending that they were deliberately planned to sabotage the new peace plan.

## REHAVAM ZEEVI IS KILLED

On October 17, 2001, Rehavam Zeevi, former minister of tourism and extreme nationalist, was assassinated in his Jerusalem hotel.[20] The PFLP claimed responsibility for the act to avenge the murder of their leader, Abu Ali Mustafa. Zeevi had resigned from Sharon's government after advocating the transfer of all Palestinians in the occupied territories and in Israel to the neighboring Arab states.

Dan Meridor, another right-wing politician, stated that Zeevi's death was partly caused by Israeli mistakes. According to Meridor, the assassination of Abu Ali Mustafa changed the rules of the game, and Zeevi's murder was the result.[21] Although the PFLP took full responsibility for the act, Sharon put the blame on Arafat. On the same day, Israel's cabinet issued an ultimatum to Arafat that essentially threatened war against the PA if Arafat did not apprehend all those involved and all the leaders of the PFLP, and hand them over to Israel. The United States, under the influence of Vice-President Cheney and his fellow neo-conservatives, allowed the Israeli aggression to continue without fear of sanctions so long as it was short and did not cause too much bloodshed.[22]

### GENERAL ZINNI'S MISSION: ANOTHER HAPLESS US EFFORT

In November Colin Powell announced that General Anthony Zinni would be sent to the Middle East to help the warring parties re-establish a ceasefire. The general arrived in the Middle East on November 26. Palestinian extremists greeted General Zinni with a series of terrorist acts, which peaked in early December. During one Sharon visit to Washington 26 Israelis were killed in one day. Sharon cut his trip short and returned to Israel. Speaking at the airport upon his arrival, Sharon placed the entire blame for the bloodshed on Arafat, although it was clear to the Israelis that the suicide missions were being carried out by Islamic extremists.[23] With little infrastructure, Arafat could do very little to stop them. The Israeli response was aggression aimed at Fatah, the PA, and Arafat himself. All the while, General Zinni was still trying to impose a ceasefire.

In mid-December the US administration recalled the general to Washington for consultations. There was a reduction in acts of terrorism at the end of 2001, and he returned to Tel Aviv on January 2, 2002. He was greeted by Israeli anxiety over the *Karine A*, the Palestinian freighter that they believed was heading to the region to bring arms and munitions to the PA. The Israelis told Zinni that they were going to intercept the ship within hours.[24] The Americans had apparently known about this ship all along, and the US navy had willingly tracked the boat on behalf of the Israelis. Zinni was planning to meet with Arafat over the issue, but he first met with Sharon, who instructed him in preparation for that meeting.[25]

Arafat claimed that the PA had nothing to do with the *Karine A*. Every word of his protest was heard by the Israelis, who had long since bugged Arafat's headquarters. At first even Israeli military intelligence admitted that Hezbollah officials had been seen on board the ship, and that they had no evidence to tie the *Karine A* to Arafat or to the PA. The official US and Israeli position, nevertheless, was that Arafat was directly responsible for the ship. Perhaps the more important question that should have been raised was why was the United States pretending to be an honest broker for peace between the two sides of the conflict. The PA was accused of trying to obtain weapons and munitions to replace their dwindling supplies destroyed by Israel, while Israel was allowed to import billions of dollars worth of America's most sophisticated weaponry. Israel wanted Zinni to remain in the region and continue the negotiations, since nothing could be more attractive to Sharon and many Israelis than endless negotiations.[26]

On March 24, 2002 General Zinni submitted a proposal for a compromise between the two sides. It was a scheme for the implementation of the Tenet plan, which was itself a scheme for the implementation of the Mitchell proposal. The Zinni proposal was considered advantageous to the Israelis, and they could not reject it. Having had the benefit of eavesdropping on Arafat's offices and knowing that the Palestinians would not respond favorably, Sharon approved it.[27]

On March 27, a bloodbath occurred at the Park Hotel in the Israeli town of Netanya. Zinni was undeterred. In an attempt to salvage his mission he demanded that Arafat immediately condemn the massacre and accept his proposal. Arafat accepted. He commanded Muhamad Dahlan, the top Fatah man in Gaza and his main lieutenant, to arrest the heads of Hamas in Gaza. But Dahlan responded that it was pointless to do so since Israel was about to reoccupy the West Bank.[28]

The failure of Zinni's mission was predictable from the beginning. This could be gleaned from Powell's speech announcing Zinni's departure, the bulk of which chastized the Palestinians for not eliminating the violence. This had been an American precondition for the achievement of a viable ceasefire. Israel's provocations, the military occupation and its consequences, were portrayed as secondary issues. Sharon was pleased with the US announcement of Zinni's mission, as not much was demanded of him. The United States made no demand to rescind Sharon's precondition of seven totally peaceful days before talks began about implementation of the Tenet plan. Sharon was confident that the PA was incapable of guaranteeing seven peaceful days. This left the Israelis free to continue with targeted assassinations, and react with outrage when Hamas or Islamic Jihad responded in kind.

## OPERATION DEFENSIVE SHIELD VERSUS THE SAUDI PEACE PLAN

Muhammad Dahlan was right. At the end of March 2002 Israel initiated an operation best known as Defensive Shield. It was designed by Israel to reoccupy the West Bank, and deliberately or inadvertently, mask the impact of the Saudi peace plan, introduced just a few weeks earlier. Thomas Friedman, who had been to Saudi Arabia in mid-February and had an audience with the Saudi Crown Prince Abdullah, first published news and details of the Saudi peace initiative in the *New York Times* of February 17. During this meeting Friedman learned that the prince intended to propose that if Israel would retreat to the 1967 borders and allow the creation of an independent Palestinian state in the West Bank and Gaza, the Arab world would end the state of belligerence and normalize its relations with Israel. This would include the establishment of diplomatic relations. The plan alluded to the thorny problem of Palestinian refugees, and suggested it would be settled by mutual agreement. According to the article, the prince said that one reason for this proposal was his desire to establish that the Arabs do not reject or despise the Israelis. They did reject the way the Israelis were treating the Palestinians.[29]

Israel generally reacted with surprise, and Sharon did not react at all. Some of his advisers believed the initiative was a gimmick. But public pressure to respond was mounting, and Sharon said he would find a way to convey Israel's position to the Saudis. Moshe Katzav, the Israeli president, proposed to fly to Saudi Arabia. This idea faced a negative reaction in the Arab media and was dropped. Editorials in *Ha'aretz* called on Sharon to examine the proposal and its significance.[30] One month later Sharon responded, stating the plan was unacceptable and even dangerous to the security of Israel, because it called for a total Israeli withdrawal from the occupied territories. He claimed this would violate UN Security Council Resolutions 242 and 338, which, according to the Israeli interpretation, merely called for Israeli withdrawal from "territories," not from "all territories."[31] Only Israel argued that the English-language version of UN Resolution 242 meant that it did not have to evacuate all the occupied territories, despite the fact that the French version clearly states that *all* territories must be evacuated.

At one point, Sharon proposed going to Beirut to present his own peace plan to the Arab League summit. This proposal was rejected by just about everybody. Some saw it as deliberately provocative. Arafat expressed his desire to attend the Arab League summit, a suggestion supported by President Bush. Israel objected strenuously because Arafat's attendance would compromise Israel's efforts to isolate Arafat. Arafat stayed at home.

The Arab League summit meeting in Beirut adopted the Saudi peace initiative on March 28. The Arab League Council's demands from Israel included:

- Israeli withdrawal from all territories occupied, including the Golan Heights and territories in South Lebanon
- an agreed-upon solution to the Palestinian refugee issue, in line with UN Resolution 184
- Israel's support for the establishment of an independent Palestinian state on territories occupied in 1967, with East Jerusalem as its capital.

In response the Arab world would undertake the following:

- enter into a peace agreement with Israel, accepting that the Arab–Israeli conflict had reached its end
- establish normal relations with Israel.

The Arab League Council called on Israel to accept this initiative to ensure prospects for peace and end further bloodshed, enabling Israel and all Arab countries to live in peace.[32]

However, the Israeli media largely ignored this proposal by a body representing the entire Arab world. Although foreign minister, Shimon Peres, actually welcomed it, a spokesman from his ministry contradictorily stated that the ultimate purpose of the Saudi initiative was Israel's destruction, with the return of the Palestinian refugees to Israel.

Displaying Israel's true attitude towards the proposal, merely one day after the details of the Arab League peace proposal were released, Operation Defensive Shield commenced. In a Ramallah under curfew, Arafat's headquarters were completely surrounded and bulldozers began destroying the walls of the Mukata'ah, the PLO headquarters and Arafat's offices. Some believed that the goal of this operation was to kill Arafat, and Arafat agreed. He proclaimed, "Allah is great, I am ready to become a martyr, and may Allah honor me as a martyr in death."

Colin Powell responded by arriving in Tel Aviv on April 11 for a
meeting with Sharon to insist that the parties talk and begin negotiations. Powell was scheduled to meet Arafat the following day. While
Powell went on a short tour of northern Israel, Sharon told reporters
that it was necessary to find a replacement for Arafat. As long as
world leaders met with him, it would be difficult to find anyone to
take his place at the head of the PLO.[33] Another suicide bombing
delayed the meeting, but much to Sharon's chagrin, Powell met with
Arafat and insisted he meet his obligations.[34] Arafat is reported to
have responded that unless Israel withdrew from the autonomous
regions in accordance with the UN Security Council resolution, there
could be no ceasefire discussion. The impasse was complete.

At a press conference immediately following Powell's return,
President Bush had this to say about Ariel Sharon:

> I do believe Ariel Sharon is a man of peace. I think he wants – I
> am confident he wants Israel to be able to exist at peace with its
> neighbor – with its neighbors. I mean, he's told that to us here in
> the Oval Office. He has embraced the notion of two states living
> side by side.[35]

In response to a reporter question whether he agreed with Sharon
about Arafat, the president had this to say: "I have been disappointed in Chairman Arafat. I think he let the Palestinian people
down. I think he's had an opportunity to lead to peace and he hasn't
done so."[36]

By mid-May, the entire West Bank was again under direct control
of the IDF. Sharon's satisfaction was deeply shared by the settlers.
Since Sharon had taken the helm of government, just a year earlier,
about 25 new settlements had been established. Officially these settle-
ment-outposts were founded without the approval of the government
and were considered illegal. They were nevertheless connected to the
electrical and water grids, and were protected by the army.[37]

In July, an assistant of Miguel Moratinos had information about a
unilateral call for a ceasefire that the leaders of a militant faction of
the Palestinian Fatah, the Tanzim, were about to publish. Sheik Ahmed
Yassin, the spiritual leader of Hamas, apparently approved this call.
But that evening, Israeli fighter planes bombed Gaza and assassinated
Salah Shehadah, a senior Hamas leader. They dropped a one-ton bomb
on his home, destroying the building and killing his entire family and
several other children who were playing with Shehadah's children at
the time. The removal of the bodies was shown on television networks

the world over. The world was shocked, and Sharon announced his satisfaction. He described it as "one of our greatest successes in the fight against terrorism." The PA responded to the bloodshed by canceling plans for the ceasefire, and Hamas announced that no future ceasefire initiatives would be entertained.

The imminent war in Iraq dominated global attention, and the Likud government looked forward to this prospect. Sharon's spokesman repeatedly said that things were about to change dramatically, that the anticipated demise of Saddam Hussein would cause a chain reaction and other enemies of Israel, primarily Arafat, would follow.

### ARAFAT IS FORCED TO RESTRUCTURE THE PA

Arafat faced increasing pressure from within and without to reform the institutions of the PA. On June 24, 2002, President Bush outlined his vision of a two-state solution to the Israeli–Palestinian conflict. This led to a multilateral initiative with the European Union, the Russian Federation, the United Nations, and the United States, which was launched on April 10, 2002, to implement a permanent two-state solution. In view of these developments, Arafat yielded to the pressure and on March 14, 2003 President Bush announced that the PA had created the position of a prime minister with, it was hoped, some real political power. Once a prime minister was installed, the road map for peace, designed by the Quartet and based on the vision expressed in June 2002, would be presented to both sides. They would then be expected to contribute to the document.[38]

Mahmoud Abbas was to become Palestinian prime minister, but Arafat was in no rush to confirm the appointment. Terje Larsen warned Arafat that if he did not move to appoint the prime minister, the next time the door opened, an Israeli soldier would be walking in to end his rule.[39] Immediately after the confirmation of the Palestinian new government, representatives of the Quartet presented the road map to Arafat as the US ambassador to Israel, Dan Kurzer, presented it to Prime Minister Sharon. Kurzer later commented that Sharon was surprised since he had believed his contacts in the United States would successfully delay this development.[40]

### THE ROAD MAP

The road map required that by June 2003, the Israelis would withdraw their forces to their pre-*Intifada* positions and stop settlement construction. The Palestinians would be required to end all violence. In the second phase, a Palestinian state would be established within provisional borders, by the end of 2003. Final status negotiations would start at the end of the second phase.

For one week, the Israeli cabinet held a marathon of debates, then it responded to the road map with 14 objections. Most were demands on the PA that it clearly could not accomplish. The United States noted the objections but said it would make no changes to the wording of the road map.[41] All the participants in the debates knew that it was not possible for the Palestinians to simply eliminate terrorism. Sharon's government accepted the plan. When challenged about this by his extreme right contingent, under the glare of television lights and cameras Sharon admitted, for the first time, that the Palestinians lived under occupation. He said, "How can you imagine keeping three and a half million Palestinians under occupation?" It was the first time he publicly used the term "occupation." One day later, appearing before the Knesset Foreign Affairs and Defense Committee, Sharon said he had been misunderstood. Some of the Europeans in the Quartet admitted that the road map was stillborn, but they felt it could serve as a template for future negotiations.

## THE AYALON–NUSSEIBEH INITIATIVE

Still in June 2003, the former commander of the Israeli navy and former head of Shabak, Ami Ayalon, and the president of Al Quds University, Sari Nusseibeh, made a surprise announcement of a new peace initiative. The plan included:

- two states for two people
- the permanent borders would be established on the basis of the 1967 lines, UN resolutions and the Arab League peace initiative
- modification of these borders would be undertaken on the basis of mutually agreed exchange
- the new Palestinian state would have territorial connections between Gaza and the West Bank
- after the borders had been determined, no settlers would remain within the Palestinian state
- Jerusalem would be the capital of the two states
- Arab neighborhoods of Jerusalem would revert to Palestinian sovereignty while Jewish neighborhoods would remain under Israeli sovereignty
- recognizing the suffering of the Palestinian refugees, Israel, the

Palestinian state, and the international community would jointly undertake compensation
- the Palestinian refugees would return only to territories within the newly established Palestinian state.[42]

Ami Ayalon was convinced that the majority of the Israeli public supported this initiative. Sari Nusseibeh apparently received a less enthusiastic response from his constituency. He was even accused of treason for his position on the right of return issue. But nothing substantial occurred after the publication of this initiative aside from a temporary opening of some checkpoints in the occupied territories.

After a short period of relative calm, suicide missions and targeted killings resumed. The deterioration of the ceasefire and his declining popularity among the Palestinians forced Mahmoud Abbas to resign in mid-August 2003. The untrusting, tense relationship with Arafat also influenced this decision. One day later Arafat asked the speaker of the Palestinian parliament, Abu Allah, to form a new government.

Hamas and Jihad extremists intensified their suicide missions in August and September, often in response to Israeli targeted assassinations. Israel retaliated with warplanes bombing the home of Mahmoud Zhara, a Hamas leader. Zhara and his wife survived but were wounded. The Israeli cabinet declared their intention to eliminate the terrorist organization, their leadership, and their infrastructure. But they continued to place the blame for everything on Arafat, who had been in house arrest for months. Israel considered Arafat an obstacle to peace, and intended to remove this obstacle.

## THE GENEVA ACCORD

In the fall of 2003, Yasser Abed Rabbo, Yossi Beilin, and an impressive group of Israelis and Palestinians announced their successful work on another agreement. Among the Israelis were former government ministers, generals, police commanders, and intellectuals. The Palestinian delegation was equally high-powered. They focused on an overall resolution of the conflict, with Israel evacuating 98 percent of the West Bank, most of its settlements, and all of the Gaza Strip. Territorial passage between Gaza and the West Bank would be provided, and Jerusalem would be the capital of both states. The Palestinian refugees would be compensated but their right of return to Israel left to Israeli jurisdiction.

This plan came to be known as the Geneva initiative in acknowledgement of the support the organizers received from the Swiss government. The official presentation took place near Lake Geneva. Sharon quickly condemned the initiative as the most serious danger to Israel since the Oslo Accords. Ehud Barak, the former Labor prime minister, supported him and described it as a maneuver sponsored by Arafat. Even Shimon Peres, the Israeli Nobel Peace Prize laureate, cautiously objected to it. On the other hand, the polls showed about 40 percent of the Israeli population in favor of the accord.

On October 12 a conference was held in Jerusalem with the participation of several well-known American neoconservatives such as Richard Perle and Daniel Pipes, American Zionist leaders and Israelis from the extreme right, including Netanyahu, the finance minister. They produced the Declaration of Jerusalem, which asserted that western civilization, its values and principles, were under threat from radical Islam. The plan sought a new way of fighting this threat, and proposed the establishment of a Council of Civilizations to replace the United Nations. The creation of a PLO state in Judea and Samaria would constitute a historical injustice of colossal proportions. The entire land must belong to the people of Israel. The declaration called on the government of Israel to stop all negotiations with terrorists.[43]

Sharon met with Elliot Abrams from the White House National Security Council in Italy, ostensibly to discuss American concerns about Sharon's settlement policy. Following their meeting, Sharon revealed to Uri Dan, his biographer and confidant, that the discussions were actually about a reawakened Syrian interest in restarting peace negotiations with Israel. According to Dan, Sharon told the Americans that it would be preferable to concentrate on one line of negotiations at a time. Since he, Sharon, was already involved with the Palestinians, he saw no reason to change.[44]

### THE GAZA DISENGAGEMENT SUBTERFUGE?

Among other moves, Sharon commenced disengagement, the withdrawal of all Israeli presence from Gaza, to deflect US pressure to reactivate negotiations with Syria.

National security advisor General Giora Eiland knew about Sharon's plans for disengagement, and explained that Sharon made the decision following the resignation of Mahmoud Abbas. The resignation supported Sharon's contention that there was no possibility of reaching agreement with Arafat in power. If nothing could be achieved in cooperation with the Palestinians, perhaps Israel could do something alone.[45] But there were other factors influencing Sharon's decision. Foremost among them was a growing unrest in many quarters of the Israeli public. Many wanted something done. The number of signatures on the Ayalon-Nusseibeh document was rising. There was growing domestic and international support for the Geneva Accord. The former heads of the Shabak issued a critical statement about the lack of a political strategy, and the police were investigating allegations of fraud by Sharon and members of his family.[46] Sharon was compelled to take some action.

On December 1, 2003, a ceremonious presentation of the Geneva Agreement was made at the Dead Sea. It was well attended by politicians and dignitaries from all over the world, eager to support Israeli withdrawal. But the Israeli right was furious, and accused the organizers of returning to the path of unilateral concessions. Perhaps as an indication of unity among extremists on both sides of the fence, Hamas, Jihad, and some members of Fatah expressed their opposition to Geneva.

In a series of planned public appearances Sharon presented his intention to take unilateral action since there was no point waiting for a Palestinian move. This should not be construed as Israeli concession but rather as steps favoring the State of Israel. Sharon designed his new policy deliberately to avoid negotiations with the Palestinians, who would obviously not concede anything beneficial to Israel. When asked by members of his own Likud Party whether his plan would involve the evacuation of settlers, he confirmed that it might involve the withdrawal of settlements. Various settler organizations demanded his resignation, and the National Religious Party (NRF), a coalition partner, threatened to resign from the coalition. The Israeli right united in condemning the plan. They concluded that by launching his own unilateral plan with concessions to the enemy, Sharon was really a traitor to the cause of Greater Israel. During a speech to the Herzeliyah Economic Forum on December 11 he said that "if the Palestinians are not making a comparable effort to resolve the conflict, Israel will take the initiative of a unilateral security measure of 'disengagement' from the Palestinians. Israel will not remain in the places where we are today."[47]

Sharon finally revealed some of the details of his plan in an interview with Yoel Markus of *Ha'aretz* on February 2, 2004.[48] He said that he had ordered the relocation of 17 settlements and about 7,500 settlers from the Gaza Strip. The plan to evacuate a militarily unmanageable Gaza was strictly to tighten Israel's grip over the West Bank. But the settlement movement responded by moving approximately 500 families back into existing settlements, particularly Gush Katif.

The violence continued undiminished. Hamas attacked the Israeli port of Ahsdod on March 6, 2004, killing 10 people and wounding 16. Israel perceived this as the straw that broke the camel's back. This time Israel did not blame Arafat but correctly marked Hamas as the attacker. Applying the rule "when force doesn't work, use more force," Israel targeted the quadriplegic spiritual leader of Hamas, Sheik Ahmed Yassin. The Shabak claimed they had evidence that Yassin was behind the attack on Ashdod, but no such evidence was ever presented. Moreover, the frail, barely audible Yassin had never been involved in operational matters.[49] He was killed on March 22 when several missiles were fired at his vehicle from an Israeli helicopter. No one could have believed this act would lead to any reduction in violence. But if they did, Arab and Palestinian leaders from Arafat to Hezbollah leader Sheik Hassan Nasrallah and the new leader of Hamas, Abd el Aziz Rantisi, dispelled this illusion immediately. Most of the 150,000 people who participated in Sheik Yassin's funeral demanded revenge. There were demonstrations of protest in Afghanistan, the Philippines, and elsewhere in the Muslim world.

The disengagement plan essentially derailed Bush's own road map, but the United States decided to support the plan. Another delegation of Americans came to the region on March 31 to insist again that the PA fight terrorism. They did not address the problem of PA participation in a process that was exclusively unilateral. The main Palestinian negotiator, Saeb Erakat, was prevented from raising the disengagement issue with the Israelis by Sharon's chief advisor, Dov Weisglass, who was apparently not authorized to discuss it.[50]

For some reason, the United States decided to reward Israel for its unilateral actions, and during Sharon's tenth visit to Washington, issued a statement signed by the president. For the first time since June 1967 the United States accepted the permanent existence of large settlement blocks in the West Bank, in its capacity as "honest broker and peace seeker." The statement concluded that all future peace negotiations would have to take this new reality into consideration. Sharon was very grateful for the generosity of the offer, which essentially allowed Israel to keep those settlements.

Domestically under pressure, Sharon reluctantly consented to a plebiscite among Likud members about the disengagement plan. He was soundly defeated, with 60 percent of Likud members voting against the withdrawal from Gaza. Despite the anti-withdrawal sentiments expressed by the Likud members, a *Yediot Aharonot* poll on May 14 showed that over 70 percent of Israelis supported the withdrawal. Given this level of public support, Sharon forced another vote on the issue, much to the displeasure of his extremist coalition partners. The cabinet now supported Sharon's position on the concept of withdrawal by a margin of 14 to 7. Sharon agreed to another vote at a future date on the specifics of the Gaza settlements.

Resignations from Sharon's coalition left him without a safe majority in the Knesset. He wanted to restructure the coalition, and needed the central committee of the Likud to approve adding the Labor Party. The committee voted against him, and Sharon had to rely on support from the left. He persisted, and presented the disengagement plan to the Knesset, where he won with 67 votes.

According to a government-appointed committee timetable, the army would start making preparation for withdrawal in July 2004. In February 2005, the cabinet would vote on the first phase of the evacuation of the Gaza settlements. The final vote would take place in July 2005, and the actual evacuation would begin and be completed by the end of September 2005.

An interview given by Dov Weisglass to Ari Shavit of *Ha'aretz* on October 8, 2004 provided a glimpse into Sharon's intentions:

> The disengagement plan is the preservative of the sequence principle. It is the bottle of formaldehyde within which you place the president's formula so that it will be preserved for a very lengthy period. The disengagement is actually formaldehyde. It supplies the amount of formaldehyde that's necessary so that there will not be a political process with the Palestinians.[51]

## ARAFAT DIES AND ABBAS RISES

Following an undetermined illness, Yasser Arafat died in a French hospital on November 11, 2004. There were widespread suspicions about the cause of death, and some Palestinians, including Arafat's personal physician, expressed their belief that Arafat had been poisoned by Israel.[52] The Israeli peace activist Uri Avnery, among others, speculated that Arafat might have been killed by the Israeli Secret Service.[53]

General elections in the PA were held immediately after Arafat's death. About two weeks earlier a group of over 500 prominent Palestinians had published a press statement asking the Palestinians to stop their armed struggle and return to a popular type of *intifada*.[54] Mahmoud Abbas also called on them to stop firing Kassam rockets. His political rivals, however, insisted that missiles continue to be launched against the Zionist colonies.

In the Palestinian presidential elections held on January 9, 2005 Mahmoud Abbas was elected with a comfortable majority. A team of international observers announced that the election was honest and transparent.

About one week later, Abbas was sworn in as the new chairman of the PA, and he stated his desire to resume peace negotiations with Israel: "I say to the people of Israel, we are two peoples destined to live side by side." He ordered his security services to prevent the launch of rockets aimed at Israeli territory. But this was more symbolic than practical, since the decimated Palestinian security services were in no position to enforce such an order. Instead, Abbas initiated talks with his political rivals about a ceasefire, and agreement was reached quite quickly. Hamas was apparently willing to move away from direct, armed struggle to focus on acquiring political power. In the municipal elections during December and January, Hamas did very well and won control over most of the municipalities undergoing elections.

The next attempt at peace making was named the Summit of Hope. It convened in Sharm el Sheikh on February 8, 2005, sponsored jointly by Mubarak of Egypt and Abdullah of Jordan. A ceasefire was declared to a large audience from the international media. Two weeks later, Islamic Jihad carried out a suicide mission in Tel Aviv, which killed several people. The Jihad declared that they were not part of the PA collaboration. Settlement construction and expansion were also continuing unabated, despite promises made by Sharon.

The evacuation of Gaza began on August 17, 2005. The number of settlers in Gaza was approximately 8,000. The Palestinian residents numbered 1.4 million. At the time of the evacuation, the settlers controlled 25 percent of Gaza, including about 40 percent of cultivated land. The settlers had access to most of the water resources available to the Strip. About 80 percent of the Palestinian residents lived far below the poverty line, existing on about $2 per day.[55]

On the first day of the evacuation seven settlements were emptied. On the second day four more settlements were emptied without any opposition from the settlers. During the evacuation of the next set of settlements, Kfar Darom and Neve Dkalim, there was some resistance but the army and police removed the residents quickly, some in handcuffs. The last day was August 22. Settlers resisted the evacuation and tried to convince soldiers to disobey orders, but they failed. The last phase was the evacuation of the Israeli security forces, which was actually completed a few days before schedule.[56]

In a recent analysis Shlaim suggests the main reason for the evacuation was the high price that Hamas and Islamic Jihad were able to exact from Israel prior to the evacuation. It was too high even for right-wing Israeli leaders, who had always been willing to pay a lot for their settlements. Sharon presented the withdrawal as Israel's contribution to peace based on a two-state solution. But within one year from the evacuation there was an increase of 12,000 settlers, without government interference, in the West Bank.[57] Shlaim further argues that disengagement was part of a plan to rearrange the boundaries of Israel by annexing the main settlement blocks to Israel.[58] It was not a step towards peace but further expansion of the Zionist project in the West Bank. In Sharon's frame of reference, the evacuation of Gaza was a basic rejection of Palestinian efforts to establish a state of their own.[59]

## ELECTIONS, ELECTIONS

Sharon resigned as prime minister following a surprise victory for Amir Peretz in the Labor Party primaries and resignation of Labor ministers from Sharon's coalition.[60] Realizing that he had also lost the support of the extreme right, Sharon left the Likud Party, which he had founded three decades earlier, to form a new party called Kadima.[61] Parliamentary elections were scheduled for March 2006. Many Likud members and some Labor members joined Sharon in his new party. Notable among them were: Ehud Olmert, Tzipi Livni from the Likud, and Shimon Peres, for many decades the leader of Labor. Sharon was not to enjoy the universally forecast victory. He suffered a stroke in December. A second, more severe stroke ended Sharon's long and controversial career. Ehud Olmert became acting prime minister.[62]

Three weeks to the day after Sharon's illness, the Palestinians held general elections to the Legislative Council of the PA and established what must be considered the only democracy in the Arab world. Hamas clearly won.[63] Given that these were democratically held elections and much effort had been made to bring democracy to the

Middle East, it would have been correct to conclude that Hamas was the choice of the majority of the Palestinian people. Some peace activists were hoping this would force Israel's hand to open a dialogue and ceasefire negotiations with the new Palestinian government.[64] But Israel refused to recognize the elected government, claiming Hamas was a terrorist organization. The United States and the European Union supported this move by Israel, and despite their dedication to democracy, their position effectively implied that they demanded the establishment of democracy. but only if the results pleased them. Sanctions were quickly placed on the Palestinians. Israel withheld the tax revenue it was collecting for the PA, and the European Union and United States withheld foreign aid. In marked contradistinction, the National Unity government formed by Fatah and Hamas following the elections moved towards moderating their extreme positions, stating that their primary goal was to negotiate a long-term ceasefire agreement with Israel. Israel, supported by the United States, refused to negotiate with this government.[65] They wanted to provoke the Fatah into an armed confrontation with Hamas, which led to the collapse of the National Unity government and drove Hamas to seize power in Gaza.

Far from the landslide predicted for Kadima under Sharon, it won only 29 Knesset seats under Olmert in the elections held on March 28. A coalition agreement with Labor placed the position of minister of defense in Amir Peretz's hands.[66] Peretz had been a union leader who won the Labor Party primaries, but journalists and Labor leaders practically pleaded with him not to accept the defense ministry. They were convinced he would become a hostage to Israel's security apparatus. Peretz did not listen, and this ended his political career.

Israel's second escapade in Lebanon was initiated by a Hezbollah attack on an Israeli patrol on July 12. The attack killed several soldiers and Hezbollah captured two soldiers who were taken prisoner in Lebanon. The war lasted more than one month and resulted in over 1,200 Lebanese casualties and 160 Israeli deaths. For the first time since the 1948 war, about half a million Israelis had to leave their homes in northern Israel to seek shelter further south. It was the first time that a major Israeli city, Haifa, came under hostile fire. Many Israelis considered the war a disaster supported by the United States, which ended in an impressive victory for Hezbollah, despite extensive damage and deaths in Lebanon.[67]

How was such a disastrous outcome possible? Israeli governments long held the position that Israel had no partner for peace, and that Israel had superior military might.[68] Therefore the endless negotiations, which were not intended to achieve peace, became the goal itself.[69] The head of the Israeli Commission of Inquiry into the second Lebanese disaster commented:

> Some of the political and military elites in Israel have reached the conclusion that Israel is beyond the era of wars. Israel had enough military might to deter others from declaring war against it ... [Thus,] since Israel did not intend to initiate a war, the conclusion was that the main challenge facing the land forces would be low-intensity asymmetrical conflicts .... Given this analysis, there was no need to prepare for war, nor was there a need to energetically seek paths to stable and long term agreements with our neighbors.[70]

Ehud Olmert has just departed the political scene. Despite his repeated declarations about reaching a painful but peaceful compromise with the Palestinians, all he accomplished was endless talks with a defeated Palestinian leader, Mahmoud Abbas. There is little reason to expect that Prime Minister Binyamin Netanyahu will do any better.

# CONCLUSION

This book attests that there is no peace in the Middle East because an equitable peace settlement was never Israel's top priority. Throughout its history, Israel often dismissed the Arabs and the Palestinian people as unworthy and weak. Recently there has been a hawkish shift in Israel, and its reluctance to make any concessions for peace is more entrenched.

Israel is a small country which has grown enormously powerful. The perception of the Israeli–Palestinian conflict generally ignores the asymmetry that exists between a country that is independent, prosperous, and possesses one of the strongest armies in the world, and a society or a nation that is and has none of these. A balanced reciprocity is never possible in these circumstances. If Israel makes no significant compromise, the Palestinians have no option but violence to end decades of occupation.

The conflict was the result of terrible wrongs. The wrongs that induced the Western Allies to give the Jews a homeland in 1948 occurred over a long period and culminated in the Holocaust of the Second World War, which cannot and should not be dismissed. So the young State of Israel was indulged and pampered, and encouraged to grow up proud. But the country the Allies gave away was not theirs to give, and resulted in other terrible wrongs, which are ongoing. The victims are largely helpless people who played no part in the wrongs inflicted on the Jews. Over 62 years, Israel has succeeded at avoiding any attempt to address these wrongs. It also resisted all attempts by the outside world to impose concessions towards ending the conflict. Israel has grown and thrived against adversity, and prides itself on its many achievements. But much of the adversity it defies is self-created, perpetuated, and cynically exploited.

Military strength is certainly one of its most recognized achievements, but Israel has practically evolved into an army that has a country. Military heroes become politicians, and politicians without a glorious military career over-compensate by becoming extremely militant. The entire country wants to see itself as a protected, mighty, and terrifying warrior, and prefers to be led by those who demonstrate the most force, the least need to compromise. Every leader who has proposed compromise, withdrawal from occupied territory, or even expressed an intention to negotiate, has had to contend with enormous pressure from within to show no weakness to the enemy. Glory and strength are the cultural good; empathy and compromise are considered weak and defeatist.

The settlement movement has been so successful because it presents itself as a purely Jewish, authentic, and valiant grass-roots force. It also provides the justification for its own existence in biblical/messianic terms, and thereby justifies all the wrongs it commits. Many Israelis want peace, and see the settlement movement as an obstacle to peace. At the same time, the majority are protective of the settlers and oppose any suggestion of dismantling the settlements.

As in many other democratic countries, there are large communities of Israelis who do not immerse themselves in politics, who do not care and prefer to remain ignorant about the occupation and the injustices that Israel commits. They want to live a pleasant life, and cannot or do not want to understand why those Palestinians are making life more difficult for them. So many other countries have conquered and ruled; so many others have destroyed the civilizations that preceded them, so why all the fuss? The conclusion many arrive at is that Israel is again being singled out because of rampant anti-Semitism. Why can the Palestinians not move to other Arab lands, they ask? But the Palestinians are not going away, and these assumptions must be eradicated. They have no basis in current geopolitical reality.

There are many distortions in a nuclear modern country, with a powerful military, that lives inside a self-imposed ghetto and nourishes its own sense of victimhood, claiming it is constantly threatened from without. It has done this so effectively that the world has not been willing to impose sanctions on Israel or take any punitive measures, or even acknowledge its wrongdoings. And the Israelis have clearly demonstrated that they are above international reprimand and beyond international law and internationally agreed boundaries. They appear eager to discuss the two-state solution (TSS) to placate the outside world, but have long made it entirely impossible to achieve. The simplest and most logical solution to this ongoing conflict is all but dead, yet Israel and its global cheerleaders still tout the virtues of TSS, as if half a million Jewish settlers do not exist in the area to be allotted to the Palestinians.

We believe that the future of Israel is bleak. Unless some dramatic change is brought about by outside pressure, demographics, public opinion, and global power shifts are working against it.

Is there any hope of a viable solution? We believe that the only option for settling the Palestinian–Israeli conflict in an equitable manner is an imposed solution by the United States, the European Union, the United Nations, or a combination of these bodies. Despite occasional expressions by world powers of frustration about the lack of progress towards peace, no willingness to impose a solution on Israel has been demonstrated. The constant talk about direct talks, proximity talks, and indirect talks is nothing but more talk. Direct or supervised talks have been going on now for almost two decades, and there has been no progress.

More recently there has been some discussion about a one-state solution (OSS). We fear that despite some very well-considered and attractive features it is no more likely to be implemented than its TSS predecessor, and it has had negligible public support.

One gets the impression that Israel is increasingly adopting a Masada complex mentality which will lead to self-destruction. We find this observation very painful because we firmly believe that Israel today is home to about 5.6 million Jews who really have no other home. However the State of Israel was born on the ashes of an indigenous Palestinian society that had lived in that part of the world for centuries. To avoid further tragedy in the region, Israel must take conciliatory steps: It must acknowledge and apologize to the Palestinian people for past wrongs. It must return the territories insisted upon by the Palestinians that were forcibly taken since 1967, and negotiate an acceptable solution to the Palestinian refugee problem. Sadly we do not expect this to happen in the foreseeable future.

At this point in time there is no formula for settling the conflict: The rhetoric used by Israel, its supporters, and some Fatah members of the Palestinian Authority in support of a TSS amounts to nothing more than rhetoric. The quest for peace in the Middle East, soon a century long, is unlikely to end in our lifetime.

# CHRONOLOGY OF PEACE

1897 The First Zionist Congress convenes in Basel, Switzerland, and announces plans to create a Jewish state in Palestine, including a plan to eject as many of the local residents as possible.

1915 McMahon–Husayn correspondence.

1916 The Sykes Picot Agreement between Britain and France about the division of the Middle East territories.

1917 The Balfour Declaration announces the intention of the British government to create a Jewish homeland in Palestine.

1918 British military rule over Palestine begins.

1919 January 3, the Weizman–Prince Faisal agreement: the leader of the Hashemite clan agrees to the establishment of a Jewish state in Palestine without consulting the local population.

1922 The League of Nations grants Britain a mandate on Palestine.

1929 The start of the Arab rebellion in Jerusalem and Hebron.

1934 Ben Gurion meets Mussa Alami to discuss an agreement between the Jews and the Arabs.

1934 Ben Gurion meets Jabri and Arslan, Palestinian nationalist leaders, in Geneva.

1936 The start of the 1936–39 disturbances.

1937 The Peel Commission, the first suggestion of the partition of Palestine. The concept of transfer forms part of the Commission's report.

1938 The Grand Mufti, Haj Amin al Husseini, flees Palestine.

1939 The British government publishes a White Paper envisaging the formation of a Palestinian state and restricting Jewish immigration to Palestine.

1939 The Second World War breaks out, leading to the Jewish Holocaust

1942 The Biltmore Conference. The Zionist leadership claims the whole of Palestine for the Jews but endorses the concept of partition.

1945 End of the Second World War, the extent of the Holocaust uncovered.

1947 Britain informs the United Nations that it will relinquish its mandate over Palestine.

The United Nations appoints a Committee on Palestine (UNSCOP). This Committee recommends the partition of Palestine.

The United Nations decides (Resolution 181) to recommend the partition of Palestine.

Violence between Jews and Arabs begins. The process of expelling the Palestinians from Palestine begins.

1948 The British Mandate ends.

February: the War of Independence – Naqba begins.

March: Plan Dalet for the evacuation of Palestinians from areas of Palestine is completed.

March–May: the coastal plain is cleared of most of its Palestinian residents.

The Arab Legion attacks several Jewish communities.

May: the Interim State Council declares the establishment of the State of Israel. Ben Gurion is appointed prime minister.

May: Count Folke Bernadotte is appointed UN mediator for Palestine.

June: first ceasefire.

July: second ceasefire.

September: mediator Bernadotte is assassinated by Jewish extremists.

November: the UN Security Council adopts Resolution 194 about the Palestinian refugees' right of return.

1949 The war ends.

February: armistice agreement between Israel and Egypt is signed.

March: armistice agreement between Israel and Lebanon is signed.

April: armistice agreement between Israel and Jordan is signed.

April–June: the Lausanne talks begin, supervised by the UN Palestine Conciliation Committee.

July: armistice agreement between Israel and Syria is signed.

December: the UN General Assembly internationalizes Jerusalem.

Peace initiative launched by Syria's Husni al-Za'im.

December: Israel establishes the Knesset in Jerusalem.

1950 The West Bank is officially annexed to Jordan.
1951 Without a bilateral agreement, Israel begins to drain the Hullah Lake.
King Abdullah of Jordan is assassinated, stopping Israeli–Jordanian peace negotiations.
1952 October: Israeli–Syrian start talks on the division of the demilitarized zone (DMZ).
1953 September: Israel starts project of diverting the water of the Jordan River.
Syria complains to the UN Security Council about Israel's Jordan project.
Johnston is appointed mediator in the water dispute between Syria and Israel.
October: the Retaliation operation on Kybia in Jordan.
December: Moshe Sharet replaces Ben Gurion as prime minister.
1954 April: Nasser assumes the post of prime minister of Egypt.
Nasser attempts peace talks with Israel through contact with Yerucham Cohen. Israel forbids any move by Cohen.
July: the *esek habish*, or the "mishap" affair in Egypt. A failed attempt to activate a Jewish sabotage ring in Egypt.
September: the Israeli ship *Bat Galim* is seized by Egypt in attempt to pass through the Suez Canal.
1955 February: the Gaza retaliation, an Israeli defense force (IDF) attacks Egyptian army barracks in Gaza.
February: Ben Gurion returns to government as minister of defense.
August: Elmore Jackson undertakes a peace mission.
September: Egypt and Czechoslovakia sign an arms deal.
November: Ben Gurion returns to government again, as prime minister.
December: the Kineret retaliation operation.
December: the Anderson initiative.
1956 October: the Suez war.
November: the USSR threatens war if Britain, France, and Israel do not stop their attack on Egypt.
November: the United States forces France, Britain, and Israel to stop the fighting against Egypt and retreat.
1957 March: Israel retreats to the armistice line with Egypt. The end of Ben Gurion's "Third Kingdom of Israel."
1963 June: Ben Gurion resigns and is replaced as prime minister by Levi Eshkol.

1964   January: Arab summit meeting in Cairo decides to divert the waters of the Jordan River.

May: the Palestine Liberation Organization (PLO) is formed.

1966   November: an Israeli operation against the village of Samu in the West Bank.

1967   May: Egypt deploys troops in the Sinai peninsula.

May: Nasser closes the Straits of Tiran to Israeli shipping.

June: the Six Day War.

June: Israel annexes East Jerusalem.

July: First presentation of the Alon Plan to the Israeli cabinet.

November: the UN Security Council passes Resolution 242.

1969   February: Eshkol dies and Golda Meir becomes prime minister.

March: the War of Attrition.

December: US Secretary of State Rogers announces the Rogers Plan.

December: Israel rejects the Rogers Plan.

1970   June: the second Rogers Plan is announced.

August: Egypt and Israel agree on a ceasefire mediated by Rogers.

September: Nasser dies and Anwar Sadat becomes president of Egypt.

1971   February: Sadat presents his initiative for an interim settlement.

February: Gunnar Jarring's initiative (the Questionnaire).

October: the third Rogers Plan is announced.

1972   May: Nixon–Brezhnev summit meeting in Moscow.

July: Sadat kicks Soviet military advisers out of Egypt.

1973   October: the October (Yom Kippur) War.

October: UN Security Council passes Resolution 338 calling for direct negotiations.

December: the Geneva peace conference.

1974   April: Golda Meir resigns and Rabin becomes prime minister.

October: Arab League summit in Rabat recognizes the PLO as the only representative of the Palestinians.

November: Yasser Arafat addresses the UN General Assembly.

1975   September: Sinai II, the Israeli–Egyptian interim disengagement agreement.

1977 May: the Likud under Begin's leadership assumes power in Israel.

October: joint USSR and US statement calls for reconvening the Geneva peace conference.

November: Sadat visits Jerusalem and addresses the Knesset.

December: Begin launches the Palestinian autonomy plan during his visit to Washington.

December: Sadat–Begin summit meeting in Ismailia, Egypt.

1978 March: Litani operation, Israel occupies part of southern Lebanon.

March: UN Security Council Resolution 425 demanding Israeli evacuation of Lebanon.

September: Camp David I is convened.

1979 March: peace treaty between Israel and Egypt is signed on White House lawn.

October: Moshe Dayan resigns as defense minister in protest over lack of progress on Palestinian autonomy.

1980 May: Ezer Weizman resigns as defense minister in protest over lack of progress towards peace.

1981 June: Sadat and Begin meet in Sharm el Sheikh.

June: Israel bombs an Iraqi nuclear reactor.

October: Sadat is assassinated and replaced by Mubarak.

December: Israel annexes the Golan Heights.

1982 June: Operation Peace for the Galilee, Israel invades Lebanon.

September: US President Reagan announces a new peace plan for the Middle East.

September: the Sabra and Shatila massacre.

1983 May: Israel and Lebanon sign an end of belligerency agreement.

August: Begin resigns and Yizthak Shamir becomes prime minister.

1984 March: the Lebanese president, Amin Gemayel cancels the Israeli–Lebanese agreement.

1985 June: Israel withdraws from most of Lebanon except for the south which remains under Israeli occupation.

October: Israel bombs PLO headquarters in Tunis.

1987 April: Peres Hussein London agreement.

1987 December: the First *Intifada* begins in the occupied territories.

1988 March: US secretary of state George Shultz announces his peace initiative.

July: King Hussein of Jordan announces the cessation of Jordanian involvement in the West Bank.

November: PLO National Council accepts UN Resolutions 181, 242, and 338.

1989 October: US secretary of state James Baker introduces his five-point plan.

1991 March: US President Bush (Senior) announces a new Middle East peace initiative.

1991 October: the United States convenes the Madrid conference on Palestine.

1991 December: Arab–Israeli bilateral peace talks begin in Washington.

1992 June: Yitzhak Rabin becomes prime minister of Israel for the second time.

1992 December: Israel deports 416 Hamas activists to Lebanon.

1993 September: Israel and the PLO exchange letters recognizing each other.

September: the Oslo Declaration of Principles is signed on the White House lawn.

1994 May: Israel and the PLO reach agreement on the application of the Declaration of Principles.

October: Israel and Jordan sign a peace treaty.

1995 September: Israel and the Palestinians sign the Oslo B interim agreement. The Palestinians assume some control over parts of the West Bank and Gaza.

1995 November: Prime Minister Rabin is assassinated. Shimon Peres becomes the next prime minister of Israel.

December: Israel and Syria hold talks at the Wye Plantation under US sponsorship.

1996 January: first Palestinian democratic elections.

April: Israel launches Operation Grapes of Wrath in South Lebanon.

April: the Palestinian National Council amends the Palestinian National Charter.

May: Binyamin Netanyahu defeats Peres and becomes Israeli prime minister.

1998 October: Arafat and Netanyahu sign the Wye River memorandum.

December: the Palestinian National Council officially abandons the goal of destroying Israel.

December: Israel suspends the implementation of the Wye River memorandum.

1999  May: Ehud Barak defeats Netanyahu in elections and becomes prime minister.
2000  June: Israel completes its withdrawal from southern Lebanon.
      October: the Second *Intifada* begins.
2001  February: Ariel Sharon becomes prime minister of Israel.
      June: a ceasefire plan proposed by George Tenet, director of the CIA.
      August: Israel assassinates Abu Ali Mustafa, the political leader of the Popular Front for the Liberation of Palestine (PFLP).
      October: Israel's former minister of tourism, Rehavam Zeevi, is assassinated by the PFLP.
      December: US General Anthony Zinni conducts an arbitration mission.
      December: the Sharon government declares Yasser Arafat "out of play."
2002  March: the Arab League approves the Saudi peace plan: the Arab world offers Israel full normalization of relations in return for complete Israeli withdrawal from all the occupied territories.
      March: Israel rejects the Saudi proposal.
      March: Israel launches Operation Defensive Shield.
      June: US President Bush declares his support for the establishment of an independent Palestinian state, but without Arafat.
2003  January: the Likud's extreme right wins a sweeping victory in the general elections.
      March: Arafat names Mahmoud Abbas as prime minister of the Palestinian Authority.
      April: the road map plan for peace is presented to Sharon and Arafat.
      June: Bush, Sharon, and Arafat meet in Aqaba.
      December: the official signing of the Geneva Initiative by Yossi Beilin and Yasser Abed Rabbo.
2004  February: Sharon informs Israeli newspaper *Ha'aretz* of his intention to withdraw from the settlements in Gaza.
      March: Israel assassinates Sheik Ahmed Yassin, the paraplegic leader of Hamas in Gaza.
      November) Yasser Arafat dies under mysterious circumstances in Paris.
2005  January: Mahmoud Abbas is elected president of the Palestinian Authority.

February: Abbas, Sharon, and Bush meet in Sharm el Sheikh, Egypt.

September: the evacuation of the Israeli settlements in Gaza is completed.

November: Sharon leaves the Likud Party and founds a new party, Kadima.

2006 January: Sharon suffers a massive stroke and slips into a coma.

January: in the legislative Palestinian elections, Hamas wins 76 out of 132 seats.

March: in Israeli general elections Kadima is the largest party and Ehud Olmert succeeds Sharon as prime minister.

July: Israel invades Lebanon, beginning the Second Lebanon War.

# NOTES

## INTRODUCTION

1   For four years between 1951 and 1959 Zalman Amit was the coordinator of the Guidance department of the Labour Youth movement. The figures and estimates above were derived from some of his still existing notes.

2   Itzhak Laor, *We Write You Our Homeland (Anu kotvim otach Moledet)*, Kibutz Hame'uchad Publishing, Tel Aviv, 1995.

3   B. Morris, *Righteous Victims: A History of the Zionist Arab Conflict 1881–2001*, Vintage, New York, 1999, p. 42; A. Gurfinkle, "On the origin, meaning, use and abuse of the phrase," *Middle Eastern Studies*, Vol. 27, No. 4, 1991.

4   I. Pappe, *The Ethnic Cleansing of Palestine*, Oneworld Publications, Oxford, 2006; Morris, *Righteous Victims*, pp. 3–36. W. Khalidi, *All That Remains: The Palestinian Villages Occupied and Depopulated by Israel in 1948*, Institute for Palestinian Studies, Washington D.C., 1992.

5   K. Marx and A. Ruge, "On the Jewish question" (Zur Judenfrage), *Deutsche Franzosishe Jahrbucher*, Paris, 1844; V. Lenin, *Lenin on the Jewish Question*, International Publishers, June 1974; J. Stalin, "Marxism and the National Question," in *Social Democracy and the National Question*, 1913.

6   A. Shapira, *Berl: The Biography of a Socialist Zionist: Berl Katznelson 1887–1944*, Cambridge University Press, 2008; S. Levenberg and B. Borochov, *Selected Essays in Socialist Zionism, 1948*; Y. Tabenkin, *Kibbutz Society* (in Hebrew), Hakkibutz Hameuchad, 1954.

7   Ofira Seliktar, *New Zionism and the Foreign Policy System of Israel*, Croom Helm, Beckenham, 1986, p. 288; R. S. Goldman, "Israel and the Arabs," *Commentary*, June 1966.

8   Choma U'Migdal, *Jewish Virtual Library Glossary* <www.jewishvirtual library.org/jsource/glossH.HTML> (accessed May 19, 2010).

9   B. Morris, *Righteous Victims*, pp. 329–43; I. A. Pappe, *History of Modern Palestine*, Cambridge University Press, Cambridge, 2004, p. 185.

10 A. Israeli, *Shalom, Shalom Ve'ein Shalom, Israel–Arabs 1948–1961*, published by the authors, Jerusalem, 1961, p. 263.

11 H. Matar, interview with Uri Avnery, previously published in *Ha'Olam Haze*, September, 2009.

12 Israeli, *Shalom Shalom Ve'ein Shalom*; *Haaretz*, September 2, 1953.

13 Yitzhak Ben Aharon, *Biography in Zionism & Israel*, <www.zionism-israel.com/bio/yitzhak_ben_aharon>(May 2010); Y. Shimshi, *The Fifth Floor: Biography of Ben Aharon* (in Hebrew), The Worker's Envoy, Tel Aviv, 1974.

14 B. Morris, *Righteous Victims*, p. 339.

15 Ibid., p. 331; E. Haber, *"Today the War Will Break Out"*: *The Reminiscences of Brig. Gen. Israel Lior* (in Hebrew), Idonim/Yediot Aharanot Press, Tel Aviv, 1987.

16 CBC (Canadian Broadcasting Corporation), Fifth Estate, "Park with no peace," October 22, 1991; I. Zayid, "Canada Park: Canadian complicity in a war crime," *Outlook*, Sept./Oct. 2001.

17 I. Pappe, *A History of Modern Palestine*, pp. 201–3.

18 M. Dayan, *Story of My Life*, Morrow, New York, 1976.

19 Morris, *Righteous Victims*, pp. 487–8.

20 Peel Commission, *Palestine Royal Commission Report*, presented by the Secretary of State for the Colonies to Parliament by Command of His Majesty. July 1937, CMD 5479.

21 T. Reinhart, *Israel/Palestine – How to End the War of 1948*, Seven Stories Press, New York, 2002, p. 22.

22 H. Agha and R. Malley, "Camp David: the tragedy of errors," *New York Review of Books*, August 9, 2001.

## CHAPTER 1 PALESTINE – HOMELAND FOR THE JEWS?

1 *Jewish Encyclopedia*, Funk & Wagnalls, New York, 1901, 1906.

2 P. Birnbaum, "L'Armee Francaise etait elle Antisimite?" pp. 70–82 in Michel Winocle, *L'Affaire Dreyfus*, Editions du Seuil, Paris, 1998.

3 Quoted from the *Economist*, December 12, 2009, p. 57.

4 R. Patai (ed.), *The Complete Diaries of Theodore Herzl*, Vol. I. T.; Herzl, *Complete Diaries*, June 12, 1895.

5 A. Hyamson, "British projects for the restoration of Jews in Palestine," American Jewish Historical Society Publication 26, 1918, p. 140; A. Garfinkle, "On the origin, meaning, use and abuse of a phrase," *Middle East Studies*, Vol. 27, 1991.

6 D. Vital, "Zangwill modern Jewish nationalism," *Modern Judaism*, Vol. 4, No. 3, 1984, pp. 243–53.

7 T. Herzl, *Altneuland,* German Seemann Nadfolger, Leipzig, 1902.

8 T. Herzl, *Der Judenstaat,* M. Breitenstein Verlag Buchhandlung, Vienna, 1895.

9 Y. Gorny, "The roots of the consciousness of the Jewish–Arab national

conflict and its reflection in the Hebrew press in the years 1900–1918" (in Hebrew), *Hatziunut*, Vol. 4, 1976, p. 96.

10   A. Elon, *Herzl*, Holt, Rinehart & Winston, New York, 1975.

11   T. Segev, *One Palestine Complete*, Abacus, 2001 p. 45, quoting from Parliamentary Debates House of Lords, 21 June 1922, vol. 50.

12   I. A. Pappe, *A History of Modern Palestine*, p. 68.

13   Morris, *Righteous Victims*, p. 75.

14   R. Sanders, *The High Walls of Jerusalem: A History of the Balfour Declaration and the Birth of the British Mandate for Palestine*, Holt Rinehart & Winston, New York, 1983, p. 639.

15   M. Bar Zohar, *Ben Gurion: A Biography*, Vol. I, Adama, Tel Aviv, 1986, pp. 303–5.

16   Pappe, *The Ethnic Cleansing*, p. 13. Segev, *One Palestine*, pp. 328–9.

17   Y. Arnon-Ohana, *Peasants in the Arab Revolt in the Land of Israel 1936–39*, (in Hebrew), Papyrus, Tel Aviv, 1982; P. Mattar, *The Mufti of Jerusalem*, Columbia University Press, New York, 1988.

18   A. Shlaim, *Collusion Across the Jordan*, Columbia University Press, New York, 1988, p. 58.

19   Ibid.

20   Ibid.

21   Bar Zohar, *Ben Gurion*, Vol. I, p. 358.

22   Palestine Royal Commission Report, CMD 5479, HMSO, London, 1937, p. 390.

23   Bar Zohar, *Ben Gurion*, Vol. I, pp. 357–8.

24   Ibid., pp. 303–4; S. Tevet, *Ben Gurion: The Burning Ground*, Houghton Mifflin, New York, p. 297.

25   Segev, *One Palestine*, pp. 403–7.

26   Vital, "Zangwill modern Jewish nationalism."

27   Bar Zohar, *Ben Gurion*, Vol. I, p. 367.

28   D. Ben Gurion to A. Ben Gurion, October 5, 1937, Israel Defence Forces Archives (IDFA) Ben Gurion correspondence.

29   Ibid.

30   M. Cohen, *Palestine: Retreat from the Mandate*, Paul Elek, London, 1978.

31   M. Oren, *Power, Faith and Fantasy*, W. W. Norton, New York, 2007, pp. 442–5.

32   J. C. Hurewitz, *The Struggle For Palestine*, Schpken Books, New York, 1976.

33   Bar Zohar, *Ben Gurion*, Vol. I, p. 355.

34   *Manchester Guardian*, May 24, 1939, p. 10.

35   T. Segev, *Yemei Hakalaniyot* (in Hebrew), Keter, Jerusalem 1999, p. 402.

## CHAPTER 2 THE PARTITION OF PALESTINE

1   S. Flapan, *Zionism and the Palestinians*, Barnes & Noble, New York, 1979, pp. 168–9.

2  Bar Zohar, *Ben Gurion*, Vol. II, p. 870.
3  W. Laqueur, *Dying for Jerusalem, The Past, Present and Future of the Holiest City,* Source Books, New York, 2006, pp. 161–2.
4  Bar Zohar, *Ben Gurion*, Vol. I, pp, 318–19; Ben Gurion's notes of his talks with the Arabs 1934–1936, CZA S25/101–88.
5  Bar Zohar, *Ben Gurion*, Vol. I, p. 320.
6  D. Ben Gurion to A. Ben Gurion, Ben Gurion correspondence, October 5, 1937, IDFA; C. Sykes, *Cross Roads to Israel*, Collins, London, 1965.
7  Protocol of the Meeting of the Jewish Agency Executive, November 1, 1936, S100/20B; N. Massalha, "The expulsion of the Palestinians: the concept of transfer," in *Zionist Political Thought 1882–1948*, Institute of Palestinian Studies, Washington, D.C., 1992, p. 37.
8  Bar Zohar, *Ben Gurion*, Vol. I, p. 357.
9  D. Scheuftan, *A Jordanian Option: Israel, Jordan and the Palestinians* (in Hebrew), Hakibutz Hameuchad, Tel Aviv, 1986, p. 48.
10  Ibid., p. 57.
11  Ibid.
12  Bar Zohar, *Ben Gurion*, Vol. I, p. 303.
13  Shlaim, *Collusion Across the Jordan*, p. 465.
14  M. Cohen, *Palestine and the Great Powers, 1945–1948,* Princeton University Press, Princeton, N.J., 1982, p. 290.
15  Massalha, "The expulsion of the Palestinians," p. 14.
16  S. Dolan, *The Polemic over Partition in the Mandatory Era* (in Hebrew), Yad Ben Tzvi, Jerusalem, 1979.
17  Bar Zohar, *Ben Gurion*, Vol. III, pp. 823–4.
18  S. Flapan, *The Birth of Israel: Myths and Realities*, Pantheon, New York, 1988, pp. 187–99.
19  Ilan Amitzur, *The Origin of the Arab Israeli Arms Race Embargo, Military Power and Decision in the 1948 Palestine War*, NYU Press, New York, 1996.
20  Bar Zohar, *Ben Gurion*, Vol. II, p. 824.
21  Flapan, *The Birth of Israel*, p. 117.
22  Pappe, *Ethnic Cleansing*, pp. 28, 39–41.
23  Flapan, *The Birth of Israel*, p. 87.
24  Salim Tamari, *The Arab Neighborhoods and Their Fate in the War*, Institute of Jerusalem Studies, Jerusalem, 1948, p. 96.
25  Dr. Alon Kadosh was keynote speaker at a meeting of the Israeli Society of Military History, Winter 2005, attended by Zalman Amit.
26  Pappe, *Ethnic Cleansing*, p. 40.
27  Avi Shlaim, *Iron Wall*, W.W. Norton, New York, 2001, p. 31.
28  Flapan, *The Birth of Israel*, p. 157.
29  I. Rabinovitch, *The Road Not Taken: Early Arab Israeli Negotiations*, Oxford University Press, 1991, pp. 172–3.
30  Ibid., pp. 174–6.
31  Bar Zohar, *Ben Gurion*, Vol. III, p. 817.

32 Protocol on Consultations on Peace Negotiations with the Arab States, April 19, 1949, Israel State Archives, Foreign Ministry Papers Israel State Archives (ISA) FM 4373/13.
33 Morris, *Righteous Victims*, pp. 264–5.
34 US Embassy, Tel Aviv, Classified Records 1949, as quoted in Morris, *Righteous Victims*, p. 264.
35 Y. Rosenthal, "Armistice negotiations with the Arab States Dec. 1948–July 1949," (in Hebrew), Jerusalem, 1983.
36 Ibid.
37 Shlaim, *Collusion Across the Jordan.*
38 Conference of Ambassadors, 3rd session, *Israel and the Arab World*, July 1950, pp. 36–9, 112–18, Israel State Archives (ISA).
39 Ibid.
40 Ben Gurion diary, February 1951.
41 Shlaim, *Iron Wall*, p. 67.

## CHAPTER 3 EARLY INITIATIVES

1 D. Ben Gurion, Speech in Knesset , January 2, 1956, Divrei Haknesset 19/672; Israeli, *Shalom Shalom*, pp. 153–8.
2 Ibid.
3 G. Shoken, "The whore from the seaports and us – thoughts on the eve of new year," *Ha'aretz*, September 30, 1951.
4 D. Ben Gurion, speech in Knesset, November 2, 1955.
5 Israeli, *Shalom Shalom*, p. 157.
6 Shoken, "The whore"; "General's word shed a new light on the Golan," *New York Times,* May 11, 1997.
7 *Documents on Foreign Policy of Israel (DPFI)*, 1951, pp. 249–50.
8 A. Gelbloom, "Global reaction to Israel's bombing in DMZ with Syria" (in Hebrew), *Ha'aretz*, April 11, 1951; Shlaim, *Iron Wall*, pp. 69–72.
9 *New York Times,* "General's word."
10 Shlaim, *Iron Wall*, pp. 73–5; *DFPI*, 1952, p. 585.
11 S. Blass, *Water in Strife and Action* (in Hebrew), Ramat Gan, Masada, 1973, pp. 183–5; Ben Gurion's *Diary*, April 17 and 23, 1953.
12 Shlaim, *Iron Wall*, p. 76.
13 Interview of Uri Avnery by Haggai Matar, Sept. 2009.
14 Y. Cohen, *The Allon Plan* (in Hebrew), Hakibbutz Hameuchad, Tel Aviv, 1969.
15 Interview of Uri Avnery by Haggai Matar, Sept. 2009.
16 *DFPI*, 1952, p. 454.
17 *DFPI*, 1953, pp. 126–8.
18 Shlaim, *Iron Wall*, p. 80.
19 Bar Zohar, *Ben Gurion*, Vol. IV pp. 1052–3.
20 Israeli, *Shalom Shalom*, p. 170; G. Flesh, Knesset Minutes, June 15, 1953, 14/1592.

21 *Ha'aretz* editorial, September 2, 1953.
22 "On your departure and return" (in Hebrew), Israel's Official Printer, January 1960, p. 20.
23 Commander E. H. Hutchison, *Violent Truce: A Military Observer Looks at the Arab Israeli Conflict 1951–1955*, Devin-Adair, London, 1955, p. 44.
24 *Le Monde*, October 21, 1953.
25 Israeli, *Shalom Shalom*, p. 165.
26 Ibid., p. 166.
27 Golda Meir, *My Life*, Time Warner, New York, 1989.
28 Ibid.
29 Shlaim, *Iron Wall*, p. 99.
30 Labor Party Archive, Minutes of Meeting of the Central Committee, April 15, 1954.
31 M. Dayan, *Milestones: An Autobiography* (in Hebrew), Idanim/Dvir, Jerusalem, 1976, pp. 191–2.
32 B. Morris, *Israel's Border Wars 1949–1956*, Clarendon Press, Oxford, 1993, p. 177.
33 Dayan, *Milestones*, p. 139.
34 M. Sharet, *A Personal Diary, 1953–1957* (in Hebrew), January 31 1954, Maariv, Tel Aviv, 1978.
35 Shlaim, *Iron Wall*, p. 106.
36 Morris, *Righteous Victims*, pp. 280–1.
37 Sharet, *A Personal Diary*, May 17, 1954; H. Eshed, "Who gave the order" (in Hebrew), 1979, quoted in Shlaim, *Iron Wall*.
38 Morris, *Righteous Victims*, quoting a speech by Sharet, November, 1957.
39 Dayan, *Milestones*, p. 122.
40 Eshed "Who gave the order."
41 Shlaim, *Iron Wall*, p. 112.
42 Israeli, *Shalom Shalom*, pp. 170–2; Flesh, Knesset Minutes, February 4, 1953, 11/1180.
43 Sharet, *A Personal Diary*, October 26, 1954.
44 E. L. M. Burns, *Between Arabs and Israelis*, Ivan Obolensky, Beirut, 1969, p. 41.
45 Shlaim, *Iron Wall*, p. 115.
46 Sharet, *A Personal Diary*, December 22, 1954.
47 D. Avni, "Report on the situation in Egypt," October 10, 1954, quoted in Shlaim, *Iron Wall*, p. 118; interview with Abdel Rahman Sadeq, quoted in Shlaim, *Iron Wall*, p. 119.
48 Shlaim, *Iron Wall*, p. 120.
49 Matar interview.
50 *New Outlook*, Oct/Dec 1974, quoted in Zeev Raphael, personal correspondence, September 2009.
51 Sharet, *A Personal Diary*, January 27, 1955.
52 G. Rafael, *Destination Peace: Three Decades of Israeli Foreign Policy*, Stein & Day, New York, 1981.

53  Shlaim, *Iron Wall*, p. 122.
54  Sharet, *A Personal Diary*, February 10, 1955.
55  Y. Shimoni, interview quoted in Shlaim, *Iron Wall*, p. 122.
56  G. Wint and P. Calvacorski, in *The Middle East Crisis*, Penguin, London, 1957, commented: "This raid that occurred in February 1955 is one of the most fateful dates in the history of the Middle East. Until that moment Egypt was the least active against Israel of all the Arab states" (p. 57, quoted in Israeli, *Shalom Shalom*, p. 172).
57  *Davar*, "Israel's statement to the UN," March 2, 1955.
58  *Davar*, March 2, 1955; *Maariv*, "The great retaliation operation against Egyptian fedayun," October 2, 1959.
59  Israeli, *Shalom, Shalom*, pp. 174–9.
60  *Maariv*, March 4, 1955.
61  Israeli, *Shalom, Shalom*, p. 177.
62  *Ha'aretz*, New York correspondent, June 20, 1955.
63  Gamal Abdel Nasser, interview with *Time*, quoted in Israeli, *Shalom, Shalom*.
64  M. Begin, Knesset Minutes, October 18, 1955–19/89.
65  D. Ben Gurion, Knesset Minutes, November 2, 1955, 19/233.
66  Israeli, *Shalom, Shalom*, p. 187.
67  *Yediot Aharonot*, December 18, 1955.
68  I. F. Stone, in *I. F. Stone Weekly*, quoted in *Al Hamishmar*, June 4, 1956.
69  A. Cohen, *Israel and the Arab World: The Political Test*, Beacon Press, Boston, 1976 pp. 177–80, quoted in Israeli, *Shalom, Shalom*, p. 200.
70  *Ha'aretz*, report from London by R. Walsh, October 14, 1956.
71  Radio Cairo broadcast on a report by *El Sh'ab*, September 15, 1956, quoted in Israeli, *Shalom, Shalom*, p. 202.
72  Radio Cairo, September 28, 1956.
73  *LaMerhav*, editorial, July 9, 1956.
74  Ben Gurion, Divrei Haknesset 20/20067, June 19, 1956.
75  *Davar*, October 21, 1956.
76  Israeli, *Shalom, Shalom*, p. 210.
77  Ben Gurion telegram to IDF troops, November 6, 1956, quoted in *Davar*, November 7, 1956.
78  Ben Gurion, Divrei Haknesset, 21/197, November 7, 1956.
79  Ben Gurion, Knesset Minutes 21/199, November 7, 1956.
80  P. Bernstein, Knesset Minutes 21/203, November 7, 1956.
81  M. Begin, Knesset Minutes 21/202, November 7, 1956.
82  M. Yaari, Knesset Minutes 21/208, November 7, 1956.
83  M. Sneh, Knesset Minutes 21/256 November 14, 1956.
84  G. Meir, Statement during visit to Washington, D.C,. quoted in *Davar*, March 18, 1957.
85  M. Rapaport, "Scoop: Moshe Dayan hatched idea of settlement in 1956," *Ha'aretz*, July 2010.

## CHAPTER 4 THE LULL IN HOSTILITIES, 1956–67

1  Ben Gurion, Knesset Minutes, 22/1235, March 5, 1957; 21/260, November 14, 1956.
2  Ben Gurion, Knesset Minutes, 22/1272, March 6–13, 1957.
3  Shlaim, *Iron Wall*, p. 187.
4  Shlaim, *Iron Wall*, p. 188.
5  Israeli, *Shalom, Shalom,* p. 372; *Ghana Evening News,* January 18, 1961.
6  U. Dan, *Ma'ariv,* May 26, 1961.
7  J. Golan, *Pages From a Diary* (in Hebrew), Carmel Press, Tel Aviv, 2006. p. 323.
8  Golan, *Pages from a Diary,* p. 202.
9  Golan, *Pages from a Diary,* p. 315.
10 Golan, *Pages from a Diary,* p. 318–19.
11 Israeli, *Shalom, Shalom* p. 374.
12 Israeli, *Shalom, Shalom,* p. 374.
13 Ben Gurion's *Diary,* February 1963.
14 Bar Zohar, *Ben Gurion,* Vol. III, pp. 1526–9.
15 Shlaim, *Iron Wall,* p. 214.
16 Rafael, *Destination Peace,* pp. 125–6.
17 Shlaim, *Iron Wall,* p. 220.
18 Interview with Ambassador Avraham Harman, quoted in Shlaim, *Iron Wall,* p. 622.
19 Shlaim, *Iron Wall,* p. 223–4.
20 Haber, *"Today War will Break Out."*
21 M. Zak, *Hussein Makes Peace: Thirty Years and Another Year on the Road to Peace* (in Hebrew), Bar Ilan University Press, Ramat Gan, 1996, pp. 41–2, p. 229, ref. 15.
22 Haber, *"Today War will Break Out,"* pp. 95–6.
23 Interview with Yitzhak Rabin, quoted in Shlaim, *Iron Wall,* p. 230.
24 A. Sela, "Arab summit conferences," in *The Continuous Political Encyclopedia of the Middle East,* ed. A. Sela, Continuum, New York, 2002, pp. 158–60.
25 D. Shaham, *Israel – 50 Years* (in Hebrew), Am Oved, Tel Aviv, 1998, p. 238.
26 M. Murakami, *Managing Water for Peace in the Middle East: Alternative Strategies,* United Nations University Press, Tokyo, 1995, Tables C-1 and C-2.
27 J. Bowen, *Six Days: How the 1967 War Shaped the Middle East,* Simon & Schuster, London, 2003, pp. 23–30.
28 Shlaim, *Iron Wall,* p. 234.
29 Shlaim, *Iron Wall,* p. 235.
30 T. Romi, "Interviews with Moshe Dayan" (in Hebrew), *Yediot Aharonot,* April 27, 1997.
31 A. Eban, *Autobiography,* Weidenfeld & Nicholson, London, 1977, p. 319.

32 Indar Jit Rikhye, *The Sinai Blunder*, Routledge, London, 1980, pp. 16–19.
33 M. Bentov, *Al Hamishmar*, April 14, 1971; M. Begin, *New York Times*, August 21, 1982; Y. Rabin, *Le Monde*, February 28, 1968.
34 A. Eban, *Personal Witness, Israel Through My Eyes*, Putnam, New York, 1992, pp. 386–90.
35 Haber, *"Today War will Break Out,"* pp. 216–21.

## CHAPTER 5 THE AFTERMATH OF THE JUNE 1967 WAR

1 M. Bentov, *Al Hamishmar*, April 14, 1971; M. Begin, *New York Times*, August 21, 1982; Y. Rabin, *Le Monde*, February 28, 1968.
2 Shlaim, *Iron Wall*, p. 242.
3 R. Alkadari, *Strategy and Tactics in Jordanian Foreign Policy 1967–1988*, D.Phil. thesis, University of Oxford, 1995, pp. 83–96, as quoted in Shlaim, *Iron Wall*; Sela, "Arab summit conferences," pp. 158–60.
4 M. Bar On, *Never Ending Conflict: Israeli Military History*, Greenwood, Westport, Conn., 2006., p. 35; T. Segev, *The Seventh Million* (in Hebrew), Keter, Tel Aviv, p. 369.
5 Segev, *The Seventh Million*, p. 369.
6 J. Wallach, M. Lissak, and S. Shamins, *Carta's Atlas of Israel*, "The Second Decade 1961–1971,*" Jerusalem, Carta/Israel Defense Ministry Press, 1980.
7 M. Bar On, *In Pursuit of Peace: A History of the Israeli Peace Movement*, US Institute of Peace, Washington, D.C., 1996.
8 R. Pedatzur, "The June decision was canceled in October" (in Hebrew), *Ha'aretz*, May 12, 1995.
9 Haber, *"Today the War will Break Out,"* pp. 275–6.
10 U. Narkiss, *Soldier of Jerusalem* (in Hebrew), Israel Defense Ministry Press, Tel Aviv, 1991, p. 346.
11 Pedatzur, "The June decision was canceled in October"; Y. Admoni, *Decades of Discretion: Settlement Policy in the Territories 1967–1977* (in Hebrew), Israel Galili Institute, 1992, p. 22.
12 Admoni, *Decades of Discretion*, pp. 51–4.
13 Admoni, *Decades of Discretion*, p. 58.
14 Haber, *"Today the War will Break Out,"* p. 282.
15 J. Kimchi and D. Kimche, *The Secret Roads: The "Illegal" Migration of a People 1938–1948*, Secker & Warburg, London, 1954, pp. 254–5.
16 A. Brown, "Moshe Dayan and the Six Day War" (in Hebrew), *Yediot Aharonot*, Tel Aviv, 1997.
17 B. Kimmerling and J. Migdal, *Palestinians: The Making of a People*, Harvard University Press, Cambridge, Mass., 1994, p. 260.
18 Kimchi and Kimche, *The Secret Roads*, pp. 254–5.
19 Kimchi and Kimche, *The Secret Roads*, p. 254.

20  M. Ma'oz, *Palestinian Leadership on the West Bank: The Changing Role of the Mayors*, Routledge, London, 1988, p. 112.
21  Ma'oz, *Palestinian Leadership*, p. 113, ref. 31.
22  S. Gazit, *The Stick and the Carrot* (in Hebrew), Zmora Bitan, Tel Aviv, 1985, pp. 143–4.
23  Morris, *Righteous Victims*, p. 340.
24  Kimchi and Kimche, *The Secret Roads*, p. 257.
25  Haber, "Today the War will Break Out," p. 271.
26  Eban, *Autobiography*, p. 435.
27  Pedatzur, *Ha'aretz*, May 12, 1995.
28  R. Stephens, *Nasser: A Political Biography*, Penguin, London, 1977, p. 523.
29  Morris, *Righteous Victims*, p. 346.
30  Shlaim, *Iron Wall*, pp. 258–9.
31  R. Pedatzur, *The Triumph of Confusion: Israel and the Territories after the Six Day War* (in Hebrew), Bitan, Tel Aviv, 1996, pp. 111–13.
32  Shlaim *Iron Wall*, p. 260.
33  Eban, *Autobiography*, p. 446.
34  M. Medzini, *A Proud Jewess: Golda Meir and the Vision of Israel, A Political Biography* (in Hebrew), Idanim, Tel Aviv, 1990, pp. 522–3.
35  Meir, *My Life*, p. 312.
36  Shlaim, *Iron Wall*, p. 285.
37  R. Rosenthal, interview with Victor Shem Tov, *Ma'ariv*, September 29, 1998.
38  Shlaim. *Iron Wall*, p. 288.
39  D. Korn, *Stalemate: The War of Attrition and Great Power Diplomacy in the Middle East, 1967–1970*, Westview Press, Boulder, Colo., 1992, p. 160.
40  Shlaim, *Iron Wall*, p. 293.
41  Shlaim, *Iron Wall*, p. 295.
42  Morris, *Righteous Victims*, p. 368.
43  D. Neff, "The Battle of Karameh establishes claim of Palestinian statehood," *Washington Report on Middle East Affairs*, 1998, pp. 87–8; B. Michaelson, "Operation Tophet, a battle on the East Bank of the Jordan" (in Hebrew), *MaArachot*, 1984, p. 292.
44  M. Karmel, Knesset Minutes 1877–1878, May 26, 1970.
45  Rafael, *Destination Peace*, p. 256.
46  Ibid., pp. 258–9.
47  Y. Rabin, *Rabin's Memoirs*, Weidenfeld & Nicholson, London, 1979, p. 162.
48  Eban, *Autobiography*, p. 488.
49  *Sunday Times*, June 15, 1969; *Washington Post*, June 16, 1969.
50  Shlaim, *Iron Wall*, p. 312.
51  A. Hart, *Arafat: A Political Biography*, Sidgwick & Jackson, London. 1994, p. 219.
52  Rafael, *Destination Peace*, p. 277.

53 Eban, *Autobiography*, p. 487.
54 M. Heikel, *The Road to Ramadan*, Collins, London, 1975, p. 205.

## CHAPTER 6 FROM YOM KIPPUR TO LEBANON

1 H. Bar Tov, *Dado* (in Hebrew), Sifriyat Maariv, Tel Aviv, 1978, p. 237.
2 A. Braun, *Moshe Dayan in the Yom Kippur War* (in Hebrew), Idanim, Tel Aviv, 1992, p. 18.
3 Morris, *Righteous Victims*, p. 438.
4 W. Quandt, *Decade of Decisions: American Policy Toward the Arab–Israeli Conflict, 1967–1976*, University of California Press, Berkeley, Calif., 1977, pp. 234, 239.
5 Shlaim, *Iron Wall*, p. 325.
6 Ibid, p. 327.
7 S. Avineri, "Leader in the grip of political constraints" (in Hebrew), *Ha'aretz*, December 1, 1995.
8 M. Shemesh, *The Palestinian Entity 1959–1974: Arab Politics and the PLO*, rev. edn, Frank Cass, London, 1996, pp. 293–5.
9 Shlaim, *Iron Wall*, p. 331.
10 Y. Melman and R. Druker, *Behind the Uprising: Israelis, Jordanians and Palestinians*, Greenwood Press, Westport, Conn., 1989, p. 130.
11 I. L. Bickerton and C. L. Klausner, *A Concise History of the Arab–Israeli Conflict*, Prentice Hall, Upper Saddle River, N.J., 2002, p, 176.
12 Shlaim, *Iron Wall*, p. 334.
13 M. Heikel, *Secret Channels: The Inside Story of Arab–Israeli Peace Negotiations*, Harper Collins, London, 1996, p. 244.
14 D. Shaham, *Israel – Fifty Years* (in Hebrew), Am Oved, Tel Aviv, 1998, p. 388.
15 Shlaim, *Iron Wall*, p. 350.
16 J. Carter, Presidential News Conference, American Presidency Project, March 9, 1977.
17 J. Carter, *Keeping Faith: Memoirs of a President*, Bantam, Toronto, 1982, p. 291.
18 Y. Meital, *Egypt's Struggle for Peace: Continuity and Change 1967–1977*, University of Florida Press, Gainesville, Fla., 1997.
19 Morris, *Righteous Victims*, p. 446.
20 M. Dayan, *Breakthrough: A Personal Account of the Egypt Israel Negotiations*, Weidenfeld & Nicholson, London, 1984, p. 38.
21 D. Kimche, *The Last Option: Nasser, Arafat and Sadam Hussein, The Quest for Peace in the Middle East*, Scribner & Sons, New York, 1991, p. 76; E. Haber, E. Yaari, and Z. Schiff, *The Year of the Dove* (in Hebrew), Zmora Bitan, Tel Aviv, 1980, p. 27.
22 A. Sadat, *In Search of Identity: An Autobiography*, Harper & Row, New York, 1978, p. 302.

23 Haber, Yaari, and Schiff, *The Year of the Dove,* p. 50.
24 I. Fahmi, *Negotiating for Peace in the Middle East,* Johns Hopkins University Press, Baltimore, Md., 1983, p. 257.
25 Ibid., p. 266.
26 Haber, Yaari, and Schiff, *The Year of the Dove,* pp. 51, 54; E. Weizman, *The Battle for Peace,* Bantam, New York, 1981, pp. 19–20.
27 Morris, *Righteous Victims,* p. 450.
28 Morris, *Righteous Victims,* p. 450.
29 Fahmi, *Negotiating for Peace,* pp. 277–8.
30 Haber, Yaari, and Schiff, *The Year of the Dove,* pp. 128–9.
31 Shlaim, *Iron Wall,* p. 361.
32 Dayan, *Breakthrough,* p. 91.
33 Haber, Yaari, and Schiff, *The Year of the Dove,* pp. 145–6.
34 A. Naor, *Begin in Power: A Personal Testimony* (in Hebrew), Yediot Aharonot, Tel Aviv, 1993, p. 152.
35 A. Benn, "In the corrals" (in Hebrew), *Ha'aretz,* May 17, 2009; B. Reich, *Political Leaders of the Middle East and North Africa: A Biographical Dictionary,* Greenwood Press, Westport, Conn., 1990, p. 148.
36 Carter, *Keeping,* p. 303.
37 Morris, *Righteous Victims,* p 459.
38 Y. Bar Siman Tov, *Israel and the Peace Process 1972–82: In Search of Legitimacy and Peace,* SUNY Press, New York, 1994, p. 96.
39 Bar On, *In Pursuit of Peace,* p. 98.
40 Haber, Yaari, and Schiff, *The Year of the Dove,* p. 286.
41 Bar Siman Tov, *Israel and the Peace Process,* p. 105.
42 Carter, *Keeping,* p. 315.
43 Ibid., p. 409.
44 Z. Brzezinski, *Power and Principle: Memoirs of a National Security Adviser, 1977–1981,* Weidenfeld & Nicholson, London, 1983, p. 287.
45 Dayan, *Breakthrough,* p. 305.
46 Shlaim, *Iron Wall,* p. 383.
47 Weizman, *The Battle for Peace,* p. 383.
48 Ibid., p. 384.
49 Morris, *Righteous Victims,* p. 489.
50 Bar Siman Tov, *Israel and the Peace Process,* pp. 219–20.
51 A. K. Hassan, *Warriors and Peacemakers* (in Hebrew), Defense Ministry Press, Tel Aviv, 1993, p. 66.

## CHAPTER 7 FROM LEBANON TO OSLO

1 G. Steinberg, "The Begin Doctrine at 25," *Jerusalem Post,* June 4, 2006.
2 A. Naor, *Begin in Power* (in Hebrew), Yediot Aharonot, Tel Aviv, 1993, p. 220.

3    Shlaim, *Iron Wall*, p. 387.
4    M. Sasson, *Seven Years in the Land of the Egyptians* (in Hebrew), Idanim, Tel Aviv, 1992, p. 145.
5    Shlaim, *Iron Wall*, p. 390.
6    Naor, *Begin in Power*, p. 232.
7    I. Peleg, *Begin's Foreign Policy, 1977–1983*, Greenwood Press, Westport, Conn., 1987, p. 191.
8    Naor, *Begin in Power*, p. 232.
9    A. Naor, *Cabinet at War* (in Hebrew), Lahav, Tel Aviv, 1986, p. 33.
10   Z. Schiff and E. Yaari, *Israel's Lebanon War*, Allen & Unwin, London, 1984, p. 375.
11   Naor, *Begin in Power*, p. 291.
12   P. Seale, *Assad in Syria: The Struggle for the Middle East*, Tauris, London, 1988, p. 365.
13   *Jerusalem Post*, August 3, 1982.
14   M. Heikel, *Secret Channels*, Harper Collins, London, 1996, p. 355; Shlaim, *Iron Wall*, p. 413.
15   Shlaim, *Iron Wall*, p. 413.
16   "Begin said to meet in secret with Beirut's president elect," *New York Times*, September 4, 1982.
17   I. Rabinovich, *The War for Lebanon, 1970–1983*, Cornell University Press, Ithaca, N.Y., 1984, p. 168.
18   Kimche, *The Last Option*, p. 174.
19   Shlaim, *Iron Wall*, p. 420.
20   L. Zitrain-Eisenberg and N. Kaplan, *Negotiating Arab Israeli Peace: Patterns, Problems, Possibilities*, Indiana University Press, Bloomington, Ind., 1998.
21   M. Medzini (ed.), *Israel's Foreign Relations: Selected Documents Vol. 9, 1984–1988* (in Hebrew), Jerusalem 1992, p. 1.
22   A. Naor, *Writing on the Wall* (in Hebrew), Edanim, Tel Aviv, 1988, p. 125.
23   A. Garfinkle, *Israel and Jordan in the Shadow of War*, Macmillan, London, 1992, p. 113.
24   Melman and Druker, *Behind the Uprising*, p. 166.
25   Ibid., p. 204.
26   Medzini, *Israel's Foreign Relation*, p. 509.
27   Y. Shamir, *Summing Up: An Autobiography*, Weidenfeld & Nicholson, London, 1994, p. 175.
28   Shlaim, *Iron Wall*, p. 450.
29   *Ha'aretz*, November 27, 1987.
30   Shlaim, *Iron Wall*, p. 451.
31   Schiff and Yaari, *Israel's Lebanon War*, p. 79.
32   Morris, *Righteous Victims*, p.562.
33   A. Shalev, *The Intifada: Causes and Effects* (in Hebrew), Yaffe Center for Strategic Studies, Papyrus, Tel Aviv, 1990, p. 24.
34   Kimmerling and Migdal, *Palestinians*, p. 259; M. Tessler, *A History of*

*the Israeli Palestinian Conflict*, Indiana University Press, Bloomington, Ind., 1994, p. 548.

35 Shalev, *The Intifada*, p. 36.
36 Shlaim, *Iron Wall*, p. 451.
37 A. Strashnov, *Justice Under Fire: The Legal System* (in Hebrew), Yediot Aharonot, Tel Aviv, 1994, pp. 50, 72.
38 D. Peretz, *Intifada: The Palestinian Uprising*, Westview Press, Boulder, Colo., 1990, p. 40.
39 Morris, *Righteous Victims*, p. 594.
40 H. Ashrawi, *This Side of Peace*, Simon & Schuster, New York, 1995, p. 156.
41 Z. Schiff and E. Yaari, *Intifada*, ed. and trans. I. Friedman, Simon & Schuster, New York, 1991, p. 315.
42 G. Shultz, *Turmoil and Triumph*, Simon & Schuster, New York, 1993, p. 1033.
43 Schiff and Yaari, *Intifada*, p. 315.
44 Tessler, *History of the Israeli Palestinian Conflict*, p.722.
45 Peretz, *Intifada*, p. 187.
46 Shalev, *The Intifada*, p. 154.
47 Tessler, *History of the Israeli Palestinian Conflict* p. 724.
48 Zak, *Hussein Makes Peace*, p. 263.
49 Shlaim, *Iron Wall*, p. 468.
50 W. Quandt, *American Diplomacy and the Arab–Israeli Conflict Since 1967*, University of California Press and Brookings Institute, Berkeley, Calif., 199 p. 389.
51 Schiff and Yaari, *Intifada*, p. 320.
52 Shamir, *Summing Up,* p. 214.
53 Ibid., p. 214.
54 Quandt, *American Diplomacy*, p. 404.
55 Y. Shamir, *Conclusion* (in Hebrew), Idanim, Tel Aviv, p. 272.
56 Quandt, *American Diplomacy*, p. 404.
57 *New York Times*, November 2, 1991.
58 Ashrawi, *This Side of Peace*, p. 200.
59 Shlaim, *Iron Wall*, p. 488.
60 Shlaim, *Iron Wall,,* p. 496.
61 Morris, *Righteous Victims,,* pp. 615–16.

## CHAPTER 8 THE PLO AS A PEACE PARTNER?

1 Reinhart, *Israel/Palestine*, p. 15.
2 Pappe, *A History of Modern Palestine*, p. 243; D. Makovski, *Making Peace with the PLO*, Westview Press, Boulder, Colo., 1996, p. 111.
3 A. Elon, "The peace makers," *New Yorker*, December 20, 1993.
4 Makovski, *Making Peace with the PLO*, p.16.
5 Pappe, *A History of Modern Palestine*, p. 243; Makovski, *Making Peace with the PLO*, pp. 21–23.

6 Reinhart, *Israel/Palestine*, p. 16.
7 Pappe, *A History of Modern Palestine*, p. 242.
8 Pappe, *A History of Modern Palestine*, p. 243; Elon, "The peace makers."
9 Pappe, *A History of Modern Palestine*, p. 243.
10 *Ha'aretz*, November 3, 1993.
11 Reinhart, *Israel/Palestine*, p. 17.
12 I. Pappe, "Breaking the mirror," in H. Gordon (ed.), *Looking Back at the June 1967 War*, Prager, Westport, Conn., p. 95.
13 *Settlement Watch Report No. 8*, Peace Now, Jerusalem, July 31, 1996.
14 UN General Assembly Resolution 194, December 11, 1949 (quoted in Pappe, *A History of Modern Palestine*, p. 244).
15 Pappe, *A History of Modern Palestine*, p. 246.
16 Shlaim, *Iron Wall*, p. 525.
17 Shlaim, *Iron Wall*, p. 528.
18 *Ha'aretz*, June 4, 1996.
19 Pappe, *A History of Modern Palestine*, p. 256.
20 Melman and Druker, *Behind the Uprising*.
21 *New York Times*, September 15, 1993.
22 E. Rubinstein, *The Peace Between Israel and Jordan: An Anatomy of a Negotiation* (in Hebrew), Jaffa Center for Strategic Studies, 1996.
23 A. Barzilai, "The sources of Yigal Amir's hatred" (in Hebrew), *Ha'aretz*, November 9, 1995.
24 *Ha'aretz*, January 22, 1996.
25 *Ha'aretz*, March 1, 1996, March 4, 1996, February 27, 1996.
26 The complete text of the Beilin–Abu Mazen proposal can be found at <www.us-israel.org/jsource/peace/beilinmazen> (accessed date?); Z. Schiff, "Beilin's final agreement" (in Hebrew), *Ha'aretz*, February 23, 1996.
27 *Ha'aretz*, June 23, 2000.
28 Lili Galili, interview with Yossi Beilin, "I want to entangle the Likud with as much peace as possible" (in Hebrew), *Ha'aretz*, March 3, 1996.
29 Reinhart, *Israel/Palestine*, p. 28.
30 U. Benziman, *Ha'aretz*, June 23, 2000.
31 *Ha'aretz*, June 17, 1996.
32 *New York Times*, September 26, 1996.
33 *New York Times*, October 2, 1996.
34 *New York Times*, January 18, 1997.
35 Morris, *Righteous Victims*, p. 646.
36 Morris, *Righteous Victims*, p. 646.
37 "Clinton trip to Gaza opens new relationship," Churches for the Middle East, *Action Alert*, March 5, 1999.
38 Morris, *Righteous Victims*, p. 649.
39 <www.knesset.gov.il/faction/eng/factionhistoryAll_eng.asp> (accessed August 31, 2010).

40  A.Margalit, "Israel: why Barak won," *New York Review of Books*, August 12, 1999.

41  J. Shaoul, "Israel's prime minister Barak forms autocratic government," <www.wsws.org/articles/1999/jul999/ isra-jog> (accessed June 19, 2010).

## CHAPTER 9 BARAK LEAVES NO STONE UNTURNED

1   For example Uri Sagie, Shlomo Ben Amit, Gilad Sher, and Yossi Beilin.

2   R. Druker, *Harakiri* (in Hebrew), Yediot Aharonot, Tel Aviv, 2002, p. 28.

3   Reinhart, *Israel/Palestine*, p. 62.

4   Reinhart, *Israel/Palestine*, p. 64.

5   *Yediot Aharonot*, December 10, 1999.

6   Reinhart, *Israel/Palestine*, p. 66; *Yediot Aharonot*, January 3, 2000.

7   *Yediot Aharonot*, January 13, 2000; *Ha'aretz*, January 13, 2000; *Al Hayat*, January 9, 2000.

8   Reinhart, *Israel/Palestine*,p. 69.

9   *Yediot Aharonot*, February 17, 1999.

10  B. Aluf, *Ha'aretz*, January 14, 2000; S. Shiffer, *Yediot Aharonot*, March 23, 2000.

11  R. Maley, *New York Times*, July 10, 2001; *Ha'aretz*, July 10, 2001.

12  A. Eldar, "On the basis of the non-existent Camp David understandings" (in Hebrew), *Ha'aretz*, November 16, 2000.

13  H. Agha and R. Malley, "Camp David: the tragedy of errors," *New York Review of Books*, August 9, 2001.

14  The authors are the Israeli Yossi Beilin and the Palestinian Abu Mazen (Mahmoud Abbas). The full text of the understanding can be found on <www.us-israel.org/jsource/peace/beilinmazen> (accessed October 22, 2010).

15  D. Rubinstein, "Two maps which are hard to accept" (in Hebrew), *Ha'aretz*, January 28, 2000.

16  N. Barnea, *Yediot Aharonot*, June 30, 2000.

17  A. Eldar, *Ha'aretz*, May 5, 1998.

18  N. Barnea, "Abu Dis and Abu Pocket," *Yediot Aharonot*, May 12, 2000; *Ha'aretz*, June 27, 2000; *Jerusalem Post*, July 27, 2000; H. Agha and R. Malley, "Camp David," *New York Review of Books*, August 9, 2001.

19  *Jerusalem Post*, August 18, 2000.

20  A. Kapeliouk, "Conducting catastrophe," *Le Monde Diplomatique*, February 2000.

21  Y. Beilin, "Beilin-Abu Mazen with full responsibility" (in Hebrew), *Ha'aretz*, November 9, 2001.

22  S. Shiffer, *Yediot Aharonot*, August 8, 2000.

23  A. Benn, *Ha'aretz*, January 15, 2001.

24  The text of UNGA Resolution 194 is at <www.un.org/depts/dpa/qpal/docs/ A_RES_194>.

25  A. Eldar, "Most Palstinians ready for deal without refugees," *Ha'aretz,* January 18, 2005.

26  The full text of the original Saudi proposal, adopted by the Arab League summit, can be found at <http://www.jewishvirtuallibrary.org/jsource/Peace/beilinmazen.html> (accessed October 22, 2010).

27  Toufik Haddad interviews Ingrid Jaradat, "Between the lines," April 2001, <www.between-lines.org>.

28  U. Shavi and J. Bana, "Everything you wanted to know about the right of return," *Ha'aretz Friday Magazine,* July 6, 2001.

29  Charles Enderlin, *The Lost Years,* Other Press, New York, 2006, p. 8.

30  Ibid., p. 8.

31  Ibid., p. 11.

32  T. Reinhart, "A reply to Benny Morris," *Guardian,* February 22, 2002.

33  Y. Ben Menachem, Israel Radio, January 20, 2001.

34  A. Benn, *Ha'aretz,* January 28, 2001; B. Kaspit, *Maariv,* January 23, 2001.

35  Barnea, *Yediot Aharonot,* December 29, 2000; Kaspit, *Maariv,* January 4, 2001.

36  Reinhart, *Israel/Palestine,* p. 214.

37  N. Strassler, "The arithmetic of war," *Ha'aretz,* February 22, 2002.

38  Reinhart, *Israel/Palestine,* p. 215.

39  Strassler, "The arithmetic of war."

40  Barnea, *Yediot Aharanot,* December 29, 2000; B. Aluf, *Ha'aretz,* January 28, 2001.

41  *Yediot Aharonot,* February 22, 2002.

## CHAPTER 10 PEACE ON A DOWNHILL SLOPE

1  Barzilai, "Ahavat Arik," *Ha'aretz,* November 29, 2002.

2  Enderlin, *The Lost Years,* p. 23.

3  Ibid.

4  <www.pna.gov.ps/subjectdetails2.asp> (accessed on July 6, 2010).

5  Barnea, *Yediot Aharonot,* March 20, 2001.

6  Enderlin, *The Lost Years,* p. 30.

7  *Yediot Aharonot,* March 30, 2001; T. Steinmetz, *Peace Index,* Research Institute for Peace, Tel Aviv University, March 2001.

8  Enderlin, *The Lost Years,* p. 39.

9  "Mubarak accuses Peres of misleading him," Kuwait News Agency (KUNA), April 30, 2001.

10  <www.state.gov/p/nea/ris/rpt/3060> (accessed on July 6, 2010).

11  Interview with General Ilan Paz, May 14, 2006, quoted in Enderlin, *The Lost Years.*

12  S. Zunes, "Is Mitchell up to the task?" *Foreign Policy in Focus,* January 23, 2009.

13  Enderlin interview with Saeb Erekat, October 30, 2005.
14  *Ha'aretz*, August 20, 2001.
15  BBC News, "Palestinian radical founder dies," January 26, 2008.
16  A. Eldar and M. Steinberg, *Ha'aretz*, January 21, 2008.
17  O. Shelah, *Ynet*, August 30, 2001.
18  Enderlin, *The Lost Years,* p. 99.
19  S. Goldenberg and J. Borger, "Furious Bush hits back at Sharon," *Guardian*, UK, October 6, 2001.
20  L. Derfner, "The assassination of a right wing Israeli cabinet member again pushes the Middle East to the brink," *US News and World Report*, October 21, 2001.
21  A. Golan, "Tis a pity they didn't speak to Gandhi," *Ha'aretz*, October 8, 2002.
22  Enderlin, *The Lost Years*, p. 108.
23  Enderlin, interview with Saeb Erakat.
24  B. Whitaker, "The strange affair of the *Karine A*," *Guardian Unlimited*, January 21, 2002.
25  Address by Sharon following the seizure of *Karine A*, Israeli Ministry of Foreign Affairs, January 6, 2002.
26  Enderlin, *The Lost Years*, p. 129.
27  Enderlin interview with Mohammed Dahlan, April 8, 2005.
28  Ibid.
29  T. Friedman, "An intriguing signal from the Saudi Crown Prince," *New York Times*, February 17, 2002.
30  *Ha'aretz*, February 26, 2002.
31  *Ha'aretz*, March 4, 2001.
32  <www.al-bab.com/arab/docs/league/peace02> (accessed on July 6, 2010).
33  "Margaret Warner examines Colin Powell's mission to the Middle East on April 11th," <www.pbs.org/newshour/bb/middle_east/jan-june02/israel 4-11" (accessed on July 6, 2010).
34  Ibid.
35  P. Slevin and M. Allen, "Bush: Sharon a man of peace," *Washington Post*, April 19, 2002.
36  J. Zacharia, "Bush: Arafat has disappointed me," *Jerusalem Post*, May 7, 2002.
37  T. Sasson, attorney, "Report on the settlements," <www.pmo.gov.il/NR/rdonlyres/OAOFBE3C-C741-46A6-8CB5-F6CDCO42465D/0/SASSON.2.pdf>(accessed on July 7, 2010) .
38  "Abbas takes up PM's post", *Middle East Economic Digest* (MEED), March 21, 2003.
39  J. Bennet, "Arafat may soon approve a premier, meeting US demand," *New York Times*, March 16, 2003.
40  L. Lahoud, "Quartet presents road map to Abbas," *Jerusalem Post*, May 1, 2003.
41  C. R. Mark, "Israel's proposal to withdraw from Gaza," CRS Report

for Congress, Federation of American Scientists < www.fas.org/sgp/crs/mideast/RS22000> (accessed on July 7, 2010).

42 <www.mifkad.org.il/en/principles.asp> (accessed on July qw, 2010); <www.peacelobby.org/nusseibeh-ayalon_initiative> (accessed on July 12, 2010).

43 Declaration of Jerusalem, in Enderlin, *The Lost Years*, p. 214.

44 U. Dan, *Ariel Sharon*, Michel Lafon, Paris, 2006, pp. 391–2.

45 "The disengagement plan," *Ha'aretz*, April 16, 2004.

46 "Sharon the survivor," *Guardian Unlimited*, January 22, 2004.

47 "Sharon addresses the Fifth Herzeliya Conference," Israeli Ministry of Foreign Affairs, website, February 16, 2004.

48 Y. Markus, interview with Sharon, *Ha'aretz*, February 2, 2204.

49 "Sheikh Yassin, spiritual figurehead," BBC News, March 22, 2004.

50 *Jerusalem Post*, February 1, 2005.

51 A. Shavit, interview with Dov Weisglass, *Ha'aretz*, October 8, 2004.

52 Enderlin, *The Lost Years*, p. 250.

53 U. Avnery, "Who murdered Arafat,"<www.rensl.com/general67>, November 9, 2005 (accessed on July 12, 2010); "Quarrel on the Titanic," May 16, 2009.

54 Enderlin, *The Lost Years*, p. 252.

55 <www.btselelm.org/english/settlements/index.asp>, 13 (accessed on July 12, 2010).

56 <www.isracast.com/article.aspx?1D=206> (accessed on July 12, 2010).

57 <www.opendemocracy.net/conflict-debate_97/democracy_sharon_3172> (accessed on July 14, 2010); <www.medea.be/index.html> (accessed on July 14, 2010).

58 A. Shlaim, "Israel and Gaza: rhetoric and reality," *Open Democracy*, July 1, 2009.

59 Shlaim, *The War for Palestine*.

60 L. Grant, "We're tired of blood," *Guardian*, March 22, 2006.

61 D. Krusch, "Kadima Party," Jewish Virtual Library, November 22, 2005.

62 Cabinet Communique, Special Session, Israel Ministry of Foreign Affairs, April 11, 2006.

63 <www.un.org/depts/dpa/ngo/history.html> (accessed on July 14, 2010).

64 U. Avnery, "Israel, Hamas and the Palestinian elections," *Counterpunch*, January 23, 2206.

65 <www.opendemocracy.org/conflict-debate_97/article_2234.jsp>(accessed on July 14, 2010).

66 B. Burston, "Lebanon II: The First War, " *Ha'aretz*, August 2, 2006.

67 Enderlin, *The Lost Years*, p. 276.

68 Reinhart, *Israel/Palestine,* p. 221.

69 Ibid.

70 Winograd Interim Report, <www.vaadatwino.co.il/press.html> (accessed on July 14, 2010), April 30, 2007.

# BIBLIOGRAPHY

## PUBLICATIONS IN HEBREW

Admoni, Y. *Decades of Discretion: Settlement Policy in the Territories 1967–1977*, Israel Galili Institute, 1992.

Arnon-Ohana, Y. *Peasants in the Arab Revolt in the Land of Israel 1936–39*, Papyrus, Tel Aviv, 1982.

Bar Tov, H. *Dado*, Sifriyat Maariv, Tel Aviv, 1978.

Bar Zohar, M. *Ben Gurion: A Biography*, Adama, Tel Aviv, 1986.

Blass, S. *Water in Strife and Action*, Ramat Gan, Masada, 1973.

Braun, A. *Moshe Dayan in the Yom Kippur War*, Idanim, Tel Aviv, 1992.

Cohen, Yerucham. *The Allon Plan*, Hakibbutz Hameuchad, Tel Aviv, 1969.

Dayan, Moshe. *Milestones: An Autobiography*, Idanim/Dvir, Jerusalem, 1976.

Dolan, S. *The Polemic over Partition in the Mandatory Era*, Yad Ben Tzvi, Jerusalem, 1979.

Gazit, S. *The Stick and the Carrot*, Zmora Bitan, Tel Aviv, 1985.

Golan, J. *Pages From a Diary*, Carmel Press, Tel Aviv, 2006.

Haber, E. *Today the War Will Break Out*, Idonim/Yediot Aharanot Press, Tel Aviv, 1987.

Haber, E., Yaari, E., and Schiff, Z. *The Year of the Dove*, Zmora Bitan, Tel Aviv, 1980.

Hassan, A. K. *Warriors and Peacemakers*, Defense Ministry Press, Tel Aviv, 1993.

Israeli, A. *Shalom, Shalom Ve'ein Shalom*, published by the authors: Jerusalem, 1961.

Laor, I. *We Write You Our Homeland (Anu kotvim otach Moledet)*, Kibbutz Hame'uchad Publishing, Tel Aviv, 1995.

Medzini, M. *A Proud Jewess, Golda Meir and the Vision of Israel: A Political Biography*, Idanim, Tel Aviv, 1990.

Naor, A. *Cabinet at War*, Lahavm, Tel Aviv, 1986.

Naor, A. *Writing on the Wall*, Idanim, Tel Aviv, 1988.

Naor, A. *Begin in Power: A Personal Testimony*, Yediot Aharonot, Tel Aviv, 1993.

Narkiss, U. *Soldier of Jerusalem*, Israel Defense Ministry Press, Tel Aviv, 1991.

Pedatzur, R. *The Triumph of Confusion: Israel and the Territories after the Six Day War*, Bitan, Tel Aviv, 1996.

Rubinstein, F. *The Peace Between Israel and Jordan: An Anatomy of a Negotiation*, Jaffe Center for Strategic Studies, Tel Aviv, 1996.

Sasson, M. *Seven Years in the Land of the Egyptians*, Idanim, Tel Aviv, 1992.

Scheuftan, D. *A Jordanian Option – Israel, Jordan and the Palestinians*, Hakibbutz Hameuchad, Tel Aviv, 1986.

Segev, T. *The Seventh Million*, Keter, Jerusalem, 1991.

Segev, T. *Yemei Hakalaniyot*, Keter, Jerusalem, 1999.

Shaham, D. *Israel – Fifty Years*, Am Oved, Tel Aviv, 1998.

Shalev, A. *The Intifada: Causes and Effects*, Yaffe Center for Strategic Studies, Papyrus, Tel Aviv, 1990.

Sharet, Moshe. *A Personal Diary, 1953–1957*, Maariv, Tel Aviv, 1978.

Shimshi, Y. *The Fifth Floor* (biography of Ben Aharon), The Worker's Envoy, Tel Aviv, 1974.

Strashnov, A., *Justice Under Fire: The Legal System*, Yediot Aharonot, Tel Aviv, 1994.

Tabenkin, Y. *Kibbutz Society*, Hakibbutz Hameuchad, 1954.

Zak, M. *Hussein Makes Peace: Thirty Years and Another Year on the Road to Peace*, Bar Ilan University Press, Ramat Gan, 1996.

## PUBLICATIONS IN GERMAN

Herzl, T. *Der Judenstaat*, M. Breitenstein Verlag Buchhandlung, Vienna, 1896.

Herzl, T. *Altneuland*, Seemann Nadfolger, Leipzig, 1902.

Marx, K. and Ruge, A. "On The Jewish Question" (Zur Judenfrage), *Deutsche Franzosishe Jahrbucher*, Paris, 1844.

## PUBLICATIONS IN FRENCH

Dan, Uri. *Ariel Sharon*, Michel Lafon, Paris, 2006.

## PUBLICATIONS IN ENGLISH

Alkadari, R. *Strategy and Tactics in Jordanian Foreign Policy 1967–1988*, D.Phil. thesis, University of Oxford, 1995.

Amitzur, Ilan. *The Origin of the Arab Israeli Arms Race Embargo, Military Power and Decision in the 1948 Palestine War*, NYU Press, New York, 1996.

Ashrawi, H. *This Side of Peace*, Simon & Schuster, New York, 1995.

Bar Siman Tov, Y. *Israel and the Peace Process 1972–82: In Search of Legitimacy and Peace*, SUNY Press, New York, 1994.

Bar On, M. *In Pursuit of Peace: A History of the Israeli Peace Movement*, US Institute of Peace: Washington, D.C., 1996.

Bar On, M. *Never Ending Conflict: Israeli Military History*, Greenwood, Westport, Conn., 2006.

Benvenisti, M. *Sacred Landscapes*, University of California Press, Berkeley, Calif., 2000.

Benvenisti, M. *Son of the Cypress*, University of California Press, Berkeley, Calif., 2007.

Bickerton, I. L. and Klausner, C. L. *A Concise History of the Arab–Israeli Conflict*, Prentice Hall, Upper Saddle River, N.J., 2002.

Bowen, J. *Six Days: How the 1967 War Shaped the Middle East*, Simon & Schuster, London, 2003.

Brzezinski, Z. *Power and Principle: Memoirs of a National Security Adviser, 1977–1981*, Weidenfeld & Nicholson, London, 1983.

Burns, E. L. M. *Between Arabs and Israelis*, Ivan Obolensky, Beirut, 1969.

Carter, J. *Keeping Faith: Memoirs of a President*, Bantam Books, Toronto, 1982.

Cohen, M. *Palestine: Retreat from the Mandate*, Paul Elek, London, 1978.

Cohen, M. *Palestine and the Great Powers, 1945–1948*, Princeton University Press, Princeton, N.J., 1982.

Dayan, M. *Story of My Life*, Morrow, New York, 1976.

Dayan, M. *Breakthrough: A Personal Account of the Egypt Israel Negotiations*, Weidenfeld & Nicholson, London, 1984.

Eban, A. *Autobiography*, Weidenfeld & Nicholson, London, 1977.

Eban, A. *Personal Witness: Israel Through My Eyes*, Putnam, New York, 1992.

Elon, A. *Herzl*, Holt, Rineheart & Winston, New York, 1975.

Enderlin, C. *The Lost Years*, Other Press, New York, 2006.

Eshed, H. *One Man "Mossad" Reuven Shiloah: Father of Israeli Intelligence*, Idanim, Jerusalem, 1988.

Fahmi, I. *Negotiating for Peace in the Middle East*, Johns Hopkins University Press, Baltimore, Md., 1983.

Flapan, S. *Zionism and the Palestinians*, Barnes & Noble, New York, 1979.

Flapan, S. *The Birth of Israel: Myths and Realities*, Pantheon, New York, 1988.

Garfinkle, A. *Israel and Jordan in the Shadow of War*, Macmillan, London, 1992.

Halper, Jeff. *An Israeli in Palestine*, Pluto Press, London, 2008.

Hart, A. *Arafat: A Political Biography*, Sidgwick & Jackson, London, 1994.

Heikel, M. *The Road to Ramadan*, Collins, London, 1975.

Heikel, M. *Secret Channels: The Inside Story of Arab–Israeli Peace Negotiations*, Harper Collins, London, 1996.

Hurewitz, J. C. *The Struggle For Palestine*, Schoken, New York, 1976.

Hutchison, E. H. Commander, *Violent Truce: A Military Observer Looks at the Arab Israeli Conflict 1951–1955*, Devin-Adair, London, 1955.

Khalidi, Rashid. *Sowing Crisis*, Beacon Press, Boston, Mass., 2009.

Khalidi, Walid. *All that Remains: The Palestinian Villages Occupied and Depopulated by Israel in 1948*, Institute for Palestinian Studies, Washington, D.C., 1992.

Kimche, D. *The Last Option, Nasser, Arafat and Sadam Hussein, The Quest for Peace in the Middle East*, Scribner & Sons, New York, 1991.

Kimchi, J. and Kimche, D. *The Secret Roads: The "Illegal" Migration of a People 1938–1948*, Secker & Warburg, London, 1954.

Kimmerling, B. and Migdal, J. *Palestinians: The Making of a People*, Harvard University Press, Cambridge, Mass., 1994.

Kimmerling, B. and Migdal, J. *The Palestinian People*, Harvard University Press, Cambridge, Mass., 2003.

Korn, D. *Stalemate: The War of Attrition and Great Power Diplomacy in the Middle East, 1967–1970*, Westview Press, Boulder, Colo., 1992.

Laqueur, W. *Dying for Jerusalem: The Past, Present and Future of the Holiest City*, Source Books, New York, 2006.

Levenberg, S. and Borochov, B. *Selected Essays in Socialist Zionism*, Rita Searl, London, 1948.

Ma'oz, M. *Palestinian Leadership on the West Bank: The Changing Role of the Mayors*, Routledge, Oxford, 1988.

Makovsky, D. *Making Peace with the PLO*, Westview Press, Boulder, Colo., 1996.

Makovsky, D. and Ross, D. *Myths, Illusions and Peace*, Viking, New York, 2009.

Mattar, P. *The Mufti of Jerusalem*, Columbia University Press, New York, 1988.

Meir, G. *My Life*, Time Warner, New York, 1989.

Meital, Y. *Egypt's Struggle for Peace: Continuity and Change 1967–1977*, University of Florida Press, Gainesville, Fla., 1997.

Melman, Y. and Druker, R. *Behind the Uprising: Israelis, Jordanians and Palestinians*, Greenwood Press, Westport, Conn., 1989.

Morris, B. *Israel's Border Wars 1949–1956*, Clarendon Press, Oxford, 1993.

Morris, B. *Righteous Victims: A History of the Zionist Arab Conflict 1881–2001*. Vintage, New York, 1999.

Murakami, M. *Managing Water for Peace in the Middle East: Alternative Strategies*, United Nations University Press, Tokyo, 1995.

Oren, M. *Power, Faith and Fantasy*, W.W. Norton, New York, 2007.

Pappe, I. *A History of Modern Palestine*, Cambridge University Press, Cambridge, 2004.

Pappe, I. *The Ethnic Cleansing of Palestine*, Oneworld Publications, Oxford, 2006.

Peleg, I. *Begin's Foreign Policy, 1977–1983*, Greenwood Press, Westport, Conn., 1987.

Peretz, D. *Intifada: The Palestinian Uprising*, Westview Press, Boulder, Colo., 1990.

Quandt, W. *Decade of Decisions: American Policy Toward the Arab-Israeli Conflict, 1967–1976*, University of California Press, Berkeley, Calif., 1977.

Quandt, W. *Peace Process: American Diplomacy and the Arab–Israeli Conflict Since 1967*, University of California Press and Brookings Institute, Berkeley, Calif., 1993.

Rabin, Y. *Rabin's Memoirs*, Weidenfeld & Nicholson, London, 1979.

Rabinovich, I. *The War for Lebanon, 1970–1983*, Cornell University Press, Ithaca, N.Y., 1984.

Rabinovitch, I. *The Road Not Taken: Early Arab Israeli Negotiations*, Oxford University Press, Oxford, 1991.

Rafael, G. *Destination Peace: Three Decades of Israeli Foreign Policy*, Stein & Day, New York, 1981.

Reich, B. *Political Leaders of the Middle East and North Africa: A Biographical Dictionary*, Greenwood Press, Westport, Conn., 1990.

Reinhart, T. *Israel/Palestine – How to End the War of 1948*, Seven Stories Press, New York, 2002.

Rikhye, I. J. *The Sinai Blunder*, Routledge, London, 1980.

Sanders, R. *The High Walls of Jerusalem: A History of the Balfour Declaration and the Birth of the British Mandate for Palestine*, Holt Rinehart & Winston, New York, 1983.

Sadat, A. *In Search of Identity: An Autobiography*, Harper & Row, New York, 1978.

Schiff, Z. and Yaari, E. *Israel's Lebanon War*, Allen & Unwin, London, 1984.

Schiff. Z. and Yaari, E., *Intifada*, ed. and trans. I. Friedman, Simon & Schuster, New York, 1991

Seale, P. *Assad in Syria: The Struggle for the Middle East*, Tauris, London, 1988.

Segev, T. *One Palestine Complete*, Abacus, London, 2001.

Sela, A. "Arab summit conferences," in *The Continuous Political Encyclopedia of the Middle East*, ed. A. Sela, Continuum, New York, 2002.

Seliktar, Ofira. *New Zionism and the Foreign Policy System of Israel*, Croom Helm, Beckenham, Kent, 1986.

Shamir, Y. *Summing Up: An Autobiography*, Weidenfeld & Nicholson, London, 1994.

Shapira, A. *Berl: The Biography of a Socialist Zionist: Berl Katznelson 1887–1944*, Cambridge University Press, Cambridge, 2008.

Shemesh, M. *The Palestinian Entity 1959–1974: Arab Politics and the PLO*, Frank Cass, London, 1996.

Shlaim, A. *Collusion Across the Jordan*, Columbia University Press, New York, 1988.

Shlaim, A. *The War for Palestine*, W.W. Norton, New York, 1999.

Shlaim, A. *Iron Wall*, W.W. Norton, New York, 2001.

Shultz, G. *Turmoil and Triumph*, Simon & Schuster, New York, 1993.

Steinmetz, T. *Peace Index*, Research Institute for Peace, Tel Aviv University, March 2001.

Stephens, R. *Nasser: A Political Biography*, Penguin, London, 1977.

Swisher, C. *The Truth About Camp David*, Nation Books, New York, 2004.

Sykes, C. *Cross Roads to Israel*, Collins, London, 1965.

Tamari, S. *The Arab Neighborhoods and Their Fate in the War*, Jerusalem, 1948/Institute of Jerusalem Studies, Jerusalem, 1999.

Tessler, M. *A History of the Israeli Palestinian Conflict*, Indiana University Press, Bloomington, Ind., 1994.

Tevet, S. *Ben Gurion: The Burning Ground*, Houghton Mifflin, London, 1987.

Warschawski, M. *On The Border*, Pluto Press, London, 2005.

Weizmann, E. *The Battle for Peace*, Bantam, New York, 1981.

Zitrain-Eisenberg, L. and Kaplan, N. *Negotiating Arab Israeli Peace: Patterns, Problems, Possibilities*, Indiana University Press, Bloomington, Ind., 1998.

# INDEX

1948 war, 28–31
1956 war, 6, 54–7
1967 war, 8, 66, 67, 70, 170
  aftermath of, 8–9, 70–84
1973 war, 84, 86, 170

## A
Abbas, Mahmoud, 152, 154, 155, 159, 162, 173
Abdullah, king of Trans–Jordan, 26, 32, 33–4, 82, 118
  assassination of, 34, 169
Abdullah II, king of Jordan, 159
Abdullan, crown prince of Saudi Arabia, 149
Abrams, Elliot, 155
Abu Dis, 120, 132–3, 138
Abu Mazen, 119–20, 136
Abu Nidal, 101
Achdut Ha'avoda Party, 80–1
Agha, Hussein, 1`33
Al–Aksa Mosque, 34
Al'Ali, 145
Al–Quds, 120, 132–3, 138
Alami, Mussa, 24, 167
Albright, Madeleine, 122
Algeria, 61
Alignment Party, 100
*Aliyah*, 27
Allah, Abu, 154
Alon, Yigal, 8, 9, 38, 58, 71–2, 77, 88
  Alon Plan, 71, 75, 83, 87, 88, 139, 170

Amer, Abdel Hakim, 64–5
American Professors for Peace in the Middle East (APME), 7
Amir, Yigal, 117
Amit, Meir, 64–5, 69
Amit, Zalman, 1–2, 6–9, 52, 175n1
Anderson, Robert, 169
anti–Semitism, 13
Aqaba, Gulf/Straits of, 44, 46, 68–9
Arab Federation, 62
Arab League
  Beirut summit (2002), 149–50
  Fez summit (1982), 105
  Khartoum summit, 76
  Rabat summit (1974), 88, 105, 170
  and Saudi peace plan, 135, 150, 173
Arab residents of Palestine/Israel *see* Palestinians
Arafat, Yasser, 89, 99, 102, 106, 108–9, 114, 121–3, 127, 131–5, 138, 141–2, 144, 147–8, 150–2, 154, 170, 173
  death, 158, 173
  headquarters demolished, 150
  house arrest, 154
Arava, 24
Arens, Moshe, 103
Argov, Shlomo, 101
armaments
  provided by Germany, 59

  provided by Soviet bloc, 28
  provided by United States, 82, 100, 148
armistice (1949), 10, 30, 33, 55, 168
Arnom, M. S., 5
Arslan, Shakib, 24, 167
Ashrawi, Hanan, 108, 110
Assad, Hafez al, 101–2, 110, 119, 128, 130
assassinations
  of Abdullah of (Trans) Jordan, 34, 169
  of editor of *Al Ahram*, 94
  of Gemayel, 103
  by Israel, 45, 107, 119, 145, 146, 149, 151, 154
  of Kennedy, 64
  of Rabin, 10, 115, 117, 172
  of Sadat, 96, 171
  of Yassin, 157, 173
  of Zeevi, 146–7, 173
Aswan Declaration, 93
Avnery, Uri, 38–9, 158
Ayalon, Ami, 153–4, 156

## B
Baghdad Alliance, 51
Baker, James, 109, 172
Balfour, Lord Arthur James, 15–16
  Balfour Declaration, 15–17, 19, 167
Bandung conference, 59
Banias River, 66
Barak, Ehud, 11, 118, 119, 124, 126–37, 139, 140, 155, 173

200

Camp David II
proposal, 132–5
quoted, 128–9
Bat Galim, 47, 48, 49,
69
Begin, Menachem, 51,
56, 71, 90–6, 99–100,
102–4, 171
Begin doctrine, 99
letter to Reagan, 102
visit to Washington,
93
Beilin, Yossi, 112, 113,
117, 119–21, 134,
136, 137–9, 154, 183
Beilin–Abu Mazen
document, 119–21,
132, 134, 138
Ben Aharon, Yitzhak, 8
Ben Ami, Shlomo, 134,
137, 139
Ben Gurion, Amos, 19
Ben Gurion, David,
19–27, 30–3, 36–7,
39–46, 49–52, 54–6,
58–9, 61–3, 68, 70,
167–9
actions after 1956
war, 7
against peace, 7–8,
10, 32
resignations, 42, 63
speeches/statements
by, 52, 53, 54–6
tendency to act alone,
32
views of, 19, 21,
23–5, 33, 43
Benn, Aluf, 135
Bernadotte, Count Folke,
31–2, 168
Biltmore conference, 21,
167
Bismarck, Otto von, 14
Black Arrow, 49
Black September, 99
Blair, Tony, 146
Blass, Simha, 37
Borochov, Ber, 5
Bourguiba, Habib, 64
Brit Shalom, 24
British Mandatory
Government of

Palestine, 1, 15–18,
22, 167
ended, 27, 168
White Paper, 22
Buber, Martin, 24
Bunche, Ralph, 32–3
Burg, Yosef, 95
Burns, William, 144
Bush, George H., 109,
110, 141–2, 144, 145,
150, 152, 172, 173

C
Camp David 1, 94–5,
99, 171
Camp David II, 11, 118,
127, 130–5
Canada, 7
Carter, Jimmy, 89, 90,
91, 93, 94–5
censorship, 4, 36, 46, 49
Center Party, 124
Cheney, Dick, 147
Choma U'Migdal, 6
Churchill, Winston, 15
Clinton, Bill, 118, 121,
123, 127–8, 130–5,
137–8
Cohen, Yerucham, 8,
38–9, 169
colonialism, 14, 58, 59
Zionism seen as, 17
conformity, pressure for,
3–4
Congress of Berlin
(1878), 14
Czechoslovakia, 50–1

D
Dahlan, Muhamad, 148,
149
Dan, Shaike, 62
Dan, Uri, 60, 141, 155
Danin, Ezra, 26
Davar, 53
Dayan, Moshe, 8–9, 26,
34, 37, 42–7, 54, 56,
66, 67, 70, 72, 73, 77,
81–3, 90–1, 93–5
resignation, 95, 171
statements, 67–8
views of, 43, 44, 58,
86, 95

Dayan, Yael, 67
deaths, violent
by assassination see
assassinations
in the Arab rebellion,
18
by Baruch Goldstein,
116
in early 1950s, 35,
42–3, 48
of Israelis, 48, 79,
145, 147, 148
of Palestinian refugees,
41, 103, 171
of Palestinians, 145
by statutory execution,
49
in violence, 121, 136
in war see wars
Declaration of Jerusalem,
155
Declaration of Principles
(1992), 113–14, 115,
172
Demilitarized Zone
(DMZ), 37, 41, 45,
67, 72, 169
demographic issues for
Israel, 1, 14–15, 27,
28, 93
see also migration
Disraeli, Benjamin, 14
Divon, Shmuel, 39–40,
48
Dreyfus, Alfred, 13

E
Eban, Abba, 7, 68–9, 71,
75–8, 82, 83–4, 86
education in Mandatory
Palestine, 1–4
Egypt
and the Arab
Federation, 62–3
arms deal with
Czechoslovakia,
50–1
attacks attributed to
by Israel, 36, 50
deal with Soviet
Union, 8
Free Officers
Movement, 38–9

lands lost to Israel, 8
nationalizes Suez
   Canal, 53
negotiations with
   Israel, 30–1, 33,
   38–40, 48, 61, 75,
   81, 90–1, 143
peace agreement with
   Israel, 11–12, 85,
   86, 95, 171
policies of, 8, 78, 98
Radio Cairo broad-
   casts, 53
relations with United
   States, 44, 65
wars/conflict with
   Israel, 30, 36, 44,
   46–7, 49–52, 54–6,
   68
Eiland, Giora, 155
Eilat, 55, 90
Eitan, Refael, 101
Eitan, Walter, 26
El Boreij, 41–2
Elazar, Dado (David), 66,
   68, 76
Eldar, Akiva, 131, 133
Erakat, Saeb, 157
Eretz Israel, 1
esek habish, 46, 48–9,
   169, 181n56
Eshkol, Levi, 63–6, 68–9,
   71, 73–5, 77, 169–70
espionage, 46–7
Etzel, 22
European Union, 161, 165

F
Fahmi, Ismail, 91–2
Faisal, Prince, 17, 167
Faisal, Amir, 20
Falluja, 38
Farouk, king, 30, 38
Fatah, 66, 147, 148, 151,
   156, 161, 165
fedayun, 35, 50, 52
First Lebanon War, 98,
   101–3
Flapan, Simha, 29
Framework for Peace, 95
France, 6, 53–5, 58
Friedman, Thomas, 141,
   149

G
Ga'hal, 140
Galilee, Israel, 84
   Galilee Document, 84
Gaon, Moshe, 127
Gaza Strip, 45, 47, 90
   demonstrations in,
      106
   division and control,
      117
   Gaza City, 52, 56
   Gaza First concept,
      107
   Hamas in power in,
      161
   International Airport,
      124
   Israel conquers in
      1956, 6, 54
   Israel occupies (1967),
      8, 71
   Israeli determination
      to retain, 109
   Israeli military opera-
      tions in, 146
   Israeli proposals for
      (1993), 114
   Israeli withdrawal
      from, 114, 155–9,
      173, 174
   negotiations over, 31
   Operation Cast Lead,
      10
   passage to West Bank,
      122, 153
   proposals for, 154
   raid (1955), 49, 169
   refugee camps, 52
   retreat from (1956), 7,
      56, 58
   settlements in, 82
Gemayel, Amin, 103,
   104, 171
Gemayel, Bashir, 102–3
Geneva peace talks/
   Initiative, 154–5, 156,
   170–1, 173
Germany, 58–9
Golan, Joe, 60–2
Golan Heights, 8, 67,
   70–2, 76, 90, 104,
   121, 128, 143

   annexed in 1981, 100,
      171
Goldman, Nahum, 60–2,
   79
Goldstein, Baruch, 116
Gorbachev, Mikhail, 110
Greater Israel Movement,
   9
Green Line, 35, 112
Gulf states, 113
Gush Emunim, 9, 72, 95
Gush Etzion, 72

H
Ha'aretz, 41, 51, 57,
   132, 135, 138, 145,
   149, 158, 173
Habash, George, 145
Habib, Philip, 102
Haganah, the, 3, 22, 28
Haifa, 29, 31, 161
Haig, Alexander, 102
Hamas, 108, 119, 144,
   146, 148, 151–2, 154,
   156–7, 159, 160–1,
   174
   activists deported, 172
   Israel's refusal to
      negotiate with, 161
Hamilton, Dennis, 62
el Hamma, 37
Haram Al Sharif, 118,
   120, 132, 136
Harel, Isser, 61, 65
Hashemite dynasty, 17,
   26
Hassan, king of
   Morocco, 89, 90, 93
Hebron, 9, 72–3, 74,
   116, 121–2, 143
Heikal, Hassanein, 61
Herut party, 140
Herzl, Theodor, 11,
   14–15
Herzog, Ya'acov, 65
Hezbollah, 106, 117,
   119, 129, 148, 161
Hirschfeld, Yair, 113
Histadrut, 1–2, 8
Historians, New,
   approach of, 10
Holocaust, the, 10, 21,
   24, 63, 163, 167–8

Hossan, 42, 43
houses, Palestinian,
   demolition of, 115
Hullah Lake, 169
Husayn, Sarif bin Ali,
   167
Hussein, king of Jordan,
   7, 63, 65, 67, 70, 75,
   76, 80–2, 88–9, 102,
   105, 107–8, 118, 143,
   172
Hussein, Saddam, 110,
   152
Husseini, Feisal, 108
Husseini, Haj Amin el,
   19, 167

I
independence struggles in
   Europe, 13
information
   Israeli government
      disinformation, 50,
      67, 128
   about Syrian airliner/
      captives incident
      (1954), 47–8
   about Suez, 52
   state control over,
      4, 41
   see also censorship
intifadas
   first, 106–7, 113, 136,
      171
   second, 118, 136–7,
      142, 143–4, 173
Iraq, 30, 44, 61, 99, 152,
   171
   and the Arab
      Federation, 62–3
Islamic fundamentalism,
   11
Islamic Jihad, 119, 144,
   156, 159, 160
Ismael, Hafez, 83
Israel
   boundaries/borders,
      16, 21, 24, 25, 27,
      28, 31, 43–4, 73,
      76, 129, 153
   considered above/not
      subject to interna-
      tional law, 28, 164

creation of, 27–30
Declaration of Inde-
   pendence, 25
desire for peace (or
   otherwise), 7–11
international criticism
   of, 58
peace agreements
   signed, 11–12
perceived as empty pre
   founding of state, 5
policy against fedayun
   attacks, 36
recognized by PLO,
   172
see also Palestine
Israeli Committee of
   Inquiry (into the
   Second Lebanon War),
   162
Israeli Society of Military
   History, 29
Istiklal, 24

J
Ja-abri, Sheikh, 74
Jabri, Ihsal al, 24, 167
Jackson, Elmore, 169
jamborees, 7
Jarring, Gunnar, 77, 78,
   81, 170
Jericho, 88
Jerusalem, 18–19, 168
   Israeli actions/changes
      in, 9, 71–2, 121
   proposals for, 31, 117,
      120, 121, 130–1,
      132–3, 138, 153
Jerusalem, East, 110
   annexed in 1967, 8–9,
      71–2
   international protec-
      tion of, 24
   Israeli annexation
      of, 96
   Mugrabi district, 9
   as potential Palestinian
      capital, 113, 132–3,
      138, 146, 150, 153,
      154
Jewish Agency, 1, 7
Jewish National Fund,
   20–1

Jews
   arguments that they
      are/are not a distinct
      people, 5
   of the authors' genera-
      tion, characteristics,
      1–4
   in Eastern Europe, 13
   history and perceived
      destiny, 4–5
   migration of, see
      under migration
   right to sovereign
      state, 21
   as target of violence,
      13
   in the United States,
      39
   'victim' status, 10
Jezreel valley, 18, 21
Johnson, Lyndon, 64,
   68–9
Johnston, Eric, 169
Jordan
   citizenship of, 75, 88
   Jordanian Legion, 79
   lands lost to Israel, 8,
      27, 71, 75
   negotiations by/with,
      33, 87, 105
   peace agreement with
      Israel, 12, 65, 118,
      172
   policies of, 98, 118
   political situation in,
      53, 82, 172
   return of land to, 118
   violence along border,
      36, 41, 47
   wars/conflict with
      Israel, 30, 45, 53–4,
      67
Jordan River, 75
   diversion of, 46, 65–6,
      170
   valley, Israeli
      proposals for, 139,
      143

K
Kabir, Yussuf al, 61
Kadima, 160, 161, 174
Kadosh, Alon, 29

Kapeliouk, Amnon, 134
Karameh operation, 79–80
Karine A, 147–8
Karmel, Moshe, 80
Katzav, Moshe, 149
Katzenelson, Itzhak, 5
Keeley, James, 32
Kennedy, John F., 63, 64
Khan Y unis, 51
kibbutz movement, 2, 3, 6
Kibya, 41
Kimche, John, 45
Kineret, 42, 169
Kissinger, Henry, 82, 86
Kreisky, Bruno, 89
Kurei, Ahmed (Abu Ala), 113
Kurzer, Dan, 152
Kuwait, 110, 113
Kybia, 169

L
Labor Federation see Histadrut
Labor Party (Mapam), 43, 56, 100, 107, 109–11, 114–15, 127, 160, 161
Labor Youth, 1–2
LaMerhav, 53
land policy, 73
    acquisition tactics, 25
    expropriation for settlements, 95, 114
    see also settlement movement
languages spoken by Jews pre Israel, 13
Larsen, Terje, 152
Laskov, Chaim, 68
Latrun enclave, 9
Lavon, Pinhas, 42, 43–9, 58
law, Ottoman, 6
League of Nations, 15, 167
Lebanon, 24, 101–3
    Meronites in, 101
    negotiations with Israel, 33, 171
    wars/conflict with

Israel, 30, 45, 99, 101, 161, 171
Lehi, 22
Lenin, Vladimir I., 5
letters from students, 79
Levi, David, 109
Levinger, Moshe, 72
Levit, Daphna, 1–2, 4, 8–9
Likud Party, 90, 99, 100, 109, 115, 118, 122, 157–8, 160, 173
Lior, Israel, 66
Litani operation, 171
Livni, Tzipi, 160
Lloyd George, David, 15
Lydda, 31

M
Ma'aleh Akrabim, 43
Ma'ariv, 50, 60, 78
Madrid peace conference, 107, 110–11, 172
Magnes, Yehuda Leib, 23–4
mahapach, the, 89–90
Malley, Robert, 131, 133
Malta, 60
Mapai see Labor Party
Markus, Yoel, 156
Marx, Karl, 5
Mayors' Initiative, 74
McMahon, Henry, 167
mehablim, 35
Meir, Golda, 26, 43, 57, 61, 77–9, 81–2, 170
    resignation, 87
    speeches and statements, 53–4
    views of, 77–8
Meretz Party, 111, 127, 142
Meridor, Dan, 147
migration
    of Arabs from Palestine, 14–16, 18, 19–20, 25, 27, 29–30
    to Palestine (pre foundation of Israel), 1, 17
    proposed restriction of Jewish, 22

and size of Jewish state, 26–7
military, Israeli
    reserves, 6
    service, 3, 6
mines, use of, 45, 67
Mintoff, Dom, 60
Mitchell Committee, 142, 143–5
Modai, Itzhak, 109
Mofaz, Shaul, 136
Moratinos, Miguel, 138–9, 151
Mordechai, Yitzhak, 124
Morocco, 61
Morris, Benny, 28
Mubarak, Hosni, 96–7, 98, 104, 107, 109, 110, 143, 159
Mugraby, 71
Murphy, Richard, 105
Muslim Brotherhood, 49
Mustafa, Abu Ali, 145, 146–7, 173

N
Na'hlin, 43
Nablus, 9
Nachal (Pioneering Combat Youth), 3
Nachshon operation, 29
Naguib, Muhammad, 38, 45
Nahal outposts, 72
Narkiss, Uzi, 73
Nasrallah, Sheik Hassan, 157
Nasser, Gamal Abdel, 8, 38–40, 45, 46, 48–9, 51, 58–63, 65, 68, 71, 76, 79, 80–1, 169–70
    death of, 81, 170
Nathan, Abie, 112
National Religious Party, 72, 87, 95, 156
National Unity Government, 104, 108
Negev, 24, 30, 31, 65
Netanyahu, Binyamin, 115, 118, 121–4, 126, 128, 155, 162, 172–3
New Historians, 10, 28–9

newspaper editors' committee, 4
Nitzana, 51, 52
Nixon, Richard M., 79, 81, 82, 170
Non-Aligned Movement, 59–60, 62
Nordau, Max, 14
nuclear program
  Iraq's, 99
  Israel's, 63
Nusseibeh, Sari, 153–4, 156

O
oil supplies blocked, 54
Okasha, Tharwat, 61, 62
Olmert, Ehud, 160, 161–2, 174
one-state solution, 165
Operation Bo-Peep, 47
Operation Cast Lead, 10, 126
Operation Defensive Shield, 149, 150, 173
Operation Field of Thorns, 136
Operation Grapes of Wrath, 172
Operation Horev, 31
Orbach, Maurice, 48
Oslo peace talks/Accords, 10, 88, 107, 112, 115–17, 123, 126, 136, 172
  Oslo II, 116–17, 119, 121
Ottoman Empire, 15

P
Palestine
  definitions of, 16
  early attempts to buy, 15
  elections in, 113
  history and geography of, 2, 5, 14
  as homeland for the Jews, 13–22
  Jewish community in 1930s and 1940s, 1
  Jewish revolt (1945), 22

Mandatory, 10, 13–22
  opposition to independent state, 155
  partition, implementation of, 23–34
  partition not the ultimate Jewish aim, 19, 24–5, 27
  partition, proposal for, 18–21
  population pre formation of Israel, 5, 14–15
  possible annexation to Jordan, 26
  as potential binational state, 23
  proposed statehood, 73, 88–9, 98, 119, 123, 145–6
Palestine Conciliation Commission (PCC), 33
Palestine Liberation Organization, 66, 87–8, 93–4, 170, 172
  confrontation with Jordan, 99
  established in Lebanon, 99
  established in Tunisia, 102
  expelled from Jordan, 105
  headquarters in Tunis bombed, 171
  Israeli policy towards, 101
  local vs exiled leadership of, 107–8
  policies of, 108–9
  as possible negotiating partner, 105, 112
  recognized by Israel, 172
  recognized by USA, 107
Palestinian Authority, 115, 133, 143, 152, 153, 157, 158–9
  elections, 159, 160–1
Palestinian Charter, 123, 124, 172
Palestinian National

Council, 108, 114, 116, 172
Palestinians
  believed to be newcomers, 5
  cost of Israeli conquest to, 6
  deaths of see under deaths, violent
  effect of Plan Dalet on, 29–30
  failure to consult (re founding of Israel), 16
  guerilla attacks by, 79–80, 94
  migration of see under migration
  not perceived as a people, 83
  numbers displaced in 1948, 29–30 (see also migration)
  pre founding of Israel, 5, 14–15
  prisoners released, 122, 124
  rebellion against Jewish immigration, 16–18, 24–5
  as refugees, 8, 32, 35, 41, 52, 71–4, 99, 103, 135, 146, 149, 153–4
  returned refugees, 33, 139
  seen as primitive by Jews, 5, 15, 18
  treatment in Israel and occupied territories, 106
  as victims, 163
Palmach, the, 3, 29
Pappe, Ilan, 28
Paz, Ilan, 144
peace
  the book's contribution to understanding, 11
  Israel's attitude to, see under Israel
  movement, 10, 94, 103, 112, 127

Peace for the Galilee,
   102, 171
Peace Now, 94
Peel, Lord William
   Robert, 18
Peel Commission, 10,
   18–21, 25–6, 167
Peres, Shimon, 9, 42, 44,
   61, 88, 89, 104–10,
   115, 118–19, 143,
   150, 155, 160, 171,
   172
Peretz, Amir, 160, 161
Perle, Richard, 155
pioneer youth
   movements, 1–3, 5
Pioneering Combat
   Youth see Nachal
Pipes, Daniel, 155
Plans A, B and C, 29
Plan Dalet, 29–30, 168
Pollack, Allan, 7
Pollard, Jonathan, 123
Popular Front for the
   Liberation of Palestine
   (PFLP), 106, 145,
   146–7
Powell, Colin, 146, 147,
   148, 151
Pundak, Ron, 113

Q
al Qaeda, 146
Quartet, the, 152

R
Rabbo, Yasser Abed,
   154, 173
Rabin, Yitzhak, 9, 66,
   68, 81, 87–9, 105–7,
   109, 111, 112,
   114–19, 124, 172
   assassination of, 10,
      115, 117, 172
   resignation, 89
   views of, 87, 105
Rabin Square, 124
Rafael, Gideon, 83
Raffah, 57
RAFI, 64
Rantisi, Abd el Aziz, 157
Rapaport, Meron, 57
Ras el Naqb, 44

Reagan, Ronald, 100,
   102, 105, 171
refugees see under
   Palestinians
Reinhart, Tanya, 114,
   120
Riad, Kamal, 30
al-Rifai, Zaid, 77
right to return, 31, 62,
   121, 131, 135–6, 154,
   168
River Wye Plantation
   agreement, 123–4, 172
   revised agreement, 128
road map for peace,
   152–3, 157, 173
roads, in the occupied
   territories, 115
Rogers, William, 78–9,
   82, 170
   Rogers Plan, 78, 82,
      170
   Rogers Plan B, 79,
      170
   Third Rogers Plan,
      170
Ross, Dennis, 11, 130
Rothschild, Edmund
   de, 62
rubinstein, Danny, 132
Rusk, Dean, 76

S
Sabha, 52
Sabra and Shatila
   massacre, 103, 171
Sadat, Anwar el, 81, 83,
   86, 89, 90–6, 100, 170
   assassination, 96, 98,
      171
   visit to Jerusalem,
      91–2, 171
Sadeq, Abdel Rahman,
   39–40, 48
Safad, 29
Said, Nuri al, 61
Samu, 67, 68, 170
Sapir, Pinhas, 84, 86
Sarid, Yossi, 137, 142
Sasson, Elias, 26, 30
Saudi Arabia, 113, 135,
   146, 149, 173
Scouts, the, 1–2

Second Lebanon War,
   161, 174
settlements/settlement
   movement, 10, 71–4,
   76, 83, 85, 87, 93, 95,
   104, 106, 110, 127,
   164
   expansion in, 114–15,
      143, 151, 159, 160
   freeze on settlements,
      90
   as major obstacle to
      peace, 116, 164
   militancy of, 117
   numbers of settlers,
      96, 115
   origins in 1956, 57
   reluctance to
      withdraw from,
      130, 134, 164
   US/Quartet demand to
      end, 144, 152–3
   and withdrawal from
      Gaza, 114, 134,
      156–7, 159–60
   within proposed West
      Bank Palestinian
      state, 120, 132,
      134, 136, 138, 160
Shabak, 156
Shafi, Abd el, 111
Shaftesbury, Lord, 5, 14
Shamir, Yitzhak, 95, 96,
   104–5, 107–11, 171
Sharet, Moshe, 26, 27,
   30–1, 34, 37, 40,
   42–9, 60, 169
   views of, 43
Sharm el Sheikh, 9, 54,
   57, 71, 78, 90, 100,
   128, 133, 159, 171,
   174
Sharon, Ariel, 99, 118,
   127, 136–7, 173
   career summary,
      140–1
   character, 140–1
   death, 160, 174
   fraud allegations, 156
   in the military, 8, 42,
      49,
   as minister of defense,
      96, 97, 101–3

as prime minister,
140–3, 146–9,
151–60, 173
resignation, 160
views, 94, 109, 140,
142, 151, 153
Shas Party, 124
Shavit, Ari, 142
Shawqi, Ali, 39
Shehadah, Salah, 151
Shehadeh, Aziz, 74
Shelah, Offer, 145
Shem–Tov, Victor, 78, 88
Sheperdstown talks,
129–30
Sher, Gilad, 134, 137
Shiffer, Shimon, 130
Shikaki, Khalil, 135
Shiloah, Reuven, 26, 34
Shishakly, Adib, 37, 45
Shlaim, Avi, 28, 49, 67,
70, 106, 160
Shultz, George, 102, 104,
107–8, 171
Sinai peninsula, 24, 40,
54–5, 78, 86, 92, 94–5
Israel conquers in
1956, 6, 54
Israel occupies (1967),
8, 70
retreat from (1956), 7,
56, 58
retreat from (1980–1),
97, 104
war see 1956 war
Sinai II Agreement, 86,
170
Sirkin, Marie, 5
Six Day War see 1967
war
Smilansky, Moshe, 15
Sneh, Moshe, 56
socialism in youth
movements, 1–2
Soviet Union, 83, 91, 169
arms deal with Egypt,
8
Stalin, Josef, 5
Steinberg, Matti, 145
Stern Gang, 32
Students Zionist
Organization of
Canada, 7

Suez Canal, 6, 39, 44,
46, 47, 65, 81
Bar Lev fortifications,
86
Egypt's nationalization
of, 53
war over, 54–5, 58,
169
suicide missions, 117,
119, 122, 151, 154,
159
Summit of Hope, 159
Sykes Picot Agreement,
167
Syria, 17, 26, 32
agreement with Israel,
32
and the Arab Federa-
tion, 62–3
conflict with Israel,
36–7, 44, 47, 52,
65–8, 86
lands lost to Israel,
8, 100
negotiations with
Israel, 37, 75, 119,
127–30, 155
policies of, 67, 101,
103, 111

T
Taba, 97, 137–9, 141, 142
Tabenkin, Yitzhak, 5
Tal, Rami, 67
Tanzim, 151
telephone strategy, 9
Ten Day Operation, 31
Tenet, George/Tenet plan,
142, 144–5, 148, 173
Tiberias, 29
Tiran see Yorvat
Tito, Josip Broz, 62
transfer to other
countries see migration
TransJordan, 26
as possible part of
Israeli state, 20
and the proposed
partition of
Palestine, 19
Tsur, Zvi, 68
Tuhami, Hassan, 89,
90–1, 93

Tunisia, 102
two-state solution,
principle of, 108, 152,
153, 164
2002 initiative, 152

U
U-Nu, 62
United Arab Kingdom,
proposal for, 83
United Kibbutz
Movement, 7
United Kingdom
and Palestine/foun-
dation of Israel,
15–16, 22, 167
and Suez, 6, 39–40,
44, 46, 47, 53–5,
58
see also British
Mandatory Govern-
ment of Palestine
United Nations, 33, 52,
165, 170
Armistice Commis-
sion, 51
end of the British
Mandate, 22
mediator, 31
observers/supervision,
37, 44, 47
Palestine Conciliation
Committee, 168
partition plan, 6, 10,
17, 22, 24, 27–8
peacekeeping force, 81
resolutions, see
separate entry
role not acknowledge
by Ben Gurion,
25–6
Security Council, 42,
50, 100
UN resolutions, 59, 86,
89, 134
no. 181, 30, 168, 172
no. 184, 150; no. 194,
135, 139, 168
no. 242, 76–7, 79–82,
88, 90, 108, 139,
149, 170, 172
no. 338, 108, 134,
149, 170, 172

no. 425, 171
  violation of, 28, 30,
    60, 151
United States
  intervention over Suez,
    169
  as mediator for peace,
    86–7, 165 (see also
    Camp David, Oslo,
    River Wye)
  policies towards Israel,
    7, 30, 89, 91, 104
  relations with Israel,
    42, 44, 47, 63,
    68–9, 82, 86, 141,
    147–8, 152
  relations with PA, 161
Usishkin, Menachem, 14

V
Vance, Cyrus, 90
village leagues concept,
    74–5
violence
  Dayan's narrative of,
    67–8
  in Egypt, 46
  and Gaza, 157
  Goldstein's atrocity,
    116
  along the Green Line,
    35–7
  in Jerusalem, 121
  by Palestinians, 43,
    48, 79, 146–7, 154
  Palmach's mode of, 29
  retaliatory, 41, 43, 50,
    79–80
  see also assassinations;
    deaths, violent;
    intifadas; Sabra and
    Shatila massacre;
    wars

W
wall and the tower,
  policy of, 6
wars see 1948 war, 1956
    war, 1967 war, 1973
    war, First Lebanon
    War, Second Lebanon
    War
  number of casualties,
    52, 67, 80, 161
  War of Attrition,
    78–9, 170
  war on tractors, 66
water
  agreement with Jordan
    over, 118
  conflict over, 37,
    65–6, 169, 170
  in Gaza, 159
Weisglass, Dov, 157, 158
Weizman, Chaim, 15, 16,
    19, 21, 22, 25, 27, 167
Weizman, Ezer, 91, 93,
    94, 96, 171
West Bank, 34
  annexed by Jordan
    (1950), 34, 169
  annexed from Jordan
    (1967), 8, 70, 72
  buffer zone in, 144
  division into three
    areas, 116, 123
  Israeli determination
    to retain, 109
  land acquisition in, 73
  limited Israeli with-
    drawal from, 122–3
  passage to Gaza, 122,
    153
  proposals/policies
    for, 71, 73, 77–8,
    104–5, 109, 120,
    130–2, 134–5, 138,
    142, 154
  reoccupied by Israel
    (2002), 149, 151
  settlement blocks

  accepted by USA,
    157
  settlers in, 160
World Jewish Congress,
    60
World Zionist
    Organization, 14

Y
Ya'alon, Moshe, 137
Yamit, 97
Yariv, Aharon, 88
Yassin, Sheikh Ahmed,
    151, 157, 173
Yediot Aharanot, 129,
    130, 145, 158
Yehud, 41
Yoav operation, 30
Yom Kipper war see
    1973 war
Yorvat, 55, 56

Z
al-Za'im, Husni, 32, 36,
    168
Zamir, Zvi, 86
Zangwill, Israel, 5, 14,
    20
Zeevi, Rehavam, 146–7,
    173
Zhara, Mahmoud, 154
Zilberstein, Tal, 127
Zinni, Anthony, 147–8,
    173
Zionism, 13, 15–18
  American, 21
  education/
    indoctrination in,
    2–4
  First Zionist
    Conference (1897),
    14–15, 167
  Zionist Congress
    (1937), 20
  Zionist Congress
    (1945), 22